D1169784

# SOUL WITHIN
# _a_ PEACH

# SOUL WITHIN
## _a_ PEACH

FLORENCE SAU KIN

SOUL WITHIN A PEACH
Copyright © 2001 by Peace Within Publishing.

All rights reserved. No part of this work may be reproduced, stored in any retrieval system, or transmitted in any way, shape or form, including electronic, digital, mechanical, recording or photocopying, without prior written permission of the publisher.

Peace Within Publishing
20238 South Danny Court
Oregon City, Oregon 97045

Cover Design by Tony Tarr

First Edition
ISBN:
Printed in the United States
of America by Thomson-Shore

PUBLISHER'S CATALOGING-IN-PUBLICATION
Sau Kin, Florence.
Soul Within A Peach / Florence Sau Kin.
— 1st ed.   p.    cm.
Includes index.
ISBN: 0-9651662-0-1

1. Spirit possession.  2. Sau Kin, Florence.
3. Therese, de Lisieux, Saint, 1873–1897—
Miscellanea.  4. Spiritual biography. I. Title.

BL482.S38 1998   291.2'15
QBI97-41441

LCCCN 2001012345

# CONTENTS

# Foreword

In 1968 Florence asked me to assist her in writing this book for God. She trusted me because I was her spiritual son and because I was a priest with a degree in theology. I promised her then that I would.

While Florence was in Jerusalem for a nine-day retreat in 1987, she telephoned me after her retreat. She asked me again on the phone if I would promise to help her with this book for God. Again I promised her that I would.

"Do you promise?"

"Yes, I promise."

"You promise?"

"I promise."

Three times I promised her on the phone that I would help her to write this book for God.

Besides having her own writings and her tape recordings, I had the privilege of living with Florence since 1969. She was a loving Christian mother to me, and I helped to care for her.

As a constant eyewitness under various circumstances for more than 30 years, I can vouch under oath for Florence: her honesty, her simplicity, her integrity, her detachment from material things, her separation from her family in order to do God's will, her fast and abstinence, her other sacrifices, her humility, her universal charity, her fidelity to her private vows to God, her saintliness.

Her writings, tape recordings and sharing of experiences and lessons were all done in the first person. I have tried to preserve her voice and tone throughout this book by letting Florence speak in her own simple, direct way.

All the ideas and lessons in this book are from Florence; any inaccuracy is from me and not from Florence. She spoke only the truth. Florence lived her whole life according to truth, justice and charity. Because of this manner of life, she was privileged to receive special guidance and assistance from a Saint.

Neither Catholic theology nor Scripture rules out an abiding influence from the spirit of a Saint. While being helped and guided by a Saint, the person retains his own identity, personality, and free will. There is no doubt in my mind that the spirit of St. Teresa of Avila had an abiding influence on the soul of St. Therese of Lisieux, because of the great love of St. Teresa for Jesus and the great love of St. Therese for Jesus. The most important factor in being helped by a Saint is how docile and generous a person is with the Holy Spirit and with the saintly spirit.

The Old Testament seems to suggest such a case of abiding influence just as Jesus Himself did in the New Testament.

In the second book of Kings 2:9-15 we read:

*When they had crossed [the Jordan], Elijah said to Elisha, "Ask what I shall do for you before I am taken from you." And Elisha said, "I pray you, let me inherit a double share of your spirit." And he said, "You have asked a hard thing; yet if you see me as I am being taken from you, it shall be so for you; but if you do not see me, it shall not be so." And as they still went on and talked, behold, a chariot of fire and horses of fire separated the two of them. And Elijah went up by whirlwind into heaven. And Elisha saw it and cried, "My father, my father! the chariots of Israel and its horsemen!" And he saw him no more.*

*...Then he took up the mantle of Elijah that had fallen from him, and went back to the Jordan. Then he took the mantle of Elijah that had fallen from him, and struck the water, saying, "Where is the Lord, the God of Elijah?" And when he struck the water, the water was parted to one side and to the other; and Elisha went over.*

*Now when the sons of the prophets who were at Jericho saw him over against them, they said, "The spirit of Elijah rests on Elisha."*

So the spirit of Elijah rested on Elisha to guide and assist him.

When an angel appeared to Zechariah to announce the birth of John the Baptist and his mission, he said, "And he will turn many of the sons of Israel to the Lord their God, and he will go before him in the spirit and power of Elijah . . . ." (Luke 1:16-17)

Jesus refers to the close relationship between Elijah and John the Baptist in Matthew 17:9-13: [After the Transfiguration]

*As they were coming down the mountain, Jesus commanded them, "Tell no one about the vision until the Son of man is risen from the dead." And the disciples asked him, "Then why do the scribes say that first Elijah must come?" He replied, "Elijah does come, and he is to restore all things; but I tell you that Elijah has already come, and they did to him whatever they pleased. So also must the Son of man suffer at their hands." Then the disciples understood that he was speaking to them of John the Baptist.*

So the *spirit and power of Elijah* (Luke 1:17) had rested on the soul of John the Baptist to guide and assist him.

The Catholic Church believes in assistance from angels and from saints. Children are taught and encouraged to pray to their guardian angels for help. Every day millions of the faithful seek the intercession and assistance of the saints in heaven and millions pray to St. Michael the archangel for protection against evil spirits.

From time to time our guardian angel and patron saint inspire us to do good. We can accept or reject the inspiration from a saintly spirit. The more we cooperate with the inspirations of the Holy Spirit and of saintly spirits, the greater influence they will have on us as we live day by day, moment by moment.

As you read this memoir, keep in mind that the Chinese, Japanese and Korean women of the author's generation were conditioned to obey and to be docile. What seems foolish or even masochistic to many Americans of the present generation was perfectly natural and normal for Asian women of earlier times, who put up with maltreatment and meanness from in-laws and from husbands.

Another fact to keep in mind is that God blessed Florence with a simple, childlike soul that lives in the present without looking back at past hurts and maltreatment. God gave her special graces to keep her from being bitter and vindictive.

The author describes the wrongs done to her not out of bitterness, but to bring out lessons that will help us to treat others with respect, fairness and compassion.

In his first epistle, St. Peter writes: "For one is approved if, mindful of God, he endures pain while suffering unjustly. ...But if when you do right and suffer for it you take it patiently, you have God's approval. For to this you have been called, because Christ suffered for you, leaving you an example, that you should follow in his steps." (I Peter 2:19-21)

As an eyewitness over the course of 31 years, I saw Florence as cheerful and outgoing with a delightful sense of humor. I never saw any manifestation of self-pity. The trait that impressed me most about Florence was her *loving kindness toward everyone.*

The people who met her were impressed by her sincerity and simplicity. They sensed that she truly cared about them. There was no hint of any bitterness in her life or of the many sufferings she had endured. For the great majority of the people she met, she came across as a lively, friendly, spiritual person. She never preached, but always gave people a lift with her positive, encouraging words.

I hope you find inspiration from her experiences and her spiritual lessons.

Father Francis Chun, S.T.L.

# Introduction

God calls each of us to be a saint, to saintly living, to be a Temple of the Holy Spirit, to allow God to live in our souls. God sent His own Son to be our Redeemer, to live in and with us, that we might see Jesus in our brothers and sisters, and that they might see Christ in us.

If you are interested in saintly living, being a living saint, this delightful book is for you. If you enjoy reading about saints, you will not be able to put this book down. If you are skeptical as I was, know that there is room for change and belief.

Florence Sau Kin was born a Buddhist, and at age ten was told that she had *sin kwat*, a Chinese term meaning *saintly bones*. Over the course of her long life, her exciting journey of faith, she was to learn what this meant.

By reading this book, you can learn the meaning of saintly living, and how the saints in heaven interact with us in the Communion of Saints. This is a book about faith and love, prayer and suffering; about Jesus and the Holy Spirit, the Blessed Virgin Mary, St. Teresa of Avila and St. Therese of Lisieux (two great Doctors of the Church), canonized Saints and everyday saints, Saints of the past millennium and a saint of the new millennium.

Florence lived in two different faith traditions, ten different decades, two different centuries, two different millennia. She was baptized in the Holy Year of 1950, and she entered eternal life in the Jubilee Year of 2000 – a woman for all seasons and a saint for our times.

St. Teresa of Avila inspired St. Therese of Lisieux, who then inspired Florence. May Florence inspire you as the Little Flower inspired her. May the Mother of Jesus inspire us all, for Jesus truly lives within each of us that we might live for all eternity with God and with all the angels and saints.

Most Reverend Kenneth Steiner
Auxiliary Bishop of the Archdiocese of Portland in Oregon

# Preface

To believe or not to believe: the choice is yours. It's up to you. With God all things are possible. Everything in this book is true.

This book is much more than a memoir. It is a book of spiritual lessons from God to help those who hunger for spiritual growth and to help those who seek peace of mind, peace of heart and peace of soul.

This book is for people of all beliefs, all ages, all social levels, all cultures, all countries.

My thanks go to *everyone* who has helped with this book in any way. I ask God to bless and reward each one for me.

I thank by name: Father Francis, who had to unscramble all my notes and organize the material for this book, Frank Amato and his team, our dedicated attorneys Mitch Wall and Marilyn Wall, and Tony Tarr, our cover designer. A special thanks to my dedicated editors Yvette S. Willis and Jennifer M. Ortiz.

My greatest gratitude goes to the three Divine Persons of the Holy Trinity: "All glory, honor, thanks and praise be to the Father Who has created us; all glory, honor, thanks and praise be to the Son Who has redeemed us; all glory, honor, thanks and praise be to the Holy Spirit Who has sanctified us; blessed be the Holy and Undivided Trinity now and forever."

Florence
A child of God

*Humility begins with the quiet acceptance*
*of the truth in humiliating situations.*

# 1

# REVELATION IN CHINA

My name is Florence. I am a child of God. I do God's will.

I never realized how hard my life was as a child and teenager until I began writing this book for God. My suffering in life began in childhood and continued throughout my life. Suffering has made me a strong woman, brought me closer to God, and taught me His spiritual lessons, which I want to share with you.

My father came from China in the early 1900s. My mother was sent from China as a "picture bride" while a teenager. Her marriage to my father was arranged through her photograph. She and my father spoke little English. I was born in Honolulu, Hawaii, in 1915. The midwife who delivered me never recorded my birth, so I never had a birth certificate. My parents then lived in Wahiawa, on the island of Oahu, where they owned and ran a restaurant. I was the second of five children, after my eldest brother, Albert. My sister Gertrude was a year younger than me. Harry and Edward were my younger brothers.

I was brought up a Buddhist, the traditional faith of my parents and their ancestors. My mother was a very religious person. She would read the Chinese bible to me while I sat on the floor. I was very interested in the many lessons from the Buddhist religion. She taught me about obedience, humility of heart, doing good to others, and never looking down on others. That is how I grew up as a practicing Buddhist, and I have carried those lessons throughout my life.

Aunt Ah Gnan was my father's sister. She and her husband did not have children and lived in a big house at Nuuanu and Iliahi streets. When her husband was sent to the tuberculosis ward of Leahi Hospital, she asked my parents to let me live with her for companionship. My parents consented, so I lived with my aunt from age five to eight.

The Chinese children of my generation were taught to obey without questioning. My time spent with my aunt was work. She made me do the dishes, dust the furniture and go on my knees to clean the wooden floor around the Chinese rugs with a dust pan and brush. If she found a dust speck, she made me dust everything again. She never allowed me to go out to play with the neighbors' children. Sometimes she punished me without reason by not giving me supper. The Chinese children of my generation were taught to obey without questioning, and God had made my soul an obedient one. So I learned to obey at a young age.

Every Saturday my aunt put me on the train at the Honolulu station, and my mother waited for me at the train station in Wahiawa. I carried my dirty clothes in a bundle, because she refused to wash them during the week. On Sundays my mother would send me back on the train with my bundle of clean clothes.

While her husband was at Leahi Hospital in the tuberculosis ward, my aunt never went to visit him. Instead she had me bring him meals in a lunch pail. When he had to go to San Francisco to receive treatment for tuberculosis, he told me, "Take good care of Auntie, now. Be good to her."

"Okay, I'll be good to her and I'll take good care of her. Will you bring me back a black doll?"

"I will; I promise."

I kept my promise by being good and by taking good care of my aunt. So when my uncle returned after his treatment, I waited and watched him as he came through the door to see whether he had a package for me, but he did not. I'm 82 now, and I still remember the disappointment I felt from that broken promise.

*That hurt taught me never to break a promise to a child. A child may remember a broken promise forever. So I always keep my promise to a child, no matter how much time and effort it takes. It's better not to make a promise to a child if we can't or won't keep that promise, or if we're not sure.*

## My Childhood Trip to China

My uncle died when I was eight years old. Ah Gnan was 24. She decided to sell her home and make a trip to China. Without my knowing about her trip, she asked my parents to allow me to accompany her to China for a visit. My parents presumed that she had told me about the trip and consented.

Secretly, she packed what little clothes I had. Then she pretended to give me a ship's tour of the American President Line. When she told me the ship was taking us to China, I started crying.

"I want to go home. I want my ma. I want to go home!"

"Climb up and look out that round window."

I saw only water. I kept crying.

"You can cry all you want. The boat won't go back. You'll never see your ma again."

Onboard the ship, whenever she felt sad or lonely, she asked me to sing some songs to amuse her.

"Up, up, in the sky, the little birds fly…"

I enjoyed singing, but when I refused to sing because I felt sad or missed my family, she wouldn't let me have any supper. She seldom left the stateroom and kept me with her the entire trip.

We visited Yokohama, Japan, during a stopover. When we stayed in a Japanese house, I was surprised that I could see the shadow and shape of a person on the other side of a wall. I stared at the wall and felt the paper with my hands.

That night we slept on *futons* (thick blankets) that were unrolled and placed on the floor. The next morning we boarded the ship to continue our trip to Shanghai. That Saturday morning, September 1, 1923, as I stood on the deck of our ship next to the pier, the great earthquake struck. Our ship was tossed outward from the pier. The big, heavy ropes snapped. The water in the bay boiled. I heard screams and saw bodies lying along the dock. Black smoke rose from the city. Our ship rocked hard. The captain ordered the ship out to sea at full speed. My aunt panicked. She yanked me from the railing and dragged me to our room. We made it out of the bay to safety. I was too young to understand what was happening.

Many years later, I learned that the earthquake, which was 8.3 on the Richter scale, killed more than 140,000 people and destroyed most of Yokohama and a large part of Tokyo, too. God saved me. He has saved my life many times. God is my Blessed Savior not only in a spiritual way, but in a physical way, too.

## Life in Shanghai

My aunt and I finally arrived in Shanghai, and we stayed with her husband's oldest brother. We lived in his three-story mansion for more than a year. The family had maids, a nanny for me, and even their own chef. Looking back some 75 years later, I now know I ate some of my most delicious meals there. I learned the language of Shanghai. I also learned about my Chinese heritage and culture: smelling and tasting the best of Chinese food, seeing and eating out of fine porcelain, seeing and wearing finely embroidered gowns of silk, looking at Chinese writing and paintings, seeing and touching jewelry of 24-karat gold, of imperial jade and of pigeon-blood ruby. The bedrooms were on the second and third floors. I could see a huge magnolia tree in bloom outside the window of the third floor.

On the ground floor were the spare room where my aunt and I slept, a large kitchen with servants' quarters, a library-sitting room with a fireplace, and a back room haunted by a ghost. That back room was between the sitting room and the toilet. The top half of the door held a glass panel with an etched design. That door was kept locked because at midnight a scary, glowing shape would come to the door. When my aunt's two nephews, university students, told us about the ghost, she didn't believe them. So they made us stay up with them near the door until midnight. Then we saw a white glowing shape through the glass panel. Her two nephews ran to their room and we ran to ours.

I saw that scary ghost with my own eyes. I was afraid to go near that locked door even during the day. When my aunt had to use the toilet at night, she woke me up and made me go with her because she had to pass that glass door next to the toilet. If I had to use the toilet at night, I asked her to take me.

Every morning while the family slept, *Mahmah* (my nanny) woke and dressed me, combed and braided my hair into two pigtails, fed me rice gruel sprinkled with salted beans, and then took me along to do the shopping. Everything had to be fresh: vegetables, eggs, chicken, pork, fish, duck, fruit. When Mahmah was free, she took me across a bridge to the International Park reserved for foreigners. She felt happy because she could enjoy the park even though she was Chinese. Our attachment to each other grew strong. I can still picture her round chubby face with rosy cheeks and her cheery smile.

I spent a lot of time with Mahmah because my aunt refused to let me go to Chinese school. My aunt went on many outings and trips, but she always left me home. I also got close to Hu Sang, the only daughter of the master of the house. Hu Sang and I were the same age, and we spent hours together after she returned from school. She taught me the Shanghai language, how to knit and how to do embroidery.

The daughters of the wealthy in China didn't do housework. They went to school and did needlework. In Shanghai I had a taste of how the wealthy lived. Hu Sang was well-behaved and gentle. I learned the best of manners at the dinner table from her mother, the mistress of the household, who managed the workers like a grand lady.

During my stay I had a severe throat infection. I couldn't swallow anything, not even water. After I stayed in bed a few days, Mahmah asked the mistress to send for the doctor. After he examined me, the doctor scolded my aunt: "You should have sent for me sooner. Her throat has swollen shut, and she could have died." He gave me some terrible-tasting medicine I had to force down several times a day. When my throat was better a few days later, I was starving. I asked my aunt for food, so she boiled two eggs for me. No boiled eggs have ever tasted better than those two eggs. I left the dish with the eggshells on the bedstand. When my aunt saw it later, she scolded me for not taking the dish down to the kitchen. Weak as I was, I got out of bed to take it down to the kitchen, then went back to bed.

While I lay sick in bed, she never checked on me. She kept going out to play mah-jongg and to visit with relatives and friends. If I had died, I wonder how she would have faced my parents about my death. My parents had trusted her to take care of me. That's why they allowed me to go with her. She was responsible for my life and health.

*Those entrusted with the care of a child should take that responsibility seriously, not only for the sake of the child and the parents, but also for the sake of God. It is God Himself who entrusts a person with that care. Persons entrusted with that responsibility will answer to Him for any mistreatment or negligence on their part.*

Secretly my aunt Ah Gnan made plans to live in Shanghai permanently. She told me Shanghai was our permanent home, so I thought I would never return to Hawaii or see my parents and brothers and sister again. But my father worried about the fighting in China and about my schooling, so he wrote Ah Gnan to tell her he was sending his mother, Popo (grandma in Chinese) and his sister Ah Kam to bring me back to Honolulu. My father borrowed the money from several persons for the steerage fares, for our traveling and living expenses and for gifts to relatives in China. When their ship docked in Shanghai, Popo and Ah Kam came to fetch me. I ran to greet Popo when she came for me. Mahmah cried as she said good-bye to me. I cared for Mahmah, too; she was kind and loving to me. Looking back, I was grateful to my father for sending his mother, Popo, to bring me back to Hawaii to my family.

## Sin Kwat

Because of the fighting in China, Ah Gnan decided to return with us to Hawaii. Popo, my two aunts and I spent the night in a hotel. The next morning we boarded a ship bound for Hong Kong. After we visited there for a few days, Ah Kam returned to Hawaii.

Popo, Ah Gnan and I boarded a junk bound for Canton. Popo wanted to visit her relatives in the Pusan area of Kwangtung Province. She also wanted to introduce me to my mother's family in a nearby village in the same province.

From Canton we traveled to Popo's village by rickshaw. I rode with Popo in one and Ah Gnan rode in another. The men pulling the rickshaws jogged until they were tired and then walked, and then jogged again. We stopped at several rest areas along the road, where people were selling things. At one rest stop Popo treated us to hot tea; at another she bought me some candy.

We finally arrived at Popo's village, where she visited many of our relatives. She gave them gifts of money and fancy fabric. Popo learned that there was a medium in that village who could predict the future and "read" people. Popo went to the medium's home to ask her about the future of her son (my father). When we walked into her parlor, the medium stared at me and told my grandmother and aunt that I had *sin kwat*, saintly bones. I heard it, but I didn't understand what she meant. Many years passed before I understood the meaning of my having *sin kwat*.

[Sin kwat, *saintly bones, can have two Chinese meanings: that the spirit of a saint has been reincarnated in the form of this person; or that this person is saintly herself.*]

While I was living in that village, an infection swelled my throat shut again. I almost died. The herbal doctor made up a remedy. Several times a day he forced down my throat some thick black muck that tasted terrible and looked like Chinese ink. The remedy worked. But the worst was yet to come, because of the flies and mosquitoes, both my legs were covered with open sores. My aunt refused to take me to the clinic in the next village, so I walked alone on footpaths through and around rice paddies to that village. At the clinic, a lady held me down while the doctor scraped the sores with a straightedge razor. I screamed while he was scraping the sores on each leg. Then he put some ointment on the sores and bandaged each leg tightly. Slowly I limped back to our village. For five days I walked alone to and from the clinic to have the bandages changed. Only then were my legs healed.

On one of my trips I saw a man in dirty, torn clothes with his left arm bandaged. He stared at me from across a rice paddy. I felt scared until I saw that he limped. Many years after my return to Hawaii, when I told my father-in-law about that man, he told me that man might have been a leper from a nearby leper camp. Sometimes lepers kidnapped girls and took them to their camp to keep as slaves to abuse them as they wished. Once again, God protected me.

After my legs healed, Popo took me to see her family's orchard. Her brother rowed us across a river to the orchard with peaches, nectarines, lychee and *lung gnan* (dragon eye fruit). The trees were low. Kau Kung, my great uncle, picked a ripe peach for me – it was sweet.

7

A little later he picked a *tau jai* (a green-colored nectarine) for me – it was crunchy and delicious.

A few days later we went to the property my father owned. I spent several days with the relative who watched over the property. She kept a pig named *Gam Lin* (Gold Necklace). *Gam Lin* was smart. She came when called and was clean. She followed me around because I petted her and slipped food to her from my meals. Ever since then I have been fond of pigs. People have told me pigs are smarter than dogs and will keep clean if given a clean pen.

A poor couple with eight children lived in a shack on the property to farm the land. They grew mainly sweet potatoes. The older children slept outside during the summer because the shack was small and hot. Their main meals were rice gruel with pieces of sweet potato in it.

One day one of the girls plucked some sweet potato vine to eat and to have me try it. It tasted like raw spinach. Later when I told my grandmother and aunt about it, they scolded me. "You shouldn't have eaten the vine; you weren't starving." Maybe they thought I had disgraced them, or maybe they knew about the human manure used for fertilizer, but they never explained why they were so angry at me.

*God used my experience with that poor family to teach me respect and love for the poor and needy. That's where I learned compassion and understanding for the poor. From then on I never looked down on people, no matter how poor or how badly they lived. Being poor is not a sin or something shameful.* I've found that most of the poor I've met are sincere people who express sincere appreciation and gratitude for the little I gave them or did for them.

In Pusan a beggar came to our door one afternoon asking for food. Ah Gnan sent me to give him the spoiled, soured rice. He thanked me politely and with a bow. I felt terrible giving him the soured rice. From that moment on I resolved never to give anyone anything that I myself would not eat or use. Weeks later, I saw that same beggar lying dead next to the wall of the gateway leading to the Buddhist temple. He lay dead in the same spot where he used to sit and beg every day.

*We should give due respect to the homeless and to beggars. Every person has human dignity. Everyone is a child of God. What we do to any person, we do to God himself. If we can't give something material, at least give respect and a prayer. Then a  sincere "God, please bless this person" is worth more than a dollar.* Those who don't believe in

God or who don't belong to any religion should nevertheless practice the Golden Rule. Show respect to others as you want others to show respect to you. Treat others as you want to be treated by others.

Popo took me to visit my mother's family in a nearby village. When my mother's sisters saw me, they said I reminded them of my mother. My uncles and aunts treated me with real kindness. There I received the usual gifts given to girls: jewelry of 24-karat gold and jade. I gave them to my mother when I returned to Honolulu.

One of my most humiliating experiences happened in that village. I was constipated. To help me, Popo put a potty in the middle of the room for me. I tried and tried, but I couldn't. Only a bit of the stool stuck out, but it wouldn't come out. They brought me hot tea, but it didn't help. Popo was worried. Neighbors and relatives came by to offer sympathy and suggestions. Everyone saw me sitting on the potty, but no one laughed at me. They felt sorry for me and were trying to think of ways to help.

Word got around the village, and others came by to see the girl from Hawaii sitting on the potty. A few of the people smiled or giggled. All the people looking at me bothered me and made it worse. It seemed as though I sat on that potty for hours. It hurt, and I didn't know what to do. Finally, with more and more hot tea, I did it. *God used that incident, one of the most embarrassing of my life, to teach me my first lesson in humility. Although I felt shame and embarrassment at first, I gradually accepted the simple truth of the situation. It wasn't my fault and there was nothing I could do. Humility begins with the quiet acceptance of the truth in humiliating situations. God taught me to be myself in any situation.* Looking back at that incident, I don't blame the people for giggling at me. It *was* a funny sight.


## My Return to Hawaii

In Hong Kong we boarded a ship bound for Hawaii, and went below to steerage class. We stayed in a hall with triple bunks on each side of the aisle. Popo took the lower bunk, Ah Gnan the middle one and I took the top one. A violent storm of three days made everyone in steerage seasick except me. Many vomited. I was the only one to show up at the long table for meals below in steerage. Ah Gnan sent me up to the kitchen for a pail of hot water so she and Popo could wash up. On the deck I felt the strong wind and saw the big black waves. I got wet from the waves splashing on the deck. When the manager of the dining room saw me carrying the pail of hot water below, he followed me down to scold my aunt.

"What's the matter with you? Don't you know the waves could have washed that girl overboard? If anything happens to her, we won't be responsible. We'll hold *you* responsible."

His words frightened my grandmother and aunt. I never went on deck again during the storm.

The seasick people in steerage did not eat during the three-day storm. After the storm they were starving. The usual amount of food served at meals wasn't enough. Ah Gnan got hungry about 8:00 in the evening, so she sent me to the kitchen to ask for extra food. The kitchen workers liked me, but they gave me enough only for myself. So Ah Gnan sent me back to steal some salted duck eggs. The kitchen boiled dozens of them and then stored them in a large barrel. While chatting with the workers, I faced them with the barrel of duck eggs behind me. I took an egg behind my back and slipped it into my pocket until I had two in each pocket. One or two workers may have seen me doing it, but they didn't stop me. Once again, I did as I was told.

Our ship was getting close to Hawaii. My long separation from my family was ending. God had reasons for allowing my five-year separation from my family from the age of five to ten, when I was staying with my aunt Ah Gnan. I think He used that separation as the first step in preparing me for future separations.

We arrived in Honolulu on December 14, 1924. Popo and Ah Gnan lived with my family in a two-bedroom cottage on Liliha Street. I was like a stranger to my family. My father could speak pidgin English, but my mother spoke only Chinese. We children spoke to them in Chinese. Since I had forgotten most of my English, I sat with my younger sister through the second half of the fourth grade at Royal School to relearn my English. The only clothes I had were from China. Some of the students teased me about my clothes and pulled my pigtails.

Because my mother used to make me run errands for her before I went to school, I was often late. My mother couldn't write a note in English for me, so I had to go to the office without an excuse. I hated doing that. One morning Mother asked me to iron my father's shirt. I knew if I did the ironing I would be late for school again. I refused to do it because I was afraid of being sent to the office without a note. I wished she had asked me to do it the evening before, or after school.

With a bamboo switch, Mother whipped my upper legs black and blue. She made sure to beat me where it wouldn't show. At school that day, my teacher noticed the black-and-blue marks when the wind blew my dress up during recess. She called in a social worker to show her the marks.

The social worker asked me, "Who did this to you?"

"My mother."

"Why did she beat you?"

"I didn't want to iron my father's shirt because I was afraid to go to the office for being late. So she beat me."

The social worker drove me home to speak to Mother. Mother looked guilty and frightened as my aunt translated the message: "If you beat this child again, I will take you to court for child abuse." Mother never hit me with the bamboo switch again. My grandmother told her, "Be careful how you treat *Sau Kin;* she has *sin kwat*, saintly bones." (*Sau Kin* is my Chinese name.)

As I look back now, I realize that my mother had many frustrations with my father. He had to close his restaurant in Wahiawa because of mismanagement. He never had a job after that and became a professional gambler. When he won, he bought groceries and sometimes treats for us. When he lost, we had little to eat because he didn't have enough money for groceries.

My mother and I were never close because of our separation for five years. Mother made me run all the errands and favored my sister. I've always loved my mother, and I helped her in many ways until she died in my arms. God trained me from childhood to accept everything that would happen in my life. *I remind all parents to check themselves on favoring one child unfairly. Parents should treat each child fairly and deal with each one individually according to the needs of each child.*

My trip to China deepened my appreciation for my Chinese culture and deepened my love for my Chinese people. God used my experiences there to prepare me for my future hardships.

*We all have a humble beginning. We are born naked and completely helpless. People should remember their humble beginnings and never treat others cruelly or harshly.*

# 2

# SCHOOL OF SUFFERING

M y life has taught me many lessons. I just live in the present from moment to moment. As I was writing this book, I realized that only with help and strength from God was I able to endure all I went through without turning hateful or bitter. God helped me to keep a forgiving and loving heart. Looking back on my life, I know I was not crazy or stupid to put up with all the mistreatment. Some may think I was foolish for doing so, but my past is part of God's plan for me. He permitted all my past experiences to bring out important lessons to share with those seeking to learn the art of living for God and with God. *My deep suffering of the past also taught me understanding and compassion so I could help others.*

When we moved to an apartment on School Street, which was across the Buddhist temple, I attended the sixth grade at Lanakila School. Mother had sewn some dresses for me by hand, and I no longer had pigtails. My aunt Ah Kam gave me the name "Florence" so I didn't have to use my Chinese name *Sau Kin* at school. I relearned my English and began to enjoy my classes. When Ah Kam saw how I was growing, she told my mother, "Sau Kin should not marry because she has *sin kwat*." She said this because the Chinese expected persons with *sin kwat* to become Buddhist monks or nuns, or remain single.

While attending Mung Lung, a Chinese-language school with late-afternoon classes, I became friends with Jean Liu, Pina Tam and Helsin Lee. They were from wealthy families, and yet they accepted me. Whenever one of them had some candy or snack to share, I received an equal share. They knew I was poor, so they never expected me to have anything to share with them.

A Chinese man who started his own Chinese school wanted me to go to his school. He tried to get my sister and me as his students by trying to persuade my mother to transfer us to his school by offering her a discount. I told Mother I didn't want to go to his school. I wanted to stay at Mung Lung School because it was an old school with high standards. I knew that a new school would not have good standards. I also didn't want to end my friendship with Jean, Helsin and Pina because they were my only friends. Mother never discussed the matter with me, and I was afraid she would transfer me, so I rebelled by rounding up my playmates in the neighborhood. I became the leader of that group of Chinese, Hawaiian and Japanese kids.

That Chinese man lived in a duplex nearby. When he was home one Saturday, each of us kids picked up several small stones. We all threw stones at his front door several times. Not satisfied with that, I found a long pole for ramming his front door. I led the pack by being at the front of the pole. We rammed his front door several times. The loud banging frightened him so much that he was afraid to open the door. He peeped out his window and saw me at the front of the pole before we ran away.

That evening he told my mother that I was the leader of the kids. Mother waited up for Father to come home from gambling. He came home after 3:00 in the morning, in a bad mood because of his losses. Mother told him what I had done and insisted that he punish me right away.

I was sleeping with my younger brother on a child's bed. My father yanked me out of bed and began beating me with a split-bamboo switch. I was terrified because I didn't know what was happening. I cried out because of the pain. Something told me to scream as loud as I could so the neighbors would hear me. When Father heard how loud I was screaming, he stopped.

*In most cases, parents should talk things over with their children, such as a change of school. Sometimes children can have important reasons for not wanting to change schools.*

*Parents should punish in the right way, at the proper time and tell the child why she is being punished. Mothers and fathers should never take out their frustrations on innocent children as though they were punching bags.*

## My Father's Death

In 1926 when I was 11, Father got sick. I was in the sixth grade at Lanakila School. The day before he died he asked Mother to keep me home from school to tend to him. The next morning while my sister and brothers were at school, Mother locked me in Father's bedroom before leaving for the Buddhist temple to pray for his recovery. Later that morning I helped Father to the bathroom next to his room. On the way back to his bed he collapsed. He lay on the floor unconscious and gasping for air. I dragged him to his bed. Somehow I managed to lift him onto the bed. I wiped the foam oozing from his mouth. Then he stopped gasping. The bedside clock read 10:28.

I ran to the door. It was locked. I pounded on the door and screamed for Mother. No answer. No one was home. I sat on the floor next to the door and cried and cried. With the dark green shade pulled over the only window, the room was dark. For two hours, terrified and crying, I just sat there on the floor of the dark room with the dead body.

Finally Mother returned and unlocked the door. What she saw sent her into shock, then hysteria. My grandmother sent me to the corner store to telephone our relatives. Mother told me to wash the rice, put it on the stove and then cut up the *lap cheung* (Chinese sausage) for steaming. Still in shock, I cut my finger. Ah Kam bandaged my finger and finished cutting the sausage.

Looking back, I don't know how I managed to drag my father back to his bed and then lift him onto it. I was only 11 and petite, and he was a big heavy man. God must have given me the strength to do it.

God must have also guided me to look at the clock when my father stopped breathing, because I didn't know the doctor had to write down the time of death. When I was asked when he died, I gave the exact time, 10:28 in the morning. God gives us extra strength in times of emergencies. God guides and helps even young children in desperate situations.

After Father's death, Mother just lay in bed grieving. She had me take over all her duties: the cooking, cleaning, laundry and care of my younger sister and brothers. My two aunts didn't help out at all. My mother lay in bed with regrets about how she had treated my father (such as not ironing his white shirts when he asked her to) and with worries because he left us poor. I did everything Mother told me to do without complaining. I obeyed her without any bad thoughts or feelings. God had trained me in obedience early on, from age five. God needed an obedient soul for a saint to take over later.

Several weeks after Father's death, Popo wanted to contact his spirit. She took my mother, my aunt Ah Gnan and me to a medium on River Street. First this Chinese lady went into a trance. Then my father spoke in Chinese through the medium: "I feel sorry for my oldest daughter; she was alone with me when I died." His words made me relive the whole scary event.

I finished the sixth grade at Lanakila School in a state of shock and depression. Words from the teacher had no meaning; words in books had no meaning. I had a blank mind. After that school year, I never returned to school again. If my teacher noticed the change in me, she did nothing about it. There were no school counselors those days. I give God complete credit for pulling me through my deep state of shock. It took me a long time to get over being locked in a room with my father as he died and with his dead body. God allowed nature to take its course and to heal me with the passing of time.

My father's death left us poor. When we moved to a cheap tenement row, Ah Gnan and Popo moved into an apartment. Mother realized she couldn't care for all five children. She decided to keep the three youngest. Ah Gnan took in Albert, the oldest, for security and running errands. Since I was the second oldest, Mother wanted to send me to a home run by the Salvation Army. I was packed and waiting for someone to come for me, when Ah Kam, my older aunt, decided to help me. She and her husband offered to take me in. They were willing to let me stay with them in their home at Fort and Kuakini streets.

While I stayed with Ah Kam, I earned my keep by doing the yard-work, the dishes, the cleaning and all the errands. Yet Ah Kam wouldn't let me sleep on a bed because she didn't want to wash an-other set of sheets. She made me sleep under the bed with my head sticking out the side, because she didn't want her husband to see me in case my nightgown shifted up to my waist. It seems my aunt didn't trust her husband, even though I knew my kind uncle would never do anything to hurt me. My uncle always left me a quarter on the table for my school lunch and for milk at recess. But my aunt always took the quarter and replaced it with 15 cents. I never told him what she did.

Ah Kam took me on walks after supper to look for pretty roses in other yards. When she saw roses she liked, she woke me at 4:00 in the morning to steal cuttings. She turned the clock in my room two hours ahead to read 6:00. I heard my uncle ask, "Why are you waking Sau Kin so early? It's only four o'clock." I realized my aunt had turned my clock ahead. Within six months I planted a complete rose garden. One morning before sunrise, she made me climb out the bathroom window on the second floor onto the neighbor's avocado tree to steal some for her. If I had fallen, I could have been seriously hurt.

Twice a week my aunt sent me to an herbal store several miles away to buy medicine for my uncle. On one trip, a man under a bridge exposed himself to me and called out to me. He scared me. I ran home but said nothing to my aunt. I relived that scary experience every time I went past that bridge. On another errand, as a Portuguese man walked past me, he hooked me between my legs with his middle finger and really hurt me. He tore my virginity. I ran home but again said nothing to my aunt. I was too ashamed to tell her, and I wouldn't have known how to tell her.

## First Job

I got my first job when I was 15 in the summer of 1930. I tried to look older in borrowed high heels, and lied about being 16. I received 15 cents an hour for summer work at the Honolulu Fruit Company. I loaded empty tin cans into trays on flatbed rail cars for the company's cannery. It was a long walk to work along a dusty road later named

Dillingham Boulevard. The manager who hired me and gave me the light job of loading empty cans later said he knew I wasn't 16, the minimum age for working. But he had known my father and felt sorry for me. I was grateful to him. Except for the 5 cents I spent on lunch every day, I gave Mother all the money I earned that summer. After working at the cannery every day, I walked to my mother's place for supper. Some days I had no supper, because Mother soaked the *fan chiu* (the half-burnt crust of rice at the bottom of the pot) in water. Rice soaked in water wasn't fit for eating.

When my summer job at the cannery ended, I was eager to return to school. I wanted to be a nurse to help people. When I was sent to bring some food to Popo and Ah Gnan, I told them I wanted to return to school. Ah Gnan didn't want me to go to school. She said I should work to help my mother support the family. I told her I wanted to return to school so I could become a nurse. As we argued about my going back to school, she got so angry that she chased me with a big Chinese cleaver. I outran her and told her, "You watch out; there's a big eye in the sky looking at you." I meant that God in heaven sees everything that happens and punishes every wrongdoing. As a Buddhist, I believed that God sees everything and is a just God. I never returned to school. I went from restaurant to restaurant looking for a job, but I couldn't get one. Maybe I wasn't hired because I was too young.

## My Popo

One day Popo asked me to hem her dress by hand because her eyesight was bad. I hurried so I could go out to play. I hemmed her dress with wide stitches and rushed outside. A few minutes later my aunt called me in to scold me. "You shouldn't do that to Popo just because she can't see well. You take it apart and do it all over again. This time you do it right." I felt ashamed and guilty for what I did to Popo, who truly loved me. She named me Sau Kin after her own mother. When she stayed with us before my father died, she used to comb and braid my hair every morning. Feeling her soft hands on my head and hair was very comforting. *Ever since I redid the hem of her dress, I have tried to do a perfect job on everything even if no one sees it. Now I know God is present everywhere and sees everything.*

Popo had a heart attack and was taken to the hospital. I wanted to visit her that evening with my aunts, but Ah Gnan made me baby-sit her adopted baby at home. Alone with the baby, I sat on the living room floor, too frightened to even go to the bathroom. Popo clung to life in the hospital and kept calling for her son, who lived on Kauai. She refused to die until he arrived by ship. She died shortly after he entered her hospital room.

Popo's death hurt me deeply. I blamed the *pu sat* (gods) for her death. I was so hurt that I went to the Buddhist temple on School Street. Crying and standing on the sidewalk, I yelled into the entrance of the temple, "Why did you let Popo die? I'll never go in your temple again." I never did. Whenever I walked past it, I wouldn't even look in.

Of all the people in my childhood, Popo loved me most. She loved and cared for me more than my mother did. I recalled how Popo combed my hair every morning with great care. She took me to the dry-goods store on Nuuanu Street to see whether any new ribbons had come in. Whenever ribbons of new colors came in, she bought some for my hair.

Popo shared her wisdom with her two daughters and my mother. Sixty-some years later I still remember some of her expressions. *Do sum* means a heart full of many desires: "Don't have a heart full of many desires, because then you'll never be happy." *Gang ago* means set in one's ways or refusing to improve. *Mao im juk* means never satisfied; such persons are never happy. *Hao sum* means having a good heart that does good to others. *Chi sum* means having a compassionate heart. *Sun sum* means a religious heart. Every person should have *hao sum, chi sum, sun sum* (a good heart, a compassionate heart, a religious heart). Popo never forgot what the medium in China said about me: "She has *sin kwat* (saintly bones)." Popo even reminded her daughters and my mother about that.

After Popo died, her two daughters, Ah Kam and Ah Gnan, sold their homes and left for China together. Ah Kam left her husband and went with her. Ah Kam's husband moved to a rooming house, and I moved back in with Mother. My mother didn't recognize me. She said my eyes had changed from black to brown, and I smelled of fresh blood as if it were seeping through my pores. Her words frightened me. She made a mixture of juices from raw watercress and from boiled *hung jao* (dried red dates) for me to drink as a remedy.

Mother tried to support us by boiling peanuts and selling them door to door. We were evicted from Hall Street and had to move into a single tenement room in the slums on River Street. The rent for the single room with a partition was $8 a month. All the tenants used the common toilet and common kitchen. Behind the partition Mother slept on a blanket over the bare bed springs because the mattress Father died on had been thrown out. My eldest brother, Albert, lived on his own in a rooming house. My two youngest brothers, Edward and Harry, my younger sister, Gertrude, and I slept on the floor on the other side of the partition.

Late the first night, a strange sound woke the four of us. The rocking chair was rocking, but no one was on it. The rocker rocked harder and harder, faster and faster. Then we saw the head of a ghost floating over the rocker. We screamed and ran behind the partition to huddle together with Mother.

"There's a ghost! There's a ghost on the rocker!"

We stayed awake all night huddled together.

The next night the same thing happened: The rocker began rocking and woke us. Then it rocked harder and harder, faster and faster. Finally we saw that head floating over the rocker. Again we ran screaming to Mother and huddled together, and she comforted us.

When it happened the third night, that was it. The next morning we told Mother we were not spending another night in that place. She refused to move out because she had already paid the $8 for the month's rent. So Albert helped me move out with my sister and brothers to a small apartment he paid for. We took along the little clothing we had.

## Hunger

Albert, 17, worked part time as a dishwasher in a restaurant, mainly for the meals and the leftover food he sometimes brought home for us. He had enough money saved for a month's rent, so he rented a one-bedroom apartment for us in a fourplex on Vineyard Street. We had no beds, no furniture, no towels, and no money. The first week there I bought a pot and some rice, eggs, bread and milk on credit at the corner store by telling the owner that my mother had sent me to get those things for her. When I couldn't pay the bill at the end of the week, I couldn't charge food anymore. Every day we waited for Albert to return from work with food for us. Some days he had none. Many nights we were too hungry to fall asleep. During the day we didn't have the energy to play. We just sat around or slept, as the days passed.

On several mornings we stole milk from different neighbors right after the early milk delivery. We stopped when those neighbors got suspicious of us. Once we were so hungry that my sister and I stole some sausage from a neighbor's icebox at two in the morning. He drove a lunch wagon that sold *bento* (hot plate lunches), and he kept food in that icebox on his porch. The next day he knew we had stolen his sausage, because the neighbors told him the smell of sausage frying came from our apartment. Albert scolded us for stealing, but we were desperate and the icebox on the porch was too tempting.

*A person must starve before knowing what starving people feel. I understand and sympathize with the poor and the starving.* I also learned about being careful not to place temptations before others.

A young newspaper reporter heard about four children living in a bare apartment without an adult, and how they charged food without paying, and then stole food. Her newspaper printed a story about us and about mother, a young widow selling boiled peanuts from door to door to support her four children. Despite the sympathetic response, the landlord evicted us children at the end of the month because we didn't have the next month's rent. But Mother found an apartment on Kukui Street so we could move in with her. No ghost there. Mother received no help from Father's brother and two sisters. One by one she sold the gold and jade jewelry she had brought with her from China as a bride. To keep paying rent and buying food, she then sold the gold and jade jewelry I had received from her relatives in China.

Mother never forgave Father's two sisters, Ah Kam and Ah Gnan, for not paying back a loan. When our Chinese restaurant in Wahiawa was doing well, Popo talked Father into lending each sister $4,000 so each could buy a home in Honolulu. Eight thousand dollars was a lot of money in the 1920s. But they never repaid a penny when we were trying to survive. Even when both sisters sold their homes several years after his death, they never repaid a penny of that loan to Mother.

Even with Mother, there were days when we children didn't have enough to eat. I recall how several times Mother made a large bowl of wide Chinese noodles, prayed over it, then left it on the table for a few

21

hours as an offering to the Buddhist gods. Four hungry children stared at the bowl of noodles often but never touched it. Then we watched Mother as she ate the whole bowl.

My mother favored my sister over me because of my being away for 5 years and because my grandma and aunt favored me. I never tattled, as my sister did. She told my mother everything she saw and heard about Popo and my aunts. So Mother took out all her frustrations on me. She made me do all the chores and run all the errands. Once Mother got so angry at me that she chased me with a kettle of hot water to scald me. I outran her and said, "When you die, I won't go to your funeral." My words came true.

The following incidents made me realize how unsafe I felt in my world:

One of the boys in the neighborhood called my sister and me "thieves," "crooks" and "bitches." My sister called him even worse names. The next afternoon he hid in an alley waiting for us. As we walked by he jumped out and punched me. I went to a policeman to report him. In court I told the judge what had happened. The judge told me, "Young lady, you should be a lawyer." He put the boy on probation and told him, "If you hurt either one of them, I'll put you in jail. You understand?"

Mr. C, who owned a restaurant in Wahiawa, told mother he might hire my sister and me to work in his restaurant. He drove us to his restaurant and showed us what to do. On the way back he sat me next to him and put his right hand on my thigh under my dress. I felt very uneasy. Then he told us he would be hiring only me. He said he would pick me up the next evening at 6:30. I told my sister I wasn't going to work for him. Instead of waiting for him on the corner, I hid behind a hedge with my sister. He stopped by and waited for about 15 minutes. My sister and I giggled behind the bushes and burst into laughter as he left.

There were cases of child molestation and rape in the 1930s as there are now. But God protected me from Mr. C. I was afraid of him even though Mrs. C, his wife, was my teacher when I returned from China. She liked me as her student. She suffered from her unfaithful husband and died of tuberculosis. Perhaps her soul saved me from her husband by making me afraid of him.

Ah Kee, with a reputation for selling drugs, was a relative on my mother's side. His father owned a restaurant near the train depot. Mother wanted me to marry him for the security it would bring her. So she encouraged me to be friendly with him. Mother thought he would marry me. Ah Kee rented a one-bedroom apartment near his own apartment for my sister and me, because our family was crowded into a small rental place. Then he gave me a jade ring and held an engagement party. I didn't even know the ring was an engagement ring and the party was for our engagement. I didn't know I was supposed to marry him.

One evening he asked to see me at his place. He drugged me with something he had put in the soda he gave me. As he was trying to rape me, I woke up and ran out, wearing only my petticoat and yelling for my mother. The police came and arrested him. I never saw him again, and Mother never mentioned him again. God had protected me from Ah Kee.

I finally found a job working weekends at a beach stand on Waikiki near the Moana Hotel. We sold hot dogs, sandwiches and soft drinks. The owner was kind to let me eat hot dogs or sandwiches before going home at closing time. Some were regulars like Duke Kahanamoku and his younger brothers, Sam and Dave. These and other regulars like Joe Hana and Joe Minor could charge what they wanted. Though respectful and kind, they never tipped. Instead they gave me the bottle caps from Coca-Cola. Under the cork of some caps was a number: 5, 10 or 25, meaning I won a nickel, dime or quarter. I dug out the corks at the end of work every weekend.

I then went to work at the Central Cafe, where my uncle was part owner, to ask for a job. Their cashier had just quit, so I was hired as cashier. My math was weak. I used my fingers and toes to count secretly, but I managed and learned. Although I had never typed before, each morning I typed out the menu by 11:00. The Central Cafe was large and had many customers. The owners always paid me on time.

## My Future Husband

My sister was a year younger than me but looked older than me. She became a taxi dancer. Men paid 10 cents a ticket to dance with the girl of their choice. Dolly K, a taxi dancer with my sister, told me I should be a taxi dancer, too. She showed me a ring and a wristwatch men had given her for "favors." I wasn't interested. Even then my world was not of this world. My sister knew me well and never asked me to join her as a taxi dancer.

One Sunday afternoon Dolly K, my sister and I took the streetcar to the zoo at Waikiki. After visiting the zoo, we sat on the grass to rest and talk. Thomas Lum and Henry Ho drove by and circled the block several times before tooting the horn at us. Dolly and my sister waved at them to get a ride. Thomas stopped and offered us a ride. He sat me in front beside him, while the others sat in the back. Later I found out that Thomas had bet his fellow workers $5 he could get me to go to bed with him. Some of them thought I was pretty and called me the "calendar girl." Thomas, my future husband, saw me working at the Empire Grill and then at the Central Cafe. He began walking me home after work every night. One night he told me that after walking me home the night before he had bought himself a new kind of ice cream in a large size.

"You ate the whole thing by yourself?"

"Yep."

That was a sign of his selfishness that I missed at that time.

Thomas graduated from St. Louis College, now St. Louis High School. He was a Catholic but he never went to church. His father was the foreman at City Mill. He gave Thomas an office job that included using the company car to collect rent from the tenants of housing owned by City Mill. Thomas knew my family was poor, so he tried to help. One evening he stole some vegetables for us from the garden of McKinley High School. At my suggestion, he bought a mattress for Mother, who was sleeping on a blanket over bare bed springs.

Thomas impressed my mother with his soft-spoken, well-mannered ways. She told me to hold hands with him in public. Her main concern was that I marry a Chinese. My sister had been going out with Filipino men. In those days, many Chinese daughters who married non-Chinese were disowned by their families.

Mr. Wedemeyer saw me working at the Central Cafe, how I treated people, and how they respected me. He was the manager of the dining rooms at the Submarine Base at Pearl Harbor.

"Florence, do you want a job as a waitress at the Sub Base? The pay there is better, you'll get three meals a day and you'll like working in the officers' dining room. I can give you a ride to work every morning, but you'll have to take the bus home. I'll even give you a monthly bus pass. Would you like to see the place?"

"Sure."

"Where do you live?"

"On Hall Street."

"I'll pick you up early tomorrow morning at 7:00 at Hall and Beretania to show you the place."

"Okay."

He drove me to the Sub Base and gave me a tour of the kitchen, the pantry, the officers' dining room, the dining room for petty officers and the counter for the sailors. The pay for serving in the officers' dining room was $45 a month. He gave me a pass for Pearl Harbor and for the Post Exchange. For meals and desserts I could order anything I wanted. The well-decorated dining room, benefits and officers impressed me. I would wait only on the officers in their dining room. So I accepted the job. It was such a blessing to have good, warm meals every day.

Captain Berry, who later became a commander, was in charge of the officers' dining room. He taught me etiquette and instructed me in the proper way of setting tables and serving officers. I learned all the insignia of rank because I had to greet and address each officer by rank.

While going with Thomas, I was loyal to him. Henry C, a true gentleman, was fond of me, too. He had been a schoolmate of Thomas, and was a practicing Catholic. His wealthy family owned a beautiful home on a large property near Koko Head. After showing me that home which his parents had given him, he gave me a large diamond ring. I accepted it with gratitude. But when he said it was an engagement ring, I gave it back. I told him I couldn't accept it because I was going with Thomas.

Henry was brokenhearted. He later married, but his marriage ended in divorce. He and his brother inherited and managed the New York Shoe Store. We remained friends through the years. If I had married Henry C and become a member of his wealthy family, my entire life would have been different. But God had other plans for me. I learned little from school and from books. God gave me wisdom and compassion through suffering.

While I was going with Thomas, his mother came to talk to my mother. She told her to stop me from going with Thomas because I wasn't good enough for him, and they already had a girl from a wealthy family for him to marry. My sister listened from the bedroom and got so angry that she entered the parlor with a broom. She whacked Thomas' mother on the behind and chased her to her car.

"Don't ever come back here again!"

Mother tried to stop my sister from chasing her with a broom because of a Chinese superstition: *You use a broom to sweep the floor and to chase away only devils.* Looking back now, my sister was right.

When I returned from work, Mother told me everything. Then she told me all about the background of Thomas' parents. When his parents were children in China, they were sold as slaves to the same wealthy family. That's how they met, married and then ran off together. They had to get away from China, so they escaped to Hawaii as illegal immigrants with forged papers. Those illegal immigrants were known in Chinese as "1,350," the price in dollars for being given fake documents and smuggled into Hawaii illegally. On the island of Kauai, Thomas' father worked in a rice paddy, and then he moved to Honolulu.

Thomas' parents had no children of their own. They adopted three sons: Thomas, Fred and Henry. Thomas was the son of a Chinese couple named Wong. Fred was the son of his father and his mistress, Ida. Henry was the son of a Japanese woman and his father. He met her in her barber shop, where she cut his hair. Her Japanese husband later divorced her. Before the divorce, once a week he brought Thomas' parents a dozen eggs for Henry.

After hearing about Thomas' parents, I wondered why they thought I wasn't good enough for their son. I later learned that while Thomas was going with me, he was also going out with Mildred J, Sarah C and other girls with the reputation of being "loose."

To make it easier for me to get a ride to the Sub Base, Thomas let me stay in a spare room near the apartment where he stayed with his parents. One morning his mother woke me up at 2:00 to question me after calling me a whore.

"Did you give birth to a boy? I heard you're hiding the boy on Kauai until after you're married to Thomas."

"Who told you that?"

"Your sister."

"No, that's not true. It was my sister who had a son from a married man. I paid the midwife who delivered the baby, and my sister gave the baby up for adoption."

Then Thomas' mother told me about her unfaithful husband, his mistress and about her problem with the law because she was caught selling opium in Honolulu and was almost deported. But her attorney won the case and kept her from being deported. They didn't have the $2,000 for the fine and his fee, but they promised to pay him $20 a month until the fine and his fee were paid. She asked me to help her pay off the fine and the attorney's fee. I felt sorry for her because of her husband's mistress and her legal problem, so I agreed to pay $20 a month to her attorney, Mr. Beebe.

## Unwed Motherhood

I didn't know anything about sex. Mother never instructed me on anything except cooking rice and steaming Chinese sausage or salted fish on top of the rice. I was truly innocent. One night Thomas took me to a hotel. He tried to have sex with me. I said "No" and resisted. But he did it to me anyway, saying, "If you loved me you would let me do it to you." Then he did it to me again. Later he did it to me again; and again, through the night. I was bleeding and hurting.

One Sunday months later, my mother stared at me and told me, "Ah Kin ( my Chinese nickname) you're pregnant. Did Thomas do something to you?"

"Yes, he did."

"You're going to have a baby."

I didn't even know I was pregnant. I was 18 years old. Mother didn't scold me. Instead, she felt sorry for me. She knew that Thomas would marry me, and she was glad about that.

I continued to work at the Sub Base until I went on maternity leave. Then Thomas lost his job at City Mill for embezzling money. He spent the money he collected from rentals instead of turning it in. I later found out he was a playboy and spent the money going out with "loose" girls. His parents kicked him out.

I asked him, "How much did you take? A hundred dollars?"

"Yeah."

27

I asked Mother to lend him the $100 she was holding for my brother so Thomas could repay the money he had taken. My brother had saved that money for his schooling. Mother worried about my brother's money, but she did lend him the $100.

Later I learned he had embezzled more than $2,000, but his parents didn't file charges against him. His parents blamed me for all the money he had spent. Actually, he had spent it on his car and on other girls. When Mother kept asking for the money back, I made sure that Thomas repaid the $100 to my brother.

Thomas made a down payment of $15 on a used car, for delivering newspapers. I rode with him to help out while I was on maternity leave. I took it like a game – as he stopped at each house, I got out and either threw the paper or dropped it on the walkway. While riding with Thomas in the car one day, I felt like vomiting because of morning sickness. I told him to stop the car so I could get out to vomit. He got angry and punched me on the thigh. He stopped the car with a jerk out of anger. I punched his leg back in anger because I couldn't help being sick. He stopped the car so I could get out to vomit.

When everybody could see I was pregnant, Albert, my older brother, said I had disgraced the family and to get out. My younger brother Edward began punching me in the stomach because I wouldn't be able to give him any more money while he finished high school. Mother told me to run and I did.

Thomas rented a room for us at the Kobayashi Hotel in downtown Honolulu. The Japanese couple who ran the hotel thought we were married. They felt sorry for us and let us stay without paying until Thomas could find a job. Then Thomas got a job as a garbage collector. While he was at work, Mother brought me rice and *lap cheung* once a day. Since that was the only meal I had all day, I was hungry most of the time. The only thing that eased my morning sickness was sipping orange soda.

As a teenager I didn't trust doctors. Once I went to a doctor who told me to return after office hours when we would be alone. I didn't return because I sensed something was wrong. Another time another doctor told me to come back in the afternoon when the nurse wouldn't be there. I didn't go back. So during my pregnancy I wanted a woman doctor, and I found Dr. Ellen Leong. She knew I wasn't married. She took good care of me and made arrangements for me at St. Francis

Hospital, because they gave a special rate of $15 a day for the poor.

I had a difficult delivery. My labor was long because the baby wouldn't drop down. Thomas never came to see me at the hospital. I gave birth to Thomas Jr. (Tommy) in January. After leaving the hospital, I cared for him in the hotel room. Two weeks after giving birth, I returned to the hospital with my baby because I had caught pneumonia in the unheated hotel. The common Japanese baths, one for men and one for women, were on the ground floor and my room was on the second floor. I waited until the bath was empty, because I was used to bathing alone. It took me a week to get well. From the hospital I returned to the hotel.

## The Devil's Instrument

Thomas' father was in China on government business as an official delegate. Embarrassed by the gossip about Thomas and the family, his mother went to see my mother out of concern for their reputation. To protect their reputation, Thomas' mother wanted Thomas, me and the baby to move in with them in a rental on Akepo Lane. So she went to my mother to ask where I was living.

"She's living at the Kobayashi Hotel."

"Tell your daughter to move in with us before my husband returns from China."

"All right."

Mother came and asked me to go with Thomas and the baby to his mother's place before her husband returned from China. I did it out of obedience to my mother. Thomas' mother came for me and the baby while Thomas was at work. She helped me to gather the few things I had and then drove the baby and me to her place. Thomas joined us after work.

Thomas' mother treated me like a slave, just as she had been treated in China. As soon as I moved in with her from the hotel, she told me to cook the rice and steam a fish. My mother had never taught me how to cook except to cook rice and to steam something on top of it. I didn't know I was supposed to remove the scales and guts before cooking the fish. I just put the fish on a plate in the pot with water to steam it. When the fish was done, my mother-in-law lifted the lid to check the fish. She screamed, "What happened to the fish?" All the scales on the fish had curled, and the whole fish had curled like a quarter moon. She took out the plate with the curled fish and hurried out to show the fish to all the neighbors shouting to them. She ridiculed me and humiliated me before all the neighbors.

I had trouble cooking on the Chinese wood stove because I couldn't control the fire and heat. Once I left the pot of rice on the stove too long. The flames not only burnt the rice, they burnt a hole in the pot. I didn't mind buying a new pot, but Thomas' mother had to show the burnt pot with the hole to all the neighbors to humiliate me again.

One day she told me she had lost her bracelet of 24-karat gold. While she was out playing dominoes, I looked all over the house for it. I finally found it in the top drawer on the right side of her sewing machine. I left it there without touching it. Excited and happy, I rushed to tell her when she returned, "I found your gold bracelet. It's in the top drawer of the right side of your sewing machine."

"Oh, good. Here, I'm giving it to you."

"No, you keep it."

"No, I want you to have it."

"Gee, thanks. Thank you. I'm so grateful to you."

I was happy, because up to then I hadn't had a single piece of jewelry. All the jewelry I had received in China was given to Mother, so she could sell it to pay the rent and buy us food. When I told my mother about the gold bracelet, she said Thomas' mother had put the bracelet in the drawer to test me. Mother was right. Months later she took back that gold bracelet while I was at work. I searched and searched, but never found it. When I asked her if she had seen it, she said no. I believed her and forgot about the bracelet.

When I returned to work at the Sub Base six weeks after giving birth, Commander Berry extended his hand to me.

"It's good to see you again, Florence. We missed you. Now I feel confident we'll be ready for our inspection every Friday."

Commander Berry gave me great respect. He told me that I was his best waitress with the best manners. Because I was so responsible in my work, he put me in charge of the other waitresses.

Thomas' mother and Ida, her husband's mistress, planned and gave a *luau* (Hawaiian feast) to celebrate little Tommy's first birthday, but Thomas and I paid for it. His mother and Ida invited all their friends and relatives. Since she always made me do the dishes and the

cleaning after meals and parties, I went to work that day to avoid doing all the cleanup after the luau. When I returned from work at 8:30
that evening, I wasn't offered any food, cake or ice cream. All the
guests gave a gift of money for Tommy, but Thomas' mother took all
the money for herself. I didn't argue with her over it.

While Thomas and I stayed at the hotel and in his parents' home, I
kept asking him, "When are you going to marry me?" He said "Soon"
or he wouldn't answer me. Even though everyone thought we were
married, I felt ashamed because I knew we weren't. Thomas finally
married me in a private ceremony before a minister 6 months after
Tommy's first birthday.

When my father-in-law returned from a trip to China, he brought
me a black Mandarin jacket full of embroidered red roses all over the
front, back and sleeves. (For the Chinese, red and black are colors of
celebration, and white is the color of mourning.) I wore that fancy
jacket for the formal custom of serving and pouring tea for my in-laws
the first time.

That beautiful jacket made me happy, but the meaning of that formal tea ceremony made me happier. I served my in-laws tea in that
ceremony to express my obedience and love for their acceptance of me
into their household. The obedience and love on my part were real and
sincere, but their acceptance of me was not. Months later I wanted to
look at my beautiful Mandarin jacket. It wasn't in my closet. I looked
all over for it but I couldn't find it. Finally I asked my mother-in-law,
"I can't find my Mandarin jacket. Do you know where it is?"

"No, I don't. I don't touch your things."

I asked Thomas if he knew where it was, but he said he didn't
know. I was puzzled, but I dropped the matter.

When I was in the ninth month of pregnancy with my second
child. My mother-in-law nagged her husband to kick me out. He
slapped a $10 bill on the table for me and told me to get out. My in-laws
waited until Thomas was at work before trying to throw me out. They
thought that Thomas would follow me if I returned to my mother.
Even if Mother could take me in, I wouldn't burden her. I was nine
months pregnant. Where would I go? How could I live on $10?

I blew up. "I won't go! I'm not leaving! You kick your son out!"

I sat on his rocker and blasted them both for an hour. I told them
how much I had helped them: the new gas stove and washing machine

I bought them, the food I bought, the cooking and cleaning I did, how their irresponsible son Thomas wasted his money on bars and on girls and never helped out with money or cleaning. They should kick *him* out. I told them how God in heaven sees everything and would punish them for their unjust ways and all the wrong they did. I told him how I gave his wife a dollar every day so she could buy him a fresh fish for dinner. He looked at his wife with shock. He could ask little Tommy about it, because I handed the dollar to Tommy to give her every morning before I left for work.

I reminded them that they had been slaves in China and were illegal immigrants. I was not born to be a slave. My father had owned a restaurant. My mother taught me embroidery and to be obedient and humble. My parents didn't sell me as a slave. If I had gone to the Salvation Army Home, they would have treated me like a human being, not like a slave. As former slaves, how could they look down on others and cut people down with words? They shouldn't mistreat the Filipino workers by charging them 25 percent interest each month on the money they borrowed. They should be fair with people and treat others with respect because they're no better than anyone else.

All my anger came out. My stern words were based on truth and justice. They thought they could make a slave out of me and then throw me out. No Chinese daughter-in-law would ever dare to bring out the truth about them and scold them for their unjust ways. No one had ever dared to speak to them like that. God gave me the special courage to stand up for truth and justice. They sat in total silence with their heads hanging in shame as I spoke. Then I went to my room. They never tried to kick me out again.

Looking back, I now realize my in-laws were criminals, because they were drug dealers. My father-in-law was smuggling opium from China on his yearly trip there, and my mother-in-law was selling it. My husband was also a criminal because he embezzled more than $2,000 from City Mill, even though he was never arrested. Wow! I was living with a bunch of criminals.

*The important lesson is that we all have a humble beginning. We are born naked and completely helpless. People should remember their humble beginnings and never treat others cruelly or harshly.* My in-laws were not thrown out even as slaves. Yet they tried to throw out a daughter-in-law who treated them with respect and kindness.

That was a very grave sin against God. Two years after giving birth to Tommy, I gave birth to my daughter, Audrey. The day after her birth, my mother-in-law came to the hospital to ask the doctor to release me the next day, Thanksgiving Day. She used the excuse of Thanksgiving Day to get me back to work sooner so I could continue paying $20 a month to her attorney. She pressured me to return to work as soon as possible. I returned to work the Monday after Thanksgiving.

My father-in-law's mistress, Ida, lived with her husband and children in a rental nearby. When they bought an old house up on Punchbowl, she told my father-in-law to buy the house next to hers. My in-laws begged Thomas and me to help with the mortgage payments. We both agreed to help with the payments every month. The two houses were so close to each other that the back door of one was just steps away from the back door of the other. Because of his mistress, my father-in-law slept in a room on the main floor while his wife slept in her own room down in the basement.

But Thomas didn't keep his word about helping with the mortgage. He kept his paycheck for going out with friends and girls. I later kept my word by turning over my entire paycheck of $45 each month.

Whatever my father-in-law brought back from China for his wife, he brought back the same thing for his mistress, Ida: a set of porcelain dishes for his wife and one for Ida, a beautiful porcelain planter for his wife and one for Ida. My mother-in-law was friendly with Ida, but took out all her frustrations on me. When her beautiful porcelain planter from China was cracked in half, my mother-in-law accused me of breaking it, because I watered the potted plant in it.

"How did you break the planter in half?"

"I didn't break it."

"You must have broken it when you watered the plant in it."

"No, I didn't break it. If I did, I would have told you right away so you wouldn't blame someone else for it. Maybe Ida broke hers and then sent her daughter over when no one was home to exchange it. You know our doors are never locked, and your husband always gives Ida the same thing he gives you."

She said nothing.

My mother-in-law called me the "garbage can" in Chinese. She said I was fit for receiving only garbage. When a relative came from China with a piece of jade for me, as he handed me the jade my mother-in-law snatched it from his hand. She told him I didn't care for such things. She kept the piece of jade for herself. I didn't make a fuss over it. Even then I was not greedy for material things, for God had made my soul hungry for spiritual things.

Ida's other daughter, Viola, took sides with my mother-in-law against me. She said cruel things to hurt me. For example, whenever I walked past, she told my mother-in-law in a loud sarcastic tone, "There goes the queen." These and other cruel words hurt me. On Viola's wedding day, she came over to visit my in-laws. I was shocked to see Viola wearing the formal Mandarin jacket my father-in-law had given me. When I asked her where she got it, she said my mother-in-law had given it to her. Seeing my jacket on Viola hurt me deeply, but I didn't fight over it, because I didn't think it was worth the trouble.

I realized my mother-in-law must have taken that jacket from my closet and given it to Viola. She lied to me when I asked her if she had seen it. I asked her, "How come Viola is wearing my jacket?" She didn't answer me, but walked out of the room. I thought that if she had taken back the Mandarin jacket, she also must have taken back the gold bracelet she had given me.

Yet I had been obedient and kind to my mother-in-law. With the pay from the Sub Base I bought her a console radio with a record player so she could listen to Chinese music. I wanted to make it pleasant for her while she took care of little Tommy and Audrey for me while I was at work.

My mother-in-law took advantage of the Filipino workers at City Mill who stacked and loaded lumber by hand. Each payday my father-in-law, their foreman, handed her the pay of those who owed her money. She deducted what they owed her plus interest before giving them the rest of their pay. She charged a dollar interest for every four dollars they borrowed. Since what they received on payday wasn't enough to live on, they had to borrow often. They were trapped by her system. I felt sorry for those workers and I was hurt by the injustice, but there was nothing I could do to help them.

I was desperate to move out, but Thomas refused to move. I saved enough for a month's rent on a two-bedroom cottage with cheap wicker furniture. I showed the cottage to Thomas, and we spent time there on our days off. But he still refused to move, so I had to give up the cottage. Thomas and I had agreed to help his parents with the mortgage, but Thomas never helped with a single cent. One payday I kept $5 to buy a pair of shoes and gave her $40. She threw the $40 at me and cursed me. "Where's the other $5?"

I was so angry at her reaction that I pushed her. "I needed a new pair of shoes for work because my old pair has holes in them. I'm using my own money for the shoes!"

She picked up the $40 off the floor after I left the room.

## Working as a Waitress

With a baby and a 2-year-old, I looked for a job closer to home. I found one in town at M's Coffee Tavern, a family restaurant, through an ad I saw in the paper. I worked there as a waitress for $45 a month. The other waitresses called me "Minnie Mouse," because I was short (5 feet), slim (90 pounds) and quick on my feet. They gave me the small tables for two or four persons. They also sent me to wait on "deadheads" or "misers" (who left no tip). The usual tip was 10 cents for lunch and 25 cents for dinner.

When I became pregnant with my third child, I suffered from severe morning sickness and vomited a lot. I didn't mind the morning sickness because I wanted a large family, and Thomas knew that. But my mother-in-law didn't want me to miss any work, because she depended on my monthly paycheck. She and Ida took me to a doctor who gave me medicine that would cause a miscarriage. When I had a miscarriage at home, I told my mother-in-law what had happened. She said nothing, but just smiled at me.

Most of our customers at M's Coffee Tavern were regulars who came every day or several times a week. A dwarf with one side of his face reddened by severe skin disease came for dinner every day. His regular table was hidden in the corner near the entrance. Even though the other waitresses called him a "deadhead," after a while he began leaving a tip for me because I treated him with respect and kindness.

Miss Lyman, a woman in her forties, came in for lunch every day and tipped me a dime. She knew the other waitresses didn't want to wait on her and treated her coldly. I always treated her with respect and kindness. On Thanksgiving Day I greeted her and took her order with my usual friendliness and cheerfulness. She surprised all of us by leaving me a dollar tip.

Every day for two years I served Mr. Campbell, a manager at the Honolulu Gas Company. When I needed a favor several years later during the war, he remembered me and helped to get a stove for me.

I treated all the customers with respect and kindness whether they left a tip or not. Mrs. Potter, the hostess, pretended to help clear my tables just to see the tips left for me. While we folded cloth napkins between 2:00 and 4:00 in the afternoon to prepare for dinner, Mrs. Potter said, "I don't know how come, but the 'deadheads' are leaving tips for 'Minnie Mouse.'"

I told them, "That's because I treat all the customers nice. You shouldn't pretend to be nice just to get a bigger tip. You should be nice to all the customers all the time."

Because I was so quick at taking orders, serving and clearing tables, I usually earned more tips than the other waitresses.

I felt sorry for Mrs. Robot, an older woman who prepared the salads, sandwiches and desserts in the kitchen. Since she never received any tips, I shared part of mine with her. I gave her at least 25 cents, usually 50 cents, and on a good day 75 cents. When Mrs. Robot did me favors by preparing my salad or dessert first, the other waitresses complained. Her answer to them was, "Minnie Mouse shares her tips with me, but none of you do."

The other waitresses were jealous of my tips from customers and of my favors from Mrs. Robot. They ganged up on me. They knew I had little schooling, so Elizabeth tricked me.

The Goulds were a middle-aged couple who owned a service station. Elizabeth urged me to make the Goulds happy. She pushed me to greet them with, "Hi, you nincompoops." I thought it was something nice because Elizabeth said so. They became so angry that they went to Mrs. Millican, the owner, to report me. I knew I was in trouble because they were longtime regulars. When Mrs. Millican came after me, I went into the kitchen. When she came into the kitchen I left quickly. Finally, before she could fire me, I went up to her and said, "I quit."

*Never trick an innocent person into doing wrong, especially a wrong that can cause a person to lose her job.*

I have understanding and compassion for waitresses and waiters because of my own experience as a waitress. They really depend on tips to help pay bills. But more important to them is being treated with the respect due to human beings. I need no reminders to treat them with respect and kindness. They have enough to put up with in their work. Besides giving a good tip, I often remind them that it is more blessed to serve than to be served, and that God will bless them for serving.

During my fourth pregnancy, Thomas and his mother pressured me into having an abortion. Thomas drove me to Kapiolani Hospital to sign the papers and then left. I was in my fourth month of pregnancy. After the abortion, the nurse couldn't revive me and thought I might die. The nurse tried calling Thomas by phone but couldn't find him. The doctor and nurse worried because I was still unconscious 4 hours after the abortion. In the evening when I regained consciousness, Eliza, the nurse, told me the 8:00 whistle of the Aloha Tower had already blown.

Eliza said, "Florence, it took you so long to regain consciousness. The doctor and I were really worried about you. And we couldn't find Thomas."

Maybe I didn't become conscious sooner because I had lost the will to live. I didn't care anymore. I was just working and bringing a paycheck home to people who didn't respect me. I didn't want to have the abortion because I wanted more children. But my mother had told me to obey my husband and my mother-in-law, so I obeyed them as she told me to. My mother-in-law forced me to have the abortion for my monthly $45. That evening, I saw my mother-in-law standing at the doorway of my room. I told the nurse, "Don't let her come near me. I don't want to see her ever again." Thomas came to get me later that night.

Thomas was a Catholic and should have known abortion was a serious sin. Maybe he did know. I know God has forgiven me for those abortions because I didn't know any better in those days. It's hard for me to explain how innocent and how ignorant of sex I was back then. I went along with both abortions out of obedience.

## Valley of Death

By refusing to move into the two-bedroom cottage I had rented, Thomas hurt me deeply. I had made it easy for him to tell his parents we were moving. He refused to move because he wanted the free room and board and didn't want to support our two children. That was the last chance I gave him for moving out of his parents' home.

I was so miserable and desperate that I wanted to commit suicide. Thomas took me for a drive and stopped at Nuuanu Pali. When we got out of the car, I was going to kill myself by jumping off the cliff. But another car pulled in and parked next to ours. Some people got out of the car, so I decided against jumping. I didn't want to kill myself in front of them.

I was depressed and desperate. I never confided in anyone about my problems, not even in my mother. I had kept all my problems and difficulties to myself. So I finally went to my mother for support and advice. Instead of showing sympathy and support, she scolded me for being quick-tempered and for not appreciating Thomas. She blamed me for all my problems because Thomas was so soft-spoken and well-mannered with her. Something inside me snapped. I pushed my mother with both hands and left. I decided life wasn't worth living.

I went to three doctors. I asked each one several times for some sleeping pills for my mother. I gathered close to a hundred pills of different sizes, shapes and colors. I wrote a long letter to Thomas and left it on the bureau. I forgot most of what I wrote, but everything was based on the truth. I told him how irresponsible and unfaithful he was, how greedy he was to live with his parents for the free room and food, and how he didn't keep his word about helping with their mortgage so that I had to turn over all my paychecks to his parents. I ended the letter with, "Thomas, I free you so you can marry your mother and sleep with her."

Thomas' own parents had described him to me like this: *Go sum di hak go mak* (his heart is blacker than Chinese black ink). I was shocked to hear that.

*Young ladies, beware of a man who is soft-spoken because there may be a vicious bite behind his soft words. Young men, beware of a soft-spoken woman who speaks too sweetly. There may be a vicious heart behind her sweet words. Such a man or woman may be silent a lot, but they can spit venom like a spitting cobra.*

Alone at home, I swallowed all the pills, a bunch at a time. I took the pills about 9:00 in the morning. They found me in my room that evening. The ambulance rushed me to Queen's Hospital. They pumped my stomach, but little came out. Dr. Pang examined me, declared me dead and signed my death certificate. While wheeling me to the morgue, the worker saw my eyelids flicker. He wheeled me back to Dr. Pang, who checked me and found me alive. Dr. Pang told me all this after I regained consciousness.

I know God saved my life by reviving me. After taking close to a hundred pills that morning and not being found until that evening, I should have been dead. Dr. Pang told me nothing came out when they pumped my stomach. He was sure I was dead when he signed my death certificate.

I regained consciousness a week later, but stayed groggy a few more days. When my mind was clear, Dr. Pang pointed at my wedding band and asked, "What's that, Florence?"

"That's my wedding ring. Thomas gave it to me."

Then Dr. Pang scolded me, "You almost caused me to lose my license. I thought you were dead and signed your death certificate, but you were still alive. You're so selfish. You only thought of yourself. What about your children?"

Dr. Pang put me in the psychiatric ward of the hospital for treatment. Dr. McNeil, the psychiatrist, asked me why I tried to kill myself. I told him about Thomas and about his mother. But it was Detective Fletcher who changed my attitude toward life. He said, "Florence, you're too young to die. You're only 26 and you have your whole life ahead of you. No man is worth killing yourself for. You have your children; you're not alone." His words shook me up.

I decided to live.

Several weeks later, Dr. McNeil called Thomas into his office to lecture him on the importance of getting me away from his mother. Dr. McNeil would not release me until Thomas found a place for us to move into. So Thomas left work at 2:00 every afternoon and came to get me. The doctor released me for the afternoon to find an apartment, but I had to return to the hospital by evening.

We found a small cottage for rent on Waiola Street. Because I weighed about 70 pounds of skin and bones and had dark brown rings under my eyes, the Japanese landlord felt sorry for me.

*Parents, pay close attention to your children and to friends. When someone is deeply troubled, it shows on the face. No one is so stupid as not to see a deeply troubled face if one looks. When you notice a big change in behavior, give more time and attention to show that you care. Sincere caring with kind words can make a big difference. You may save a life.*

From my own experience of trying to commit suicide, I have deep understanding and compassion for those who commit suicide or try to. Because of my own experience of being depressed and desperate enough to try killing myself, God used me years later to save several women from committing suicide. *Those who suffer deeply can have a special compassion and understanding for helping others who suffer. Ever since my baptism, I prayed daily to God: "Please save those who are thinking of suicide. Give them a new outlook on life and a new lease on life."*

Words cannot describe my happiness as Thomas and I moved into the unfurnished cottage on Waiola Street. We slept on the floor until Thomas bought a bed. Then he charged a stove, a used refrigerator, and later some cheap furniture. I was finally free of my mother-in-law. I had escaped from hell. I sent Thomas to bring Tommy, Audrey and our things from his parents' place. He brought our things and Audrey, but his mother kept Tommy and his things. Thomas let his mother keep Tommy and didn't fight for him, because Thomas was a coward and he didn't want to support another child. I had to go to court to get Tommy back.

At the hearing in the judge's chambers, I told him, "I'm Tommy's mother; I bore him. She didn't bear him; she's not his mother. I want him back because he's my son and I want all his clothes. But he can stay with her on weekends when she wants."

The judge gave Tommy back to me. For second time a judge said to me, "Young lady, you would make a good lawyer."

When I became pregnant again, I went about the cottage singing for joy because I knew I would be having and keeping my baby. But I found out later that Thomas had been going with another woman while I was pregnant. A Japanese neighbor had seen them together several times downtown. Thomas worked the late shift, so he was free in the afternoons. That elderly neighbor I called *Babang* (Japanese for grandma) didn't want to hurt me by telling me about Thomas and his girlfriend during my pregnancy.

For about two weeks I was paralyzed from the waist down by my pregnancy. *Babang* telephoned my mother to ask her to come over to help, since I was paralyzed. My mother never came. So *Babang* came over to help me while I was paralyzed. Once I had to crawl to the door to let Thomas in at 3:00 in the morning because he hadn't taken his house key with him to work. I gave birth to my third child, Stephen, in August 1941. After I gave birth, *Babang* telephoned my mother again to ask her to come over and help. My mother refused to come, so *Babang* used to help me with the baby and my other two children.

One day she called Thomas into the bedroom, closed the door and scolded him for going out with another woman while I was home with a baby and two small children. She scolded him so loud that I could hear her. I was deeply hurt. Only then did I discover why Thomas had bought himself two-tone shoes, flashy shirts and a sport jacket. I hadn't suspected anything. I was happy that he looked good in his new clothes, because he wore only khakis and boots to work.

Then one Saturday when Tommy was in the third grade and Audrey in the first grade, while I was sitting on the rocker with baby Stephen in my arms, Tommy asked me, "Mama, how come Daddy takes us and the lady to the park for a picnic, but he doesn't take you with us?" Hurt and angry, I yelled at Thomas.

I found out that he had been going with a Japanese girl named Sally, who was a receptionist in a dental office. I made Thomas drive me to her office and call her out to the car. Then I sat in the back seat with her. With Stephen in my arms, I told her, "You stay away from my husband." Then I punched her on the knee. Sally got out of the car and ran back into the office.

I told Thomas, "If you want to fool around with Sally, you should marry her. I'll never trust you again as long as I live!" I realized then how he had neglected us while spending his money on new clothes and on Sally. Sometimes the refrigerator was empty and we had only bread and jelly.

(Wives, beware when your husband suddenly buys flashy clothes without any apparent reason. Find out the real reason.)

I thought about suicide again. Then I recalled Dr. Pang's words: "You're so selfish, Florence. What about your children?" Sitting on the rocker with Stephen in my arms, I prayed, "God, please let me live to care for my children until Stephen is at least 16." I didn't want a step-mother to raise my three children. Yet I never once thought of divorcing Thomas because he never abused me physically, the children needed his support, and I loved him.

Any woman who has suffered from an unfaithful husband knows

how I felt and what I went through. But I stayed with mine because I didn't want my small children to be raised and mistreated by a step-mother. I knew many stepmothers mistreated or neglected their step-children, and I didn't trust Thomas to protect his children from mistreatment. I was a good mother to them.

My baby Stephen was a joy to me. He saved my life by erasing my thoughts of committing suicide again. I realized that my first duty was living to raise my three children.

Although I stayed married to Thomas because of the children, I would have left him if he had physically abused me or the children. *A woman with a husband or boyfriend who physically abuses her or her children must leave him. To such a woman I say, "Have courage. Leave him." There are now many secret shelters for battered women. God will provide for you through good persons who serve as His instruments to help you.*

When Stephen was two months old, a detective came to arrest me. "Your mother-in-law has accused you of stealing her diamond ring."

"I didn't take her ring. I never saw it."

"I'm sorry, but you'll have to come with me to the station."

"Wait till I put on my shoes and get a bottle for the baby."

With Stephen in my arms, I was taken to the police station. When Detective Charles Chan (his friends called him "Charlie Chan") saw how frightened I was in the police car, he tried to reassure me. "Are you Chun Chiu's daughter?"

"Yes, I am."

"I was a friend of your father; we used to gamble together. He was a good man. When he won, he was generous to the needy. Don't worry. Nothing's going to happen to you."

I told Detective Chan about my mother-in-law's cruelty, my at-tempt at suicide, my going to court to get my son Tommy back, and to check with Dr. McNeil the psychiatrist, and Detective Fletcher who spoke to me at Queen's Hospital, and the judge. The detective already knew about her bad reputation in Chinatown.

At the police station I was fingerprinted and taken to a room. Af-ter Detective Chan made some phone calls and talked to his chief, he came and told me his chief was dropping the charge against me. While he drove me and Stephen home, I thanked him for believing me and releasing me. I was so relieved. Being arrested and fingerprinted for a crime I hadn't committed shocked and scared me.

One day a bill for Thomas came from Detor's Jeweler on Fort Street. It was for a monthly payment on a diamond ring. I was stunned and hurt. I thought that ring was for his secret sweetheart. The only thing Thomas ever gave me was my wedding band. When I angrily asked Thomas about the ring and the bill, he said his mother had forced him to buy that diamond ring for her. That was the ring she had accused me of stealing.

Fifteen years later my mother-in-law came to visit me at our home on Noah Street. Because of the cruel treatment I had received from her, my heart used to pound whenever I saw her. Yet I welcomed her with sincere kindness, as I always did. I had nothing to serve her for lunch. So I telephoned my neighbor at her workplace to borrow a can of crab meat from her kitchen. She told me to take anything I needed. I promised to buy her another a can of crab meat. She told me to help myself and to forget about it, but I did buy another can of crab meat for her. I knew crab was my mother-in-law's favorite, so I served her a crab omelet with rice and tea for lunch.

As she was leaving, I gave her my last dollar bill for her bus fare. When she opened her purse to put it away, her handkerchief stuck out of her purse. Then I saw a diamond ring fall out of her handkerchief and heard the "plop" as it landed on the wooden floor in front of the Enthronement altar – the diamond ring she had accused me of stealing 15 years ago. I had been arrested and fingerprinted for that "crime." Yet the first time I ever saw that ring was there on my living-room floor. When her ring fell out, her eyes got big, her mouth dropped, her face turned white. I saw the guilt, shame and fear in her face, so I picked up the ring, shoved it into her purse and told her to hurry because her bus was coming. I wanted to spare her further humiliation and embarrassment.

She never came to visit me again after that incident. Years after my mother-in-law had falsely accused me of stealing her diamond ring, God humiliated her in front of me by revealing the truth before our altar. That's how God justified and cleared me of her false accusation.

*That incident teaches the serious lesson of never accusing an innocent person of a crime. The injustice of innocent persons wrongly convicted and imprisoned must be corrected. The police or prosecutors who suppress or falsify evidence to convict the innocent will be judged most severely by God, the Final Judge, before and after death. God is a God of truth and justice.*

In November 1941 our Japanese landlord gave notice that all the tenants of his cottages and apartments had a month to move out. He never gave a reason. But God had compassion on me. I saw an ad in the paper about a small house for sale on Wela Street for $3,300. Mr. Augustine, the real estate agent, was a Catholic who had graduated from St. Louis High School. I still looked terrible, weighing about 75 pounds. I told him that our landlord was forcing everyone to leave and that we had to find another place to live. I told him about my mother-in-law's cruelty, my attempt at suicide and the reason the psychiatrist wouldn't release me until I found a place to move into.

Mr. Augustine was selling that house near Fort Ruger for an Army officer who was being transferred to the mainland. When Mr. Augustine explained my suicide attempt and my situation to the officer and his wife, whom I never met, she didn't even ask for a down payment on the house. She asked for only the monthly mortgage payments of $35. She turned over the keys and deed to Mr. Augustine for me right away, and even cleaned the house completely, including the windows, so I wouldn't have to do any cleaning after moving in.

Then Mr. Augustine telephoned Thomas and his father and told them to come to his office. When they came, Mr. Augustine was angry. He lectured them about taking care of me. He told them, "This is a matter of life and death. I don't want her to try suicide again. The next time she'll be dead. If anything happens to her, I'll hold you responsible and I will come after you." Mr. Augustine made my father-in-law cosign for the mortgage loan. In those days, the alumni of St. Louis stuck together. They not only helped each other, they also tried to straighten each other out when they found out one of them did wrong.

Even today I still ask God to reward Mr. Augustine for his kindness and his trust, and for being such a good Catholic as to lecture Thomas and his father for my sake. I owe my life to all those whom God used as instruments to save my life: Dr. Pang, Dr. McNeil, Detective Fletcher, the Japanese landlord, Mr. Augustine and the Army officer and his wife.

I remember the date we moved into our first home: December 7,

1941. We had just moved our first load into the house that morning when we heard the news on the radio around 9:00 that the Japanese were attacking Pearl Harbor. All naval workers were to report immediately to Pearl Harbor. Thomas left for work right away and didn't return for several days. I worried about him and prayed real hard for him, because he worked under dangerous conditions.

Moving into our own home on Wela Street made me the happiest I had ever been. We had a home of our own. A week after we moved in, while Thomas was at work, I sat on the bare floor of the empty house singing aloud.

One evening, while Thomas was at work, I joined a group of our neighbors who were outside talking about husbands being unfaithful. They told me, "You're lucky Thomas is so faithful."

The very next afternoon Thomas drove home in a Navy pickup truck. In the front seat with him was a Portuguese girl. I saw her, and so did some of the neighbors.

When Thomas came into the house, I asked him, "What are you doing home? You're supposed to be at work."

"I have to buy something for work."

"You're lying. The Navy doesn't need you to buy something for them. And you shouldn't be driving that girl around with you, especially bringing her here."

Thomas left without saying anything.

Afterward some of the neighbors teased me about his affair with that Portuguese girl. The neighbors gossiped about Thomas and teased me about not being able to hold on to my husband. I was humiliated and hurt.

I was so hurt that I took the bus to Kaimuki to see the head of all the civilian workers at Pearl Harbor. I cried as I told him and his wife about Thomas driving home during work in a Navy truck with a girl sitting beside him.

A few days later I asked Thomas, "Why did you marry me?"

"I never loved you. I married you out of pity."

He never knew how deeply those words wounded my heart. For I truly loved him.

## Breakdown

Tuberculosis struck my mother hard. During her last weeks, I cared for her as best as I could in my sister's home. Soon after I began caring for my dying mother, Thomas' mother sent him to deliver a message to me. Afraid of catching tuberculosis, Thomas stood on the porch and yelled, "My mother sent me to take you home. She says if you keep caring for your mother, you can't come home. I won't let you in the house. You're going to catch TB and pass it on to me and the children. Then the children will pass it on to my mother. So I want you to come home right away and forget about taking care of your mother."

His message shocked, confused and hurt me. Instead of asking whether there was something he could do to help, he told me to stop caring for my dying mother and threatened to lock me out of my own home if I did stay to care for her. He gave me the choice either of caring for my dying mother or caring for my three small children.

Hurt and angry, I yelled at him, "You go and tell your mother I don't give a damn. I'm going to take care of my mother!"

The day she died, my mother asked me to comb her hair and to roll it into a bun at the back of her head. I combed her hair, but I didn't roll it into a bun because I didn't know how to do it properly. I gave her my only coat to cover her. She asked for some cream of mushroom soup, so I sent my sister to buy a can. But Mother was too weak to eat it when we warmed it for her. Coughing up blood and struggling for breath, my mother died in my arms.

When I got home, I collapsed on the floor but remained conscious. Several neighbors came over to help. I could feel the stiffening moving slowly up my legs and arms. I thought if the stiffness reached my brain I would die. So I told them to massage my legs and arms to prevent the stiffening from spreading. They worked hard at massaging my legs and arms. Then I was taken to the hospital. I remained conscious, but I had a complete physical breakdown. The heartaches Thomas caused me, his threat to lock me out of my home and away from the children, the lack of sleep and food while caring for my mother, and the shock of her death broke me down. The nurse told me that I weighed only 70 pounds when I first came to the hospital. I was in the hospital for more than a month. My mother was buried while I was there. What I said to Mother when she chased me with the kettle of hot water had come real many years later. I had said to her, "When you die, I won't go to your funeral."

Thomas' mother cared for the children while I was in the hospital. When she came to see me in the hospital, she asked me to sign one of my blank checks. I told her I wasn't crazy, and I wasn't going to sign that blank check for her. Days later Thomas told me his mother tried to persuade him to have me committed to the state mental hospital, but he refused to sign the papers.

The doctors and nurses restored my health with vitamins, tonics, and a special diet. When my mind was finally clear after two weeks, I began cheering up other patients and playing cards with some of them. My friendliness and kindness helped some of them get well so they could leave the hospital. Several nurses told me, "Florence, you're here to help us cure people so they can go home."

The house on Wela Street held too many painful memories for me. I told Thomas we had to move to another house. So we sold that house in 1944 and bought a lot on McCully Street to build a new home. During the three months it took to build our home, we lived in a basement apartment we rented for $50 a month. Even though we offered to pay rent to our in-laws, they refused to let us stay in their basement.

God had saved me from the earthquake in Yokohama, from the two throat infections in China, from the Japanese soldiers and the Communists in China, and from my suicide, because He had special plans for me.

*I now know how precious is the gift*
*of free choice from God.*

# 3

# WITH GOD ALL THINGS ARE POSSIBLE

I was nine years old when my grandmother took my aunt and me to see a lady medium in Pusan, China. When the lady saw me, she told my grandmother and aunt I had *sin kwat,* saintly bones. I didn't understand. God slowly revealed the full meaning of those words to me these past 73 years.

## A Bargain with God

God began revealing the meaning of "saintly bones" to me after I became a Catholic. As a young woman, I was a practicing Buddhist who prayed and went to the temple to consult God about important matters. My relatives and friends asked me to pray for them at the temple. Some even asked me to consult God for them on important decisions. I had compassion toward others, and I tried to be of good heart.

My conversion to Christ began when I enrolled my eldest son, Tommy, in St. Louis School. Even though I wasn't a Catholic, I wanted him in that school because some students at his public school were beating up other students for money. My brother-in-law Fred bet me $5 I would fail, because he knew how strict Brother Hammond, the principal, was. I accepted the challenge. I made an appointment and met with Brother Hammond. He set a date for Tommy's entrance exam for the seventh grade.

A week after the exam, Thomas and I met with Brother Hammond in his office. He showed us the test results.

"We can't accept Tommy because he failed the test. He did all right except for the religion section."

I said, "But he's not Catholic. How can my son learn about your God and your religion if you don't give him a chance? Just give him a chance and I'll make sure he'll study for his religion class. Don't you want others to learn about your religion?"

He paused, then said, "All right, we'll let him try it out for six months. If he can't pass all his classes, he'll have to leave."

"Thank you, Brother. You won't regret it. All I want is a chance for Tommy to come to this school. If he can't pass his classes, then I'll take him out."

I asked Thomas to get the package from the car. When he returned with a box in a brown paper bag, I handed the package to Brother Hammond and said, "Here's a box of cigars for you. I didn't want to give it to you before you decided about Tommy, because I didn't want you to think I was trying to bribe you. I would have given you the cigars even if you had said 'No.' Honest."

Brother Hammond thanked us for the cigars, his favorite treat, and we chatted. When he learned Thomas had graduated from St. Louis, he said, "Why didn't you tell me he's an alumnus? That would have made a big difference."

"My husband's brother Fred is an alumnus, too, but I didn't want to use them to get Tommy enrolled. I wanted him to get in on his own. Fred bet me $5 I wouldn't get within five feet of you. I'm going to collect that $5 and use it to cover the cost of the cigars."

Brother Hammond and Thomas laughed aloud. Thomas didn't know about my bet with Fred.

I also told Brother Hammond, "If I become Catholic, I want to be good from the inside, not from the outside."

He nodded and said, "I have faith in you, Florence."

The next day I collected $5 from Fred. With the money I bought three pictures of flowers: one of hibiscus, one of ginger, one of orchid. Each picture had a frame of bamboo.

I was so proud of Tommy. He did well in all his classes. The following year, he asked me to sign a consent form so he could become a Catholic. He was in the eighth grade and he needed my consent because I was a practicing Buddhist and he was so young. I told him, "You can become Catholic, but be sure to be a good one and to practice your religion." He said he would. But while receiving instruction for baptism, he caught rheumatic fever, which can cause permanent damage to the heart.

I remember the day Tommy came home from school with rheumatic fever. He brought home an order of *gau gee* (special, larger won ton), which he had bought with his own money. It was a surprise treat for me. His face was flushed with fever.

I took him to a Japanese doctor who diagnosed him with rheumatic fever. He taught me how to care for Tommy and prevent any strain to his heart, I carried him to and from the bathroom on my back. (I'm 5 feet tall and I used to weigh about 90 pounds.) I called a taxi for his weekly blood test. The taxi driver carried Tommy into the clinic and waited for us. Then he carried Tommy back to the car to drive us home.

During Tommy's illness, Brother Leo came after school to tutor him so he wouldn't lose a year of schooling. Father M, the school chaplain, continued to instruct him in the Catholic religion.

When Father M saw a big picture of my Buddhist God in our parlor, he said, "You should be a Catholic, Florence."

"No, I like being a Buddhist because I don't have to get up early on Sundays to go to church. I just pray anywhere."

Father M said nothing, but his face showed surprise which turned into irritation.

During those long quiet nights of Tommy's illness, I cried and prayed to God for my son's life and health. A Brother had given me a picture of Jesus and one of Mary. I replaced the photos of my husband's parents with those two pictures in a small dual frame. I thought Mary was the wife of Jesus. I got a crochet needle and some string, and I asked Mary to teach me how to crochet so I wouldn't go crazy from worrying. She did. (Since then, I have crocheted more than 100 items, from doilies, caps and scarves to fancy sweaters.)

Father M baptized Tommy into the Catholic Church at our home. Tommy stayed in bed while Father baptized him. I wasn't Catholic and I didn't know how important his baptism was. I was not in his room when Tommy was being baptized. I missed his spiritual birth.

About 2:00 one morning I opened our front door, pushed open the screen door, looked at the black sky and made a bargain with God: "God, if you save my son's life and health, I will join his Church." I didn't tell anyone about my bargain with God.

Tommy recovered completely, without any damage to his heart. When it was time for his confirmation, I watched him as he left for church in his dress shirt and tie. I wish I had witnessed his confirmation, too, even though I wasn't Catholic.

## My Spiritual Birth

During the months after his recovery I forgot about my bargain with God. So God used a Marianist Brother to remind me of it. Stephen, my youngest, went with Tommy to and from school by bus every day. If Tommy stayed at school for some reason, I went by bus to bring Stephen home. One afternoon while I was waiting for Stephen outside his second grade classroom, his teacher, Brother Edward Strauss, came out to greet me. Because it was September 8, the birthday of Mary, the mother of Jesus, I gave Brother a dollar to light a candle in her honor.

"Florence, this is the second year you remembered to honor our Blessed Mother on her birthday even though you're not Catholic. When are you going to be baptized a Catholic?"

He didn't know about my bargain with God. No one did. So his words scared me. I took those words as coming from a powerful God. I hurried to the school chapel. I felt so ashamed for not keeping my bargain with God that I didn't go inside. I knelt just outside the chapel entrance with my head bowed low in shame. I told God I wanted to be baptized right away, that moment.

The moment I reached home I telephoned Tommy's parish church.

Father P, the pastor, answered the phone. I blurted out, "Father, I want to be baptized a Catholic right now." He recognized my voice because he used to bring Communion to Tommy during his illness.

"Who do you think you are, wanting to be baptized right away when you don't know anything about the Catholic Church?" Then, in a quieter tone he told me he would assign a priest to instruct me for baptism. I was to go for instruction on Tuesday and Friday evenings from 7:00 to 8:00.

Father P was right. I knew nothing about the Catholic Church. I was a 35-year-old Buddhist who thought Jesus and Mary were husband and wife. I knew nothing about Jesus or the Holy Spirit.

Father J used the children's catechism to instruct me in September 1949. I was set to be baptized on December 24 and to make my First Communion on Christmas Day.

Father J had trouble teaching me because I had so little schooling, but he was kind and patient with me. At the first session, Father J began by asking me, "Who is the Holy Ghost?" When he mentioned the Holy Ghost, I became frightened because of my past experiences with ghosts and because I had to walk home alone in the dark.

"Don't talk to me about ghosts."

I was so scared that I just stood up, left his office and hurried all the way home. He arrived at our home by car shortly after I did. When I told him about the ghost I saw in Shanghai and the ghost in the rocker at our tenement room on River Street, he finally understood why I was so scared. After that he never talked to me about the Holy Ghost. A few years later, the Church changed the title *Holy Ghost* to *Holy Spirit* for the third person of the Holy Trinity.

Our sessions went smoothly for the next few weeks. Then some scary incidents happened. We didn't have a car. From our home on McCully Street I walked to and from Sacred Heart Church, a distance of more than two miles each way. On the way home from instruction, sometimes a pack of barking dogs came after me. I froze, then yelled for help. I could see people looking out their windows, but no one came out to help. I thanked God for protecting me from those dogs.

Some nights a stranger in a car slowed down near me and told me to get in. I would run into someone's yard and hide behind a hedge or bush. When the car left, I hurried all the way home. One night I was so frightened by the stranger following me in his car that I ran back to tell

Father J. So he drove me home that night and for several nights after that incident. (I wondered later if the devil was trying to stop me from being baptized.)

During one instruction Father J shocked me by telling me he had a sweetheart. I thought, "How can a priest have a sweetheart when priests aren't allowed to marry?" So I asked, "You, Father J, have a sweetheart?" Then he reassured me by showing me a picture of St. Therese of Lisieux and saying she was his sweetheart. He was so devoted to her that he loaned me his copy of her autobiography to read, and later suggested that I take her name for my confirmation.

I took the book home because I didn't want to hurt Father's feelings. I could read the book, but I didn't understand what I read. So each night I turned a few pages as though I was reading it, and then put the book under my pillow. That's how I finished "reading" the book before returning it to Father J.

He didn't meet with me some Fridays. I was always on time. A priest saw me waiting for Father one Friday evening as I sat on the bench outside the rectory. He told me Father J was at a dinner engagement. So I went home.

The next Friday evening another priest asked me at 7:30, "Why are you sitting there?"

"I'm waiting for Father J to instruct me for baptism."

"Father J is a Scout leader and goes to a Scout meeting on Friday evenings."

"Every Friday evening I've been walking from home and waiting for him until 8:00. Please tell Father I won't be coming for instruction anymore."

*We should always be considerate of others by keeping our appointments and being on time. We have telephones to inform others if we can't keep an appointment. Our main responsibility to God is to help one another find God and gain heaven with His help.* By doing first things first, we allow God to help us fulfill our day's work in an orderly way. The examples we set can lead souls to a good way of life or to a bad way of life. *We have to set good examples for others to follow if we are to live for God.*

Once Father told me to go into the church and just sit there and look at the large crucifix about the altar. I didn't question him; I just obeyed. I went into the church and sat down.

God drew good from my obedience. I didn't know how to pray then. As I sat in church, I remembered helping Stephen learn the *Our Father*, the *Hail Mary* and the *Glory Be*. I didn't know the *Our Father* because it was too long for me to memorize. Even the *Hail Mary* was too long for me to memorize. I remembered only the first two words of the *Glory Be*.

So I repeated "Glory be" over and over again as I pondered the meaning. I began with that prayer because it was the shortest and easiest for me to learn. God read my thoughts and saw my desire to learn and understand that prayer. He gave me the rest of the words. They just came together: "Glory be to the Father, and to the Son, and to the Holy Spirit, as it was in the beginning, is now and ever shall be, world without end. Amen." God taught me the prayer and also gave me the meaning of the prayer.

I had learned my first prayer! I didn't know how to give the credit to the Holy Spirit then. I was so happy and so proud of myself for learning that prayer all on my own. I thought I had done something great. I was so excited about learning my first prayer on my own that I just left the church and went home.

(Since I couldn't memorize the *Our Father* and the *Hail Mary*, I had to read those prayers at my baptism and afterward until I finally learned them. The *Glory Be* is the favorite prayer of the Carmelites on Trinity Sunday. These three prayers are the ones that make up the prayers of the rosary).

That was my preparation for becoming a Catholic. Looking back on my baptismal instruction, I think God arranged to have Father J instruct me the way he did. If Father had instructed me the way he was supposed to, he might have distorted some of the lessons or I might have misunderstood them. All the credit for my religious knowledge must go to the Holy Spirit, my one and only teacher. The Holy Spirit was pleased with my obedience and took me under His wing.

Father J sensed something about me. He later told a friend about me: "I have never met a person with such deep faith." That friend telephoned to tell me what Father had said about me. My faith in God was so deep, as a Buddhist and then as a Catholic, that I simply believed without understanding.

Even though I stopped going for instruction in November, my baptism was still set for Christmas Eve and my First Communion for Christmas Day. I looked forward with excitement to the best Christmas of my life. Father J asked for volunteers to clean the church for Christmas. I said I would do it for Jesus for his birthday, since the church was his house. So on December 23, the day before my baptism, I worked in the church from 8:00 in the morning to 4:00 in the afternoon. After several boys dusted the pews and lifted the kneelers, I swept the floor and mopped it. Without being asked, I waxed the floor and then buffed it with the heavy buffing machine. I did all the cleaning willingly and cheerfully for Jesus.

That same evening, the evening before my baptism, Father J telephoned me.

"Hello, Florence? I can't baptize you tomorrow."

"What?"

"I can't baptize you tomorrow."

"Why can't you baptize me tomorrow?"

"I'll explain it to you later."

I slammed down the phone. I was hurt deeply because I thought I wasn't good enough to be a Catholic, and I thought Jesus was rejecting me after I had worked so hard and long in cleaning the church and waxing the floor for Him. I went to the living room and knocked down the Christmas tree full of ornaments. Thomas and the children were stunned by my wild behavior. I began throwing the Christmas presents out the front door, but my children stopped me and brought back those I had thrown out.

I told Thomas and the children what Father had told me on the phone. I said, "I will never become a Catholic!"

After New Year's Day, Father J came to see Thomas. He wasn't home, so while Father waited for Thomas he explained to me that he couldn't baptize me until my marriage to Thomas was validated. I didn't understand. Father said that since our marriage had been performed by a minister, it wasn't valid in the eyes of the Church. I still didn't understand what he was talking about. Father explained it to Thomas when he came home. I stopped going to Sunday Mass because I was so hurt and confused. I had lost my desire to become a Catholic. After all I had gone through, the Buddhist way of living seemed so much simpler, I thought. It seemed to treat people with more respect and honesty.

But God made sure I kept my bargain with Him. The following Good Friday, my daughter Audrey asked whether I was going with them to Sacred Heart Church for the Good Friday service. I thought, "Why should I go when I wasn't good enough to be a Catholic?" So I told her I was going to give Grandma a treat by taking her to visit a friend. That evening around 7:00 Father J telephoned me. I recognized his voice, so I said, "Now what do you want, Father?" I was surprised to hear from him, because the last time I had spoken with him was the day after New Year's Day, when he came to speak to Thomas about fixing up our marriage.

"Florence, I'm calling to let you know you'll be baptized tomorrow afternoon at 1:00 sharp. If you're one minute late, the church door will be locked."

The joy his message brought erased the disappointment I felt when I was not baptized on Christmas Eve.

## A New Life for God

The next day a taxi drove Thomas, our two sons and me to Sacred Heart Church by 12:30. Audrey stayed home because she was sick. We were early, so I went into the church. Then I thought of Stephen. He wasn't baptized. Tommy was baptized, and Audrey was baptized while attending Maryknoll School. I thought, "If Stephen dies, he won't go to heaven."

I began crying loudly in church. Mrs. Muraki, my sponsor, heard me crying and came over to lead me out of the church.

"We don't cry loud like that in church, Florence. What's wrong?"

"I'm going to be baptized, and I want Stephen to be baptized, too. I don't want to go to heaven if Stephen can't go."

Then I looked for Father J. He was talking to a young couple whose baby he was going to baptize.

I said, "Father, Stephen isn't baptized, and I want him to be baptized, too."

"Let's baptize you first. Stephen isn't ready for baptism. He didn't receive any instruction."

(Stephen wasn't even dressed properly – barefooted, he wore *puka puka* pants, pants torn at both knees.)

Brother Edward Strauss saw me crying and came over to us. "What's the matter?"

"Father won't baptize Stephen because he's not ready. But I want him baptized, too."

Brother Strauss told Father J, "I've been teaching Stephen the Catholic religion every day at school for nearly two years now, so he's ready for baptism."

"All right, don't cry, Florence. I'll baptize you and Stephen. Now let's get ready for the baptism. I'm going to baptize you *Florence*."

"I want the name *Mary* in honor of Blessed Mother."

"Take *Florence*; it's a good Christian name."

"No, I want *Mary* for my baptismal name."

Brother Edward heard me arguing and came over to us again to ask what was wrong.

"Father J won't baptize me *Mary*."

Brother Edward told Father, "She's free to choose her own name; let her have the name *Mary*."

"All right, but I'm going to baptize you in Latin, so I'll use *Maria* instead of *Mary* – don't you cry then."

"Okay, I won't cry."

I chose the name *Mary* in honor of my spiritual mother, the only true mother I had ever had, because my birth mother was only a guardian. I knew Mary would become my mother in the spiritual life through baptism. I cherished her name, a name sacred to me. I wanted her name on my baptismal certificate, but I would never use it because I didn't want anyone to abuse her name out of anger at me. I didn't mind people saying, "That damned Florence," but I didn't want them to say that with the name *Mary*. I wanted to be like her: "Like mother, like daughter." Choosing her name meant following Mary's example in the Christian way of living for God and with God.

*I now know how precious is the gift of free choice from God. When Jesus came to teach and save us, He never forced anyone to do His will. So we must allow others to use this precious gift of free choice from God. We should never tamper with God's gift of free will in anybody.*

*We should use this gift of free will to accept and cooperate with God's graces. All the money in the world, all the gold and silver in the world cannot buy any of God's gifts and graces. We have to cooperate with God's graces by practicing virtue and living up to the teachings of Jesus Christ. Yet we must use our minds to think wisely before making our choices. We should put doing God's will first.*

On Holy Saturday, April 8, 1950, the *Holy Year*, at 1:00 in the afternoon, I was baptized into the Catholic Church with my son Stephen.

Thomas and I returned to church that evening so he could go to Father J for confession. Thomas had been away from the Church since graduating from high school 18 years ago. Thomas' confession seemed to last more than an hour. I thought maybe some of his sins would not be forgiven. While waiting I told God, "Please forgive all his sins. Let me take his place in hell if his sins are not forgiven."

After the confession, Father J asked Thomas, "Did you remember to bring a witness?"

"No, Father, I didn't."

Father J validated our marriage in a short ceremony in the rectory with Father Henry as the witness. Only then could our entire family receive Communion together the next day, Easter Sunday.

Thomas and I returned home after Father J validated our marriage. As I was falling asleep, I heard a woman's voice calling me gently from the foot of my bed: "Florence, Florence, Florence." I opened my eyes and saw a lady in white who disappeared so quickly that I didn't see her face. Shortly after that I fell asleep.

Months later, when I told a Catholic friend how I had asked God to let me take Thomas' place in hell during his long confession, she said, "You shouldn't pray like that, Florence. It's not right." I had just been baptized and I didn't know any better. But God read my heart and knew I really meant what I said. God saw how true and complete my love for Thomas was.

Through my baptism, God baptized Stephen and brought Thomas back to the Church after being away 18 years. I was so happy and excited about being a Catholic and about my First Communion that I wanted to attend the first Mass at 6:00 in the morning. I told Father I was going to that Mass because "the early bird catches the early worm."

While instructing me, Father J did his best to teach me about Holy Communion. He even showed me a large host and a small host to help me understand, but I just couldn't understand the meaning of the "Real Presence" of Jesus in Holy Communion. I told Father, "I don't understand, but I believe."

At the 6:00 Mass that Easter morning, with the church full of people, I followed my husband and children to the altar rail and watched the person receiving before me so I would know what to do. I was so afraid of making a mistake that as I walked slowly in line to the communion rail I repeated to myself, "Monkey see, monkey do; do what they do."

I didn't understand the full meaning and sacredness of Holy Communion, but I knew I was receiving Jesus in a real way. I was happy just being at Mass and believing with all my heart that Jesus was real in that church. I believed without any doubt that God sees and knows all things, so he saw and knew the love and gratitude in my heart that Easter morning. I told Jesus that I wanted only His love and His wisdom. I told God that my biggest desire was to love Him and to please Him. He flooded my soul with spiritual joy for weeks after my baptism, the beginning of a new life for God.

Even though we were in debt and in danger of losing our home, I didn't ask Jesus for money. Even though Thomas wasn't a loving husband, I didn't ask for his love or my children's love. I told Jesus I wanted only His love and His wisdom. I also told Him, "Jesus, let me have eyes only for you. Don't let anyone come between Your love for me and my love for You." Jesus accepted my desires as prayers from my heart, and He granted my prayers.

After my baptism, I waited for Sundays so I could go to Mass and receive Communion. I told my daughter, Audrey, "I'm so anxious for Sunday so I can go to Mass and receive Jesus."

"You don't have to wait till Sunday, Mom. There's Mass every morning at 8:00 in our church. You can come to it."

So I walked to school with Audrey every morning to attend daily Mass. I have been going to daily Mass and Communion ever since, unless I was sick or Mass was not available.

The Holy Spirit moved Henry Chock, Tommy's classmate, to teach me a prayer I have used for 48 years since my baptism: "O Sacrament most holy, O Sacrament divine, all praise and all thanksgiving be every moment Thine." I say this prayer slowly with meaning every time I genuflect before the Blessed Sacrament and also every time I pass a Catholic church. I recommend this practice to every Catholic who wants to deepen their faith in the Blessed Sacrament.

I was taught to make a *Morning Offering* to begin each day. That was a prayer from a leaflet or prayer book that offered to God my entire being, body and soul, everything I had and everything I did, even all my sins, so Jesus could use them in any way He wanted for the honor and glory of the Father. The *Morning Offering* I used was similar to this one, because it has been updated:

**O Jesus,**
through the Immaculate Heart
of Mary I offer You my prayers,
works, joys and sufferings of this
day in union with the Holy Sacrifice
of the Mass throughout the world.

I offer them for all the intentions
of Your Sacred Heart: for the salvation
of souls, reparation for sin, the reunion
of all Christians.

I offer them for all the intentions of
our Bishops and all Apostles of Prayer
and in particular for those recommended
by our Holy Father this month.  Amen.

## First Confession

The bishop was coming to Sacred Heart Church for confirmation the next month, on May 7. Father J sent me to confirmation class for instruction once a week for the next three weeks. After the classes were over, he asked me, "Florence, have you pick a name for confirmation yet?"

"No, Father."

"Why don't you take the name *Therese?*"

"Okay."

Father J also told me to go to confession the day before my confirmation. On Saturday evening, May 6, I walked to church and stood in line for my first confession. When I stepped into the dark confessional and knelt in silence, Father Flick, an elderly priest with a hearing aid, told me to begin.

"Bless me, Father, for I did not sin."

"Would you repeat that."

"Bless me, Father, for I did not sin."

"Is that you, Florence?"

"Yes, Father."

"Stay right here. I'm going to my room, but I'll be right back."

He left the confessional and I waited for him. When he didn't return after a few minutes, I thought of the people waiting in line. So I opened the door, stuck my head out to face them and said, "I think Father has diarrhea and went to the toilet, but he'll be back."

Some of the people in line smiled. I knelt again and waited for Father Flick. After he returned, he told me he wasn't hearing properly, so he had to change the battery in his hearing aid. He asked me to begin my confession.

I repeated louder, "Bless me, Father, for I did not sin."

Then he said in anger, "What kind of confession is that? I changed the battery in my hearing aid because I thought it wasn't working right. But I did hear you right. Now you go to my office and stay there until I finish hearing confessions."

I was scared as I walked slowly to his office. I sat and waited for more than 30 minutes before he finally came.

"Florence, I know you were baptized recently. Don't you know how to confess your sins?"

"I just used the Ten Commandments: I didn't kill, I didn't commit adultery, I didn't steal, I didn't lie. That's why I said, 'Bless me, Father, for I did not sin.' This is my first confession."

"Who instructed you for baptism?"

"Father J."

Father Flick started smiling, but stopped when he saw how scared I was. I was scared because I had caused him so much trouble and because I thought I would be thrown out of the Church. He spoke in a kindly tone as he stood up from his desk: "Florence, I want you to come on Monday so I can teach you how to go to confession."

"Okay, Father, I'll come on Monday as you say."

He winked and smiled at me as I got up to leave. Ever since then, whenever we met he winked at me.

On Sunday, May 7, 1950, Bishop James Sweeney confirmed me as *Therese*, the name Father J had suggested for my confirmation.

A few weeks later Tommy told me what Father J had said to him: "Your mother is a saint, but tell her to come back for more instruction." I remembered the skipped appointments and other difficulties during my instruction, and I thought of the baptismal certificate I had received by mail. So I told Tommy to tell Father I wasn't going back for more instruction, because I had already graduated (been baptized) and I already had my diploma (my baptismal certificate).

Looking back now, I wonder whether Father Flick had told Father J to give me more instruction.

Several months after my confirmation, Father J came to our home one afternoon. As I welcomed him in, he told me that I should look for a spiritual director. I didn't know what he meant by a spiritual director. In my ignorance I blurted out, "Father, I already have a spiritual director.

"Who's your spiritual director?"

"You, Father."

He looked puzzled. Then he scratched his head, turned around and walked out the door. I was just as puzzled because I didn't know what a spiritual director was or why I needed one. I said he was my spiritual director because he had instructed me and baptized me. I learned a year later that a spiritual director guides you in doing God's will and helps you in your spiritual life.

A friend had repeated to me what Father J had told her, "I have never met a person with such deep faith." Perhaps that was the reason he thought a spiritual director could help me.

## Special Signs

From the start of my Catholic life, I began hearing an "inner voice" that taught and guided me. I still do. This "inner voice" is not like a real voice or like I'm thinking to myself. I can't explain it. For example, it teaches me how to spell words, it gives me the meaning, and it shows me how to use each word in a sentence, all in a flash. From time to time this "inner voice" instructs me, directs me, reveals things to me, and even upbraids me when I fail to practice certain virtues. Often it consoles and reassures me in times of sorrow and suffering.

I know some of the mentally ill do "hear voices." Recently, the "inner voice" taught me the difference between mental illness and the "inner voice" that is the Holy Spirit. Very few souls truly "hear that inner voice" with the "ears" of their souls. Just as the "eyes" of the soul can "see" visions from God, the "ears" of the soul can "hear the voice" of God. The "voices" that the mentally ill "hear" come from their brains and bring confusion and fear. The "inner voice" I hear comes from the Divine Indwelling of the Father, Son and Holy Spirit in my soul (in my heart area) and sets me at peace with gentleness and clear understanding.

At first I thought that everyone hears an "inner voice" from being baptized. But I soon realized that others didn't have an "inner voice" to guide and help them as I did.

The "inner voice" instructed me to surrender my free will completely to God as a total offering of myself to Him, so that I would be completely free to do His will. I did that to do God's will instead of doing my own will. I meant it from my heart. Ever since I surrendered my free will to God, I have been trying to do *His* will in everything.

*I always check and double-check before doing something to make sure I'm doing God's will and not my own will.* I don't doubt God, but I don't trust myself. I tell Jesus, "Let me drop dead or stop me at any cost if I'm about to do something against your will." Then I let the Holy Spirit guide me while I remain at peace. By trying to do God's will all the time, things have always turned out well for me. The timing turned out right and things worked out smoothly.

Now I see that I must have had special help from the Holy Spirit to surrender my free will completely to God. It was so soon after my baptism that I couldn't have thought of that by myself. As I keep trying to do God's will instead my own will, by and by there'll be no more Florence. Surrendering my free will to God was one of the most important things I ever did in my entire life.

It's the hardest thing in life to try to do God's will in everything instead of one's own will. It's a real struggle every day. But thanks to the help of the Holy Spirit, I have continued to try to do God's will instead of my own will these past 48 years.

I dare say the Holy Spirit has been my only true teacher and guide during my entire Catholic life. I let the Holy Spirit inspire me with His lessons on the spiritual life to share with others. I want to share these lessons with those who want to learn the art of living with God and for God.

Several months after my confirmation, I was listening to the radio while ironing. A song about a mockingbird caused a strange feeling and image in me. I pictured a nun coming out of a burial tomb in a convent and coming alive in me. I felt like I was that nun coming out of a cocoon the way a butterfly comes out of its cocoon. It seemed and felt like that nun became me. I can't describe that mysterious experience, which happened again weeks later when I heard that same song on the radio and had the same feeling and image.

The first Christmas season after my confirmation, the song *O Holy Night* caused another strange experience in me. That song carried me back in time and to the place where I used to live. I felt and pictured myself as a nun walking back and forth in the corridor of a convent. I was saying my prayers from a prayer book as I walked along a cloistered garden. That song took me back in time, and I was no longer me but that nun in her convent. That feeling and picture came to me every time I heard the song *O Holy Night*.

In Pusan, China, a medium said I had *sin kwat*, saintly bones. A song on the radio made me feel and see a nun coming out of a burial tomb in a convent to come alive in me. The song *O Holy Night* made me feel and see myself as a nun walking back and forth in the corridor of a convent while praying from a prayer book. Then the words of a Passionist priest gave me a clear, complete picture: A saint had an abiding influence of my soul. I would receive many more signs of this saintly influence.

*Let me explain this saintly influence as I understand it. My body is like a peach, which has a skin with fine fuzz on it. My skin has fine hair on it, too. My soul is like the pit of the peach. The Saint in my soul is like the kernel in the pit. So the Saint is hidden in my soul, which is hidden in the flesh of my body, the way the kernel (her soul) is hidden in the pit (my soul), which is hidden in the flesh of the peach (my body).*

Yet, I never revealed this secret to anyone for 38 years until Christmas Day 1993, when I told my spiritual son Father Francis my secret at the Holy Rosary Convent in Jerusalem. The only reason I revealed it to him was for the book for God. Otherwise I would never have revealed this secret to anyone. I wanted to take this secret back with me to heaven. Even though Father Francis had promised me more than three times that he would write the book for God, he didn't take the book and his promises seriously by ignoring my writings and tapes. He just put them aside. The "inner voice" told me to reveal the secret of my being influenced by a saint so he would begin working on the book for God. There was no other way to move him to begin.

So the "inner voice" urged me to reveal my secret to Father Francis, so he would begin work on the book. This book is the book of the Saint in my soul. This book is her idea and her way to share her spiritual lessons with others. The Saint in my soul wants to use this book to gain souls for God and to win love for love. Two months before her death, Saint Therese said, "If God answers my desire, my heaven will be spent on earth until the end of the world. Yes, I want to spend heaven on earth in doing good." I know of no other saint who asked to spend heaven on earth to continue working for God.

His attitude toward the book changed after I revealed my seccret to him. He left his teaching job and went into seclusion to work on this book full time. If the "inner voice" hadn't instructed me to reveal my secret to him, I never would have told him my secret. I never wanted to reveal the special graces God gave me, because I didn't want to get special treatment or special favors from others. I wanted people to accept me and deal with me as me, and to keep treating me the way they always treated me.

*Whatever we do for the honor and glory of God must be done with sacrifices. Father Francis had to go into seclusion to concentrate on writing the book for God. Without sacrifices, nothing worthwhile is achieved.* There are many kinds of books. But the hardest books to write well are about the spiritual life, the things of God and the spirituality of a soul. Everything Father Francis has written is based on the truth.

## Spiritual Guidance

With the guidance of the Holy Spirit and with the help of Blessed Mother, I have lived my way of life in union with Jesus Christ. With Jesus in my soul I have tried, through my words and behavior, to bring out the best in everybody. Those who saw my spirituality saw the love and kindness of Christ shining through me. I lived the gospel lessons every day, and I made those lessons come alive in my prayers, conversations and actions.

My responsibility as a Catholic has been to live my life as the Father, the giver of life, wants it to be lived. Soon after my baptism I knew I should use my free will to live according to God's will. So I surrendered my free will to God for love of Jesus. It was so soon after my baptism that I couldn't have thought of that by myself. The idea of surrendering my will to God must have come from the Saint in my soul.

I had many failings, but the Holy Spirit corrected me and set me back on the right track. I was docile and obedient to Him. All credit for my spirituality must go to the Spirit of Jesus Christ.

I accepted and lived by the words of Jesus Christ: "You have one Father and you have one teacher." I took God the Father as my true and only Father. My earthly father was only my guardian. I said the *Our Father* with deep love and gratitude. God the Father, the giver of all life, was my lifeline for living the spiritual life. I took the Holy Spirit as my only teacher, the best of teachers.

I added to the words of Jesus. I have only one mother: Mary, the perfect mother and the best of mothers. Her motherly love, care, protection and guidance were a big gain for my spiritual life. She taught me about motherhood and how to maintain the dignity of womanhood. She taught me how to dress modestly and how to behave politely with self-confidence in public, so I wouldn't disgrace her, my spiritual mother.

Our earthly mothers are only guardians. Some mothers have died; others are far away. But our Blessed Mother is always with us in spirit. She has never failed me. Whenever I prayed, "Blessed Mother, help me," I felt comforted and my peace of soul returned. The peace and comfort I felt were the touch of a loving mother, unseen but present.

Blessed Mother is a human being. God is God, above all. By giving us Mary to be our spiritual mother, God showed us that the human soul never dies. Our souls will go on living just like the soul of Blessed Mother.

Call on your spiritual mother and address her as Blessed Mother. That title keeps the devil away. Call on her in your hour of need with "Blessed Mother, help me." Call on her with the belief that she is your mother and will help you.

While Father Francis did the writing, I cooked lunch and dinner for him, even though I was almost completely blind. With God, all things are possible. Without God I'm nothing. But with God, with his strength, guidance and help, I could still cook. I had to use my memory to remember where everything was located in the kitchen.

*Never underestimate blind persons. They can do a lot with God's help.* They use their memory to remember where everything is. At times memory can be the most important part of our minds. As I stir-fried some food, I remembered to put in all the ingredients in the proper order. God helped me. At the end of the day, I thanked Jesus for his help. When I went completely blind, Father Francis finally did all the cooking, with me directing him.

*If you're struggling with some kind of disability, don't make excuses, be lazy or seek pity. God helps those who help themselves. And show gratitude to God for His help. The more you thank God, the more help He gives you.*

I first thought of writing a book the year I was baptized. When I mentioned this to Brother Leo , Tommy's teacher, he laughed and said, "You, Florence, write a book?" He knew I had little schooling so I wasn't offended or surprised by his disbelief. I knew if God wanted me to write a book giving Him full credit for my life, He would help me do it – with God anything is possible. I had such confidence in God even with my little amount of schooling.

During these past 48 years, no matter where I was or how busy I was, the urge to write a book giving full credit to God for His gifts and blessings kept nagging me. Again and again the "inner voice" kept reminding me to write this book.

## Lessons for Living

I lack education and I'm not a writer. I can't quote the Bible, because I don't understand what I read in it. I learn best from example and from guidance from the "inner voice." I write with love for all, and I ask God to bless anyone who takes the time to read my writings. I write about my experiences not as a memoir, but in order to bring out important lessons for improving one's life. *Unless we strive to become more honest and more just everyday, we will not grow spiritually.*

I'm asking God to use the lessons in this book to help you readers become better persons. I also thank God for allowing me to share them with you. These lessons can be stepping stones to living for God and with God.

I tried writing this book more than 20 times in different places these past 40 years. But I always held back because I didn't want to bring out the ugly truth about my family and my friends. Then the "inner voice" taught me to put truth and justice before loyalty to family and friends. So I must put obedience to God before loyalty to them.

I once told Brother Joseph Dangel, "If one of my children committed a crime, I would be the first to report it."

Surprised, he stared at me.

I'm kind and gentle; God made me like that. But God also made me a fighter for truth and justice. *Justice* is my middle name.

Brother Dangel respected me so highly that he enrolled me in the Society of the Little Flower and gave me the certificate of enrollment. The members of this society share in the prayers of each other because of their devotion to St. Therese.

I write without bitterness. I write not to blame or to criticize, but to bring out lessons for spiritual growth. I learned about spiritual growth from the practice of virtues and not from books. Through the faults and failings of others, God taught me many lessons on the art of living for God. He wants me to share these lessons, learned the hard way through suffering, with those who want to grow spiritually. These lessons can lead a person closer to God and to peace of mind, peace of heart and peace of soul.

I'm grateful to everyone I have met during my lifetime for providing me with all the lessons I am sharing with others. Each of you is dear to God. I didn't want to use the names of those who wronged me. Just think of the persons mentioned in this book as actors playing a role on stage so I could have lessons to share.

It's important for me to write this book with a loving heart, without a grudge against those who provided me with so many lessons by their pride and selfishness. Only by the grace of God could I have forgiven every person who wronged me.

But I cannot forget the hurt each one caused me. Scars remain. God did not say to forget; He said to forgive. Following the teachings of Jesus Christ, I must prove my love for God by truly forgiving each and every one. I forgive with sincerity of heart, because I loathe pretending.

*Because of pride, people pretend a lot by wearing a different mask to suit each occasion. The sin of pride behind this pretense is our worst enemy because it keeps us far from our God of Truth. Jesus Christ (the Way, the Truth and the Life) has called Christians to a closer union with Him in the Father by way of humbleness. This humbleness makes us truthful and gentle, and only the truth will set us free from a life of pretending and deceiving.*

I gather everyone I met since childhood to serve as the pages in my book of knowledge. Each one contributed lessons for the art of living for God. So I thank God for each and every one of them, because He had a purpose for bringing each of them into my life.

Everything God permits to happen in our lives has a purpose. Accepting everything He permits to happen gives us peace of soul and helps us to control our emotions. After we learn such acceptance, we never say, "Why me?" or "Why did this have to happen?" Whatever happens, we can rise above it with God's help.

*Whenever we face a problem, we are being tested on our faith and trust in God. Try to see things from His point of view. Everything God allows to happen to us is a chance to grow in the spiritual life. Every cross we have is a blessing in disguise, because it is a test of our faith and trust in God.*

*Whenever I start to worry, I remind myself that worrying goes against my faith and trust in God. The only thing we should worry about is offending Him. God will give us the strength and courage to go on, and He will restore our inner peace. Worry belongs to the devil's department. Worry is the devil's trick to weaken our faith and our trust in God.*

This earth is a battleground between the devil and God. The devil uses evil and weak souls as his instruments to cause wars and to disturb souls. There's so little peace in the world and in souls because of these instruments of the devil. So be aware of the devil's dirty tricks and be alert to them.

Belief in God and prayer protect us from the problems that come from the devil. Living in God's presence also keeps the devil away. Just be aware that God is watching over us all the time. Turn to Him in prayer. Our powerful God will always give us all the help we need.

To his followers Jesus did not say, "Try to be perfect." He said, *"Be* perfect as your heavenly Father is perfect." *Being perfect means getting a passing grade on our daily tests on humility and charity. Even though we fail, we must keep trying the way a law student keeps trying to pass the bar exam. The good example we set helps others much more than books and sermons. For those who seek the spiritual perfection that brings inner peace and eternal happiness, the finishing school is the School of Christ.*

I am not trying to convert anyone to the Catholic faith. There is only one God. All believers worship and pray to the same God. Whatever church or faith you belong to, your faith is the foundation of your inner peace. Only God can give this gift of faith, which money cannot buy and which no one can take from you. You alone can lose or reject this gift of faith. Your faith in God is your first step into God's peace.

Whether you are a Hindu, a Buddhist, a Jew, a Christian, a Muslim or some other seeker of God doesn't matter. We are all children of the same God. We all need His help; we all seek His peace. *Knowing that God respects the free will of everyone, I also respect everyone's free choice. We are not doing God's will when we prevent others from using their free will. We may disagree with the choices of others, but we should not tamper with their free will.* We should never argue about religion. We can share our thoughts, but not to argue over who's right.

God didn't say, "You *must* do My will." He does not force anyone to do His will. He simply asks and invites us to do so. God has too much respect for each of us to tamper with our free will.

I try to be like God in respecting the free of every human person. I am a Catholic who believes that abortion is wrong and goes against God's will. But I respect the free choice of women to have an abortion, even though I disagree with that choice. I let God judge them for that choice.

I respect every woman's free will, but I know having a child is better than having precious jewelry. Every human life is precious to God. For the sake of God the Father, the Giver of life, women thinking of having an abortion should pray to the Holy Spirit for help in making the right choice. The Holy Spirit is all love, and He will never inspire anyone to hurt herself or another person. Pray before deciding about an abortion. Pray to Mary, the Mother of Jesus.

The devil, our worst enemy, is out to destroy lives and souls. No one should be an instrument of the devil in destroying life. Besides destroying human life, I think abortions also destroy the dignity of womanhood.

Our God of love is so loving that He wants everyone to make the right choice. If you're thinking about having an abortion, ask God for the courage to have your child. If you can't keep your baby, give your baby up for adoption. So many good couples are seeking to adopt a baby. God will always provide for your needs when you do His will.

## Tests from Neighbors

When we first moved into our new home on McCully Street in Honolulu in 1944, we became friendly with all the neighbors. The Ls were our next-door neighbors. Mr. L was from China. He was a chef at the Wagon Wheel Restaurant in Waikiki. Mrs. L was a Hawaiian lady everybody called *Amu* (Chinese for "lady"). I respected her and treated her with love and kindness as if she were my mother. On Mother's Day I bought her a triple-strand lei of *pikake* (jasmine) flowers. I was hungering for a mother's love.

But shortly after we moved in, Thomas ruined everything. Because of him, Amu ruined my joy of living in that home. She had seven low-growing Samoan coconut trees along our property. Their low branches hanging over our property were in the way when Thomas had to make a driveway leading to our garage at the back of the house. One afternoon while I was cooking dinner, Thomas, without asking me or Amu, cut off all the branches hanging over our property. The coconut trees looked terrible with all the branches cut off on one side.

When Amu saw her trees with all the branches cut off on one side, she screamed and yelled at us. Thomas just yelled back at her with foul language. Amu telephoned her eldest son, Joe, and her eldest daughter, Dorothy, to come over to see what Thomas did to her trees. Joe and Dorothy stood on the porch with Amu as she yelled at us, and Thomas swore back at her.

Even though I had treated her with respect and kindness, and she knew Thomas was the one who had cut off the branches on our side of the property, she blamed me and held a grudge against me for years. She never gave me the chance to tell her Thomas did it on his own. If I had known Thomas was going to do it, I would have stopped him, and I would have told him to talk it over with Amu first.

From my terrible experience with Amu, I learned the importance of having good neighbors. A bad neighbor can make life miserable for us, while a good neighbor can come over to help in an emergency even before our family members can arrive. Before moving into a neighborhood, it's important to check it out and also the people living there, for the peace of your family.

When we moved to our new home up St. Louis Heights, we gave none of the neighbors our new address. We didn't even tell them we were moving. Several years after we moved, I met Amu at a bus stop on King Street. We greeted each other.

*Many people hold grudges against the other members of a family when someone commits a crime. This is unfair to the innocent. Never blame the innocent members of a family for the wrongdoing of one person. What we do to the innocent we do to God Himself. Never pick on an innocent person for what someone else did.*

*Many people care only about
their physical appearance: their face, hair,
body, weight, clothes. What about their souls?*

# 4

# SPECIAL GRACES

After my baptism, I slowly realized that God gave me special graces. I am sure that God gives special graces to every newly-baptized person. Here are some of the special graces God gave me soon after my baptism.

## The Enthronement

One of my happiest events happened on December 21, 1950. This is how God led me to having the Enthronement to the Sacred Heart of Jesus in our home.

Since I couldn't understand the Bible, I went to the Catholic bookstore for simple books I could understand. Bagley's used to be the religious store on Merchant Street. I told Mrs. Bagley I wanted to learn more about my religion, and she showed me several books that I looked at but couldn't understand. Then I saw the little black book

*Come Holy Spirit,* which cost only $3.95. The book was simple enough for me to understand. That was the best book for gaining true devotion to the Holy Spirit. It can help all priests, even the pope, to a close relationship with the Holy Spirit if it is used with a deep desire for His guidance and help and used every day.

That book taught me all about the Holy Spirit and how to pray to Him. As the Spirit of Jesus Christ, the Holy Spirit dwells in us to teach, guide, help, inspire, strengthen and console us in our spiritual life. When I read about His Seven Gifts (wisdom, understanding, counsel, fortitude, knowledge, piety, fear of the Lord), I wanted them with my whole heart. When I read about His Twelve Fruits (charity, joy, peace, patience, kindness, goodness, generosity, gentleness, faithfulness, modesty, self-control, chastity), I wanted them, too. I was so determined to receive His Gifts and Fruits that I began the novena to the Holy Spirit given in the book the very next day. (A novena is nine straight days of special prayers for a special intention.)

I walked to the Sisters' chapel after attending daily Mass at St. Patrick Church to begin the novena to obtain the Gifts and Fruits of the Holy Spirit, but I didn't know how to make the novena. After the same opening prayers for each day, there was a different reading and a different prayer for each of the nine days. Instead of doing the reading and prayer for each day, I did all the readings and said all the prayers for all nine days each day. It took me almost an hour to do all the readings and prayers each day, and I did it with attention and fervor because I was so anxious to receive the Gifts and Fruits of the Holy Spirit.

I treasured that small book on devotion to the Holy Spirit with its many prayers, because it taught me true devotion to the teacher and guide of my soul. This book has been my favorite and most valuable book. *The secret to living the spiritual life fully to achieve holiness is having true devotion to the Holy Spirit. This true devotion means praying to Him for guidance every day, and relying on Him for help every day in matters big and small.*

On the last day of the novena, I walked across the street from the church to the chapel of the Sacred Hearts Sisters. There I did all the readings and said all the novena prayers and then spent time in silence before the Blessed Sacrament. Then the "inner voice" told me to have the "Enthronement of the Sacred Heart of Jesus" in our home. I had never heard of the "Enthronement." I was excited over the request, so I rushed home before I forgot what the "inner voice" had told me.

As soon as I got home I telephoned Father J. I told him what had happened, and asked whether he knew about such a thing as the "Enthronement of the Sacred Heart of Jesus." Father said, "Yes, there is, Florence. Father Mateo Crawley-Boevey, a Sacred Hearts priest, began and promoted this devotion." I was relieved and happy to hear that there was something called the Enthronement.

Father asked, "When do you want it done, Florence?"

"I'll leave it up to you, Father."

"Let's see. Let's have it on December 21 at 3:00 in the afternoon. I'll write to the Center for the pamphlets."

"Okay, Father."

The "inner voice" revealed the meaning of the Enthronement to me: This ceremony welcomes Jesus into our home, where we enthrone Him as king and head of our family. As Lord, Master, King and God, Christ reigns mainly in our hearts as we serve Him by serving others. With the King of kings enthroned in our hearts, we don't need an altar to worship Him. We can worship Christ enthroned in our hearts wherever we are, at any time. This meaning of the Enthronement was real for me. What helped me to understand the Enthronement of Jesus as king in our home was a custom and saying of the ancient Chinese: "To welcome the emperor into one's home and then enthrone him as emperor of the house." So I knew the Enthronement was a *big* event. Jesus was coming into our home to reign as king, and I wanted to give him the place of honor.

Because Jesus and His enthronement were so real to me (now more than ever), I tried my best to prepare our home and my heart for welcoming the King. After giving the house a complete cleaning, I had it painted inside and out. I bought a small table-like cabinet and turned it into an altar. The two front sliding panels were mirrors that distracted us when we knelt to pray the family rosary, so I replaced them with sliding wooden panels. I bought a large picture of Jesus, with His Sacred Heart showing, from Sister Damien Joseph at the Sacred Hearts gift shop. Brother Ralph Smith framed it, but he wouldn't accept payment for his time and materials when we picked it up the day before the ceremony of Enthronement.

The Sacred Heart represents the human and divine love of Jesus for us. It tells me that everything must flow from the heart, from love. My devotion to the Sacred Heart of Jesus began then. Later I offered myself to God as a little victim soul of the Sacred Heart for the salvation of souls. I was also reminded of what my grandma told me: "We must have a good heart, a compassionate heart, and a religious heart."

It was raining heavily the evening Thomas and I brought the picture home. When I took off the wrapping in front of my family, the picture of Jesus came alive before my eyes for several seconds.

"Can you see Jesus? He's alive."

No one spoke. I began describing Jesus as I saw Him come alive. Then everyone stood silent as I hung the picture on our living room wall above the altar I had bought for the Enthronement. (Today, 48 years later, I still treasure that picture of Jesus and His Sacred Heart which came alive for me.)

On the day of the Enthronement, my invited friends came to share in the joy. At 3:00 in the afternoon Father J performed the blessing and recited the formal prayers of the Enthronement. Afterward I served our guests chow mein from a Chinese restaurant and jasmine tea. After we had eaten, a friend told me in private, "You're going to suffer like hell, Florence." I didn't understand why she said that or what she meant. Brother Strauss, the last to leave, also said to me as he was leaving, "You're going to suffer, Florence." His words puzzled me, but I didn't ask him what he meant.

The memory of that joyous event has lingered in my mind and heart these past 48 years. I use pleasant memories to help me serve God with calmness of heart in times of trials and suffering. I know He loves a cheerful giver not only in good times, but at all times.

Father J returned to our home about 7:30 that evening to visit. He stayed till after 10:00. I think he sensed something special about our home. Perhaps he felt the presence of God and His special peace.

I was the last to go to bed. Everybody was asleep by 11:30. Then Jesus gave me a sign that He had come to our home and had accepted my welcoming Him as the king and head of our family.

As I got into bed I felt and heard a loud thud like an earthquake, and I heard a horrible cry of anguish from a man in agony, a cry loud enough to shake the walls.

"Thomas, wake up. Something happened."

"Huh?"

"I heard a man cry out."

"It's the neighbors. Somebody's drunk." He fell asleep again.

I felt a deep peace. I looked at the alarm clock. It was just after midnight. I got out of bed and was guided to the living room where the Enthronement ceremony had taken place just hours ago. I went to the picture of Jesus above the altar and asked, "What's the matter, Jesus?" I pulled up a chair and sat in silence to be with Him. I sat there for a while, and then went to bed.

When I woke up that morning, the thought came to me that I should make a holy hour before the Enthronement altar once a month. Jesus was inviting me to do that. I recalled what He asked His disciples on Holy Thursday at the Garden of Gethsemane: "Could you not watch one hour with Me?" I wanted to make up to Jesus because His disciples didn't stay up with Him for an hour.

Later that morning I telephoned Father J.

"Hello, Father, this is Florence."

He sighed loud enough for me to hear and asked, "Now what?"

"Is there such a thing as making a holy hour in reparation for sins before the Enthronement?"

"The booklet says some generous souls spend a holy hour before the Enthronement altar once a month. Do you want a specific hour and day of the month for this?"

"I prefer to let Jesus choose the time and day of my monthly holy hour."

When Father J wrote the Enthronement Center to enroll me as a member, he also asked for a day and time for my monthly holy hour. The Center surprised me with the day and time it assigned me: the twenty-second of each month from 11:00 to midnight. I had heard the loud cry of agony on December 21 at midnight, and I spent the first part of December 22 with Jesus in front of His picture. *In the spiritual life there are no coincidences. I believe that everything is governed by Divine Providence.*

That loud cry of anguish revealed the extent of Christ's suffering on the Cross. It was loud enough to shake the whole house. I pictured Jesus crying out in agony when men dropped the Cross with Jesus nailed to it into the hole that held up the Cross. The Cross with Jesus on it dropped into the hole with a thud. The jolt must have made Him cry out in agony. God used that cry of agony to teach me, a new Catholic with little schooling, how our sins made Jesus suffer and how much He loves us. I never told my family or anyone what I experienced that night of our Enthronement. Today, 48 years later, I can still hear how that loud cry of agony sounded.

That's why Jesus is so dear to me. Any Christian who heard His cry of agony would willingly accept suffering to make up to Him for His suffering on the Cross. It would be a privilege to do so. If He loved me so much, how could I not love Him in return? Ever since then, for love of Jesus I accepted my suffering in silence and in secret.

*I applied the words of Jesus – "Don't let your left hand know what your right hand does" – not only to the good I did for others, but also to the sacrifices and suffering I offered to God. I also applied those words to special blessings that I kept as secrets between me and God.*

Each of the roses I bought for our Enthronement ceremony got as big as a rice bowl and lasted more than a month. When people asked me where I had bought the roses, I told them. But the roses others bought from the same florist never got as big or lasted as long. I took that as a sign of Jesus' love for me. For weeks after the Enthronement I felt intense joy.

*The more we love God, the more He blesses us. He loves us all, and He asks for only our love. But we have to prove our love for Him. We have to do all things out of love for God, and not to please self or to gain praise from others.*

When others learned about the Enthronement in our home, they also asked for it in their homes: Mrs. C, Mrs. Mary Lum, Mrs. Boles, Mrs. Shimabukuro and Mrs. Spencer.

Father J asked Helen Woodall, one of our parishioners, to invite me to a retreat. He knew those retreats would continue to teach me about the Catholic religion. Helen and I used to work together as waitresses more than 15 years ago. Half an hour before she telephoned me, the "inner voice" told me I would be invited to a retreat and to accept the invitation. I didn't know then what a retreat was.

As I listened to the radio while ironing, once again a song about a mockingbird gave me a strange feeling and image. I saw and felt myself as a nun coming out of a tomb in a convent, the way a butterfly comes out of its cocoon. I felt as though I became that nun. Again, I can't explain that mysterious experience. It passed quickly.

As I continued ironing that quiet morning, the phone rang and I picked it up. Helen told me who she was and that she had heard about my recent baptism. Just as the "inner voice" had predicted, she invited me to be her guest at a Sunday retreat sponsored by the Catholic Women's Guild. I told her how happy I was to hear from her, and I accepted her invitation with gladness, but without telling her that the "inner voice" had prepared me for her invitation.

On the morning of the retreat, Helen drove me to St. Francis Convent for the retreat. She introduced me to the retreat master, the priest who would give several talks. Between those talks there were periods of silence for reflection, spiritual reading and personal prayer. Even though I listened carefully, I couldn't understand the talks because the priest used many difficult words I didn't know.

I suppose I did gain something from that first retreat by just being there and trying to learn. *I now know that God reads our hearts and rewards us according to our intentions and efforts.*

My longing to learn about Jesus and how to please Him moved me to accept more invitations to retreats and lectures. A few weeks after that first retreat, Helen invited me to a lecture on Mary, the Mother of Jesus, at the hall next to the Cathedral of Our Lady of Peace. Again, I couldn't understand what the priest was talking about, but I continued to listen along with the other ladies. When they clapped, I clapped; when they laughed, I laughed. After the lecture I joined some ladies in thanking the priest for a wonderful lecture.

Then I went into the cathedral to pray. As I sat in silence before praying the rosary, the "inner voice" told me someone was waiting for me at the side door. I recited the rosary slowly while pondering the mystery of each decade of beads. Normally a person would turn around out of curiosity to look or even go out to meet the person. But I had faith in the "inner voice." Instead of being distracted, I prayed with attention because that was the reason I went into the church. I also prayed slowly to test the patience of the person waiting for me. (I enjoy being playful with people.) If she thought I was good enough to be her friend, she would wait. I never went looking for friends.

I finished the rosary and went to the side door. A Chinese lady was waiting for me. She was the lady who had sat next to me at the lecture, but we never spoke to each other.

"I saw you at the lecture and followed you. I'm Ruth C."

"I'm Florence. You must be a schoolmarm."

"Who told you I was a school teacher?"

"Nobody."

She was surprised that I knew even though we never met. She said, "I used to teach at Punahou School and I also taught Chinese at Mung Lung School. My husband is Dr. R. C., a general practitioner."

"I knew someone was waiting for me, so I prayed the rosary slowly, as I usually do, to test your patience and to see if you thought I was good enough to be your friend. You passed the test."

She smiled.

I continued, "I didn't understand what the priest was talking about during his lecture, so I clapped or laughed whenever the other ladies clapped or laughed."

We both laughed.

"I never heard of such a thing. Then why did you come to hear this lecture?"

"Because I wanted to learn more about Mary and the teachings of the Catholic Church. I just became a Catholic not long ago."

She asked for my address and phone number.

I gave them to her and said, "Call before you come because I do volunteer work and may not be home."

I didn't make Mrs. C wait because I wanted to finish my rosary first or just to play a game with her. God gave me the wisdom to read a person's character. I gave her the respect due her as a school teacher and as a doctor's wife. Because she waited for me, I knew she didn't look down on me. Lots of people looked down on me because I had no education and no profession. But I didn't look for new friends; I was content being a wife and mother.

I took the precaution of studying a person when she wanted to become friends with me. With Mrs. C, I took it as part of God's plan to bring us together. God used our friendship to teach me many lessons on human nature and the spiritual life.

No one was home the first time she came, bringing a can of ham. She left the ham with a note on our porch. When I returned home, I telephoned to thank her for the ham, and reminded her to call before she came.

When she returned another day, I started telling her about my

childhood experiences. She listened and then told me how much I reminded her of the Little Flower, St. Therese of Lisieux.

"Did you read her autobiography, *The Story of a Soul*?"

"No, I don't read books, because I can read words but I don't understand the meaning of what I read."

"How you remind me of the Little Flower in the words you use
and in the way you say things."

"I don't know what or how I say things to remind you of her."

When Mrs. C came the next day to visit me, she told me, "I told my
husband how you reminded me of the Little Flower. Afterward, he
told me to ask *Little Florence* for her prayers. We need your prayers because he has to move into a new office so he can be on his own."

After that Mrs. C came every day. We spoke about religion and the
spiritual life. She began reading the autobiography of St. Therese to
me. I wasn't interested, but I kept quiet because I didn't want to hurt
her feelings.

One day she drove me to St. Francis Hospital, where I did volunteer work. We went early so we could visit a while. She began reading
to me from the autobiography of St. Therese as we sat on a bench on
the hospital grounds. I lost interest after several minutes. She was being a school teacher to me. I was bored because I wanted to talk about
God, but she kept talking about the Little Flower. So I began chasing a
red cardinal bird on the lawn. She slammed her book shut and never
read to me again.

I have never read a book about St. Therese. I have never bothered
to learn more about her because I never had the desire and I had
trouble understanding what I read in books. But I did choose her as my
patron saint by being confirmed as "Therese" because Father J suggested that name for confirmation.

## Predictions by My First Spiritual Director

A Marianist Brother, back in Honolulu for a visit with his family,
told me I should have a spiritual director to guide me in doing God's
will. He suggested that I see Father Colloton, a former Trappist monk
who had transferred to the Sacred Hearts Order in Hawaii because of
his health. I ignored his suggestion. Then someone else telephoned to
tell me about a very spiritual priest she had met – the same priest the
Brother had recommended.

I went to see Father Basil Colloton at St. Patrick Church. His smile and kind words put me at ease. I answered his questions truthfully because I knew there must be trust and openness between the soul and her spiritual director. When I told him I was guided by an "inner voice", he believed me.

"Florence, Jesus loves you very much."

"Jesus loves everybody, Father."

"No, Jesus loves His Blessed Mother more than anyone. He loves you very special. Florence, all Jesus asks of you is to love Him and to pray for everybody. Some day you'll change. People won't recognize you. There'll be no more Florence. You're going to be just like Job."

I didn't understand what he meant. I wondered about what he said. I thought that he meant some day I was going to die and there would be no more Florence.

His words about the love of Jesus for me deepened my desire to love Jesus more and to please Him more. I understood about praying for people and loving Jesus, but I didn't understand the rest of what he said. It took me another 46 years to understand what he meant. I don't know how he knew, but his predictions came true.

These past 48 years, the Saint in my soul began to take over my life more and more. Is this what Father Colloton meant by "Someday you'll change and there'll be no more Florence?" For everything I gave up for love of Jesus, He returned much more to me. I guess that's what Father meant by "You're going to be just like Job."

I told him how quick-tempered I was. So my first lesson in the spiritual life was learning to control my temper. That was hard to practice because of my three children and my irresponsible husband. By nature I am a peaceful person. I never start an argument to hurt anybody. My quick-tempered ways were triggered by others, and made worse when I couldn't find the right words to explain myself. God sees all and knows all, so He knows I'm telling the truth.

As my first spiritual director, Father Colloton spent hours guiding me on how to live as a good Catholic and how to please Jesus. I reported to him twice a month, and I told him how hard it was for me to control my temper. Even though I failed many times, I kept trying. *My determination to love Jesus and to please Him helped me to govern my words and to be more lenient with others. The first step in controlling one's temper is to govern one's words and to live in the presence of God,*

*Who sees everything. With God's help and lots of practice over time, I did overcome my quick-tempered ways.*

God helped me to make progress in the spiritual life by leading me from the natural level to the supernatural level. *The most important practice leading to a closer union with God is living in His presence. To remind myself of His presence, I placed images of Jesus or of Mary in every room of our home,* even in the bathroom: either a crucifix, a picture or a statue. I found this method more helpful than reading about the saints. *Whenever I saw the crucifix, picture or statue, I became aware of God's presence and said a prayer. But all the sacred images in the world will not help if we don't see them and then become aware of God's presence.*

When the pastor came to bless our home, he saw the religious pictures and statues. He said, "Florence, your home is worse than a church." He even told some of his parishioners that I was a religious fanatic. He thought I was trying to appear religious, but I really used those sacred images to remind myself of God's presence and to pray for others.

Now I no longer need sacred images to remind me of God's presence, because now He is so real to me. I believe and know that God is here, there, and everywhere. Being aware of His presence makes it easier to cope with daily difficulties. *It's rewarding to have God as one's constant companion. If more people lived in His presence, there would be fewer complaints about loneliness.*

Father Colloton suggested that I go to confession weekly to the same confessor. I prayed to God to help me find a good one. Then I learned about Father Victorinus, an elderly priest who spent hours hearing the confessions of hundreds of Catholics from all over the island of Oahu. I went into his confessional, told him about Father Colloton's suggestion and asked him to be my confessor. So Father Victorinus became my confessor in 1951. Every Saturday after the noonday Mass at the cathedral, I stood in line waiting for my turn for confession with this wise, kindly priest.

During one confession Father Victorinus told me, *"Whatever you do – eating, sleeping, working, talking, praying – do all for the honor and glory of our heavenly Father." Ever since then I have tried to do everything for the honor and glory of the Father.*

With God's help and guidance from Fathers Colloton and

Victorinus, I gradually overcame some of my failings. *I would hear the "inner voice" giving me recipes for ridding myself of certain faults. For example, whenever someone did me wrong and then an uncharitable thought against that person came to mind, I should think of something nice that person did for me. Then I should force myself to ask God repeatedly to bless that person. It was like a game to trick the mind into thinking good thoughts about those who stir up uncharitable ones. This recipe also helped me to pray more often.*

*To prevent me from thinking that I was better than others who did wrong, the "inner voice" inspired me to pray, "Blessed Mother, please don't let me commit that same fault" or "Please don't let me be like that." These were two of the many recipes the "inner voice" gave me. Each person and each situation are different. But if you seek guidance from the Holy Spirit, He will inspire you with the proper course of action for you in your situation.*

Looking back at my beginning years as a Catholic, I thank God for His love and wisdom in giving me Father Colloton as my spiritual director and Father Victorinus as my confessor.

Weekly confession was like going to a doctor for a checkup. My confessor checked the state of my soul and the progress I made on the virtue he gave me to practice for the week. With fatherly concern he corrected me or instructed me according to my need. He answered my questions about right and wrong and about the spiritual life. Along with trying his best to guide and help me, Father Victorinus' best quality was his sense of humor.

Father Colloton gave me lots of spiritual guidance. When he was helping out at St. Francis Hospital, he advised me to make a total consecration of myself to the Immaculate Heart of Mary. To prepare me for this personal consecration, he explained its meaning and read sections from a thick book. I didn't understand most of what he read to me.

It was the "inner voice" that revealed the deep meaning of this total consecration: surrendering my entire being, body and soul, my free will and all I had to God *through* Mary. This consecration allowed Blessed Mother to dispose of everything of mine as she pleased for the greater honor and glory of God. No one knows how to please God better than Christ's own mother. This consecration simplified my life, so I could serve God wholeheartedly with spiritual freedom.

I thought of how a mother can tidy up and gift-wrap a present for her child before presenting it to someone. If I offered up all my good deeds and sacrifices to Jesus through my spiritual mother, she could purify my offering before presenting it to Him on a silver platter. (I thought of a silver platter because the wife of a TV repairman had given me a roasted turkey on a silver platter for Thanksgiving.) So I often served others or made secret sacrifices for God with "All for Jesus through Mary."

On the day of my consecration to Mary, I knelt before the crucifix in Father Colloton's cottage to recite the consecration prayer with deep love for Blessed Mother and with complete trust in her. Being a lady of my word, I tried my best to live up to the consecration. I wanted to belong completely to God with the help of my spiritual mother.

## Visions

On New Year's Day the children were out. As Thomas and I drank coffee in the kitchen, for no reason at all he said, "You'll never go to heaven."

His words cut deep. I thought, "Then why be baptized? What's the use of being a Catholic?" I asked Thomas why I wouldn't go to heaven, but he never told me why. One of the cruelest things a person can say to another is that she will never go to heaven. And of all days, on New Year's Day, the first day of the new year.

The next day while Thomas was at work and the children were at school, Mrs. C came for a visit. As she and I talked in the living room, I recalled Thomas' words and I started crying. I cried hard because his words made me think I had offended Jesus in a serious way. I cried so hard because I loved Jesus and I wanted to face Him after death with no regrets.

Suddenly a man in a white robe stood before me as I sat facing Mrs. C. With His arms out to welcome me, He stood facing me with his back to her. He looked down at me with the most loving eyes I have ever seen. I have never seen such a kind face and merciful eyes. He was not a white man. He had dark eyes and olive skin. Then I realized that it was Jesus. I stopped crying, wiped my tears with the bottom of my red and white floral muumuu, and began giggling. Jesus appeared and disappeared in a blink. But the image of His kind, merciful face and eyes is printed in my soul.

Mrs. C didn't see him, and something prevented me from telling her what I saw. She was surprised by my sudden tears and then by my sudden giggles. She said, "Oh, Florence, I thought I hurt you by something I said." I told her no.

That night she telephoned to tell me what she had told her husband: "Florence is just like a child; crying one moment and then laughing the next."

I think Jesus appeared to me to reassure me that He had forgiven all my sins. He set me at peace and made me happy again. I saw His entire body in a simple white robe, but in a flash He was gone. I'll never forget that vision of Jesus. I saw Him from head to foot and with His arms out to welcome me. I can still picture Him. His love, kindness, gentleness and mercy all showed in His eyes. No painting or picture of Jesus has come close to resembling the face and eyes I saw. No artist can paint His face and those eyes.

Jesus appeared to me in my living room. He appeared and disappeared in a flash, but He gave me a complete understanding of His merciful love. I still remember exactly how He looked. Anyone who saw Him as I did would love Him above all others on earth.

The following August the "inner voice" inspired me with the thought, "Where there is a king, there must be a queen." I felt that something was missing; I loved Blessed Mother and wanted her for my queen. So I telephoned Father J. When he recognized my voice, he asked, "Now what?"

"Is there such a thing as enthronement to welcome a queen into the home?"

"No, there isn't. But there is a consecration of the home and family to the Immaculate Heart of Mary. We could do that. When do you want the Consecration done?"

"I'll leave that up to you."

"Let's see. Let's do it on the feast of the Immaculate Heart of Mary, August 22, at 7:00 in the evening. You can go and get a large picture of the Immaculate Heart of Mary from Sister Damien Joseph."

"What about the leaflets for the ceremony?"

"Ask Sister Damien Joseph. She must have some."

I was happy that Father J had chosen the Feast of the Immaculate Heart of Mary.

When I told Thomas and the children that I found out there was a Consecration to the Immaculate Heart of Mary, Thomas looked at the children and asked, "Now what?" Tommy also said, "Now what?"

I went to Sister Damien Joseph to buy a large picture of Mary pointing to her heart. I bought the last one she had that matched the big picture of Jesus, and some leaflets for the ceremony. I took the picture to a shop for framing, because I didn't want to take advantage of Brother Ralph Smith, who wouldn't charge us for the materials and for his work.

As I did for Christ the King, I did my best to prepare home and heart for His mother the queen. Guided by the "inner voice," I wanted to welcome Mary into our home and into my heart as queen. Even though she is humble and our spiritual mother, she is still queen because her son Jesus is King.

On the day of our Consecration to the Immaculate Heart of Mary, I went to an early Mass and then to Watanabe, wholesaler of cut flowers. I bought two dozen roses of all colors. That evening at 7:00, members of the Junior Chinese Catholic Club and other guests packed our home. Father J brought Father Gallagher, a missionary who had served in China. Even my father-in-law came. Dr. and Mrs. C kept everyone waiting and delayed the ceremony to 7:30 by being 30 minutes late. After Father J consecrated our home and family to the Immaculate Heart of Mary, he led us in praying the rosary in her honor. Then we celebrated with cookies and soft drinks the guests had brought. That special evening filled everyone with spiritual joy.

Jesus had crowned His Blessed Mother Queen of heaven and earth. Mary is also the Queen of Martyrs and the Queen of All Saints. So I wanted her to be the queen of our home and the queen of my heart. I was the mother of our home, and Mary was its queen mother. I relied on her in my cooking and cleaning. I cried to her whenever I had problems. She was a mother who listened to my problems and consoled me.

*Anyone who honors His mother, Jesus will bless in a special way.* My father-in-law came alone on the bus because his wife didn't want to come. Jesus rewarded him years later by giving him the gift of faith before he died at age 81.

After the Consecration to Mary, I told Father P, the pastor, that I wanted to go to China to teach the Chinese people about Jesus. He said nothing, but he gave me a strange look. At that time I didn't know anything about the Communists taking over China and stopping the practice of religion. Later someone told me what Father P had said about me: "A new broom sweeps clean; but when it gets old, it'll just stay in the closet. We'll wait and see." I didn't know what he meant by that.

Years later someone explained that Father P had meant that I had the first fervor and enthusiasm of being a new Catholic, but they would eventually fade away. Father was wrong. Today, 48 years later at age 83, my love for God is a thousand times stronger. So is my desire to do God's will and His work. My prayer life has reached out to everyone on earth and to all the dead. I pray for all the needs of the Church and of the world.

Because of the Enthronement and the Consecration, the "inner voice" told me to pray the family rosary. So I told the family we would pray the family rosary every evening. Since I was the only one who knew all the mysteries, I had to lead the rosary. We knelt before the altar to pray the family rosary every evening. My husband and three children never resisted or grumbled. If anyone planned to go out for the evening, then we prayed the rosary together earlier.

The family rosary was promoted by Father Patrick Peyton, a Holy Cross priest. His motto was: "The family that prays together stays together." The family rosary can help to prevent divorce and keep the family together. It will also help the children to keep the practice of their faith and to have true devotion to Mary, their spiritual mother. Even when the children grow up, leave home and marry, the family will still be together in spirit.

But parents should detach themselves from their grown children, who belong to God. Parents should not be possessive and interfere with the marriage of their children. Children should also detach themselves from their parents after marriage, and avoid running home with every problem. I encourage Catholic families to pray the family rosary together every Sunday. But this practice must begin when the children are small. As the children grow older, arrangements can be made for the teenagers. Even if some have to leave after one decade of the rosary, the rest of the family can finish the rosary.

*I suggest that every Catholic mother lead her family in praying the rosary together every Sunday. If not on Sunday, then once a week when the family can pray together. Blessed Mother will protect and help the families that pray the rosary together. She will ask her son Jesus to grant many blessings to these families.*

With its crucifix and all its prayers, the rosary is the best weapon Blessed Mother uses to defend the family and the Church against the devil. That's why she asked Bernadette at Lourdes and the three children of Fatima to pray the rosary and to ask others to pray the rosary. Those who honor their spiritual mother by following her request to pray the rosary will be blessed by God. We Catholics believe that all graces come to us through Mary, because of the big part she played in the life of Jesus, Who loves her, honors her and grants all her requests.

The rosary deepens our faith and prayer life, because the Creed is a profession of faith in all our main beliefs, and the "Our Father" is a complete prayer. We also salute Mary with the words of the archangel Gabriel and of her cousin Elizabeth, and then ask for Mary's prayers. We end each decade with the "Glory Be" to glorify the Holy Trinity.

*All glory must go to the Father, the Son and the Holy Spirit. Many of us steal glory and honor from God when we seek praise for ourselves. We forget that we live and breathe and move and have our total being in God.* We Christians forget that Christ is the Head of His Mystical Body and we are only His members.

If we ponder the mystery of each decade with love for Jesus and Mary, the rosary will never become boring. At times we may be distracted, but Jesus will bless our effort to recall the important events of His life. Praying the rosary links us to Jesus and Mary. When done to honor Christ and His mother, and lived up to, the Enthronement and Consecration will bring many special blessings. Because of God's presence in the home and Mary's prayers, each family member will have peace and protection.

I hope and pray that the practice of these devotions will continue and spread throughout the world. Catholic families should learn and think about having the Enthronement and Consecration in their homes to honor Jesus and His mother.

One day two young missionaries of the Mormon Church knocked at my door and introduced themselves. I told them I was a Catholic, but they wanted to come in anyway. When they saw my large picture of the Immaculate Heart of Mary, one asked, "Why do you Catholics worship Mary along with Jesus Christ?"

"We don't worship Mary. She's a human creature. We worship Jesus because He's God. We honor Mary because she's the mother of Jesus. Here, take out your wallet."

"What?"

"Take our your wallet and show it to me."

When he took out his wallet, I pointed to the picture of his mother in his wallet and asked, "Do you worship your mother as God because you love her and carry her picture in your wallet?"

He laughed and said no.

"See. We Catholics love and honor Mary because she's the mother of Jesus, not because she's God. She's also our spiritual mother, because Jesus on the cross gave her to us when He said, 'Behold thy mother.'"

(Forty-six years later, I realized how Jesus kept His word when He said, "I will not leave you orphans." We were not left orphans for an instant before the Holy Spirit descended on the Apostles on Pentecost, because before dying on the cross Jesus gave us His own mother to be our spiritual mother. So we were not orphans even for an instant.)

I also told them, "When my children want something from their dad, they often come to me and have me ask him for them. They know I can get things and permission for them. That's why we Catholics go to Mary – to have her ask her son, Jesus, for us. Jesus loves and honors His mother, and He will always grant her requests.

As they were leaving, they asked to come again because they found me so interesting.

I usually lay down about 3:00 in the afternoon to rest and to meditate. I closed my eyes, kept silent, and then prayed: "Holy Spirit, teach me and guide me. Draw me to the top of the mountain where I can be alone with God and contemplate His love for me and for all mankind. Teach me what I ought to know." I wanted to hear the word of God, to keep His word, and to be a doer of His word.

On September 15, about 3:00 in the afternoon, as I lay half awake in bed, a woman with a black veil over her face and dressed in black appeared to me. She pointed to a beating heart while she gave me the thought, "This is my son you have sinned against." Then the vision disappeared. I saw only a live beating heart, pinkish in color, without the body. It was not a painted heart. I saw a real, live human heart. Later while I was cooking dinner, I realized it was the Feast of Our Lady of Sorrows, and the woman I saw in black was her. I never saw her face.

Catholics believe that no woman ever suffered as much as Mary the Mother of Jesus because of her anguish when she saw her son carrying his cross and stood at the foot of the cross as he suffered and died an agonizing death slowly. All artists have painted Mary, Our Mother of Sorrows, dressed in black.

From the time I heard the loud cry of agony from Jesus on the night of the Enthronement and months later when I saw the vision of Our Lady of Sorrows with the beating heart of her son Jesus, I thought of making reparation to the Sacred Hearts of Jesus and Mary for our sins. When someone came to me for spiritual help, I often suggested accepting trials and suffering to make up to God for one's own sins or the sins of others.

For weeks after I saw Our Lady of Sorrows, I felt terrible because I took her words to mean that my sins alone made Jesus suffer on the Cross. Only weeks later did I realize that the "you" meant "you humans." During the months after the vision, I kept asking Jesus, "What makes Your heart tick so perfect?" I asked so I could be like Him, so my heart would tick as perfect as His heart. Then one day while waiting for a bus, I got the answer to what makes the heart of Jesus tick so perfect: His love, wisdom, goodness and compassion.

## Detach from Creatures

Once a year the Catholic Women's Guild sponsored a weekend retreat, which began Friday evening and ended Sunday afternoon. A retreat of one day was also called a day of recollection. Once a month on a Sunday the Guild sponsored a day of recollection, which began at 8:00 in the morning and ended at 3:00 in the afternoon. Since I was eager to learn about Jesus and the spiritual life, I went to many of those days of recollection.

One Sunday retreat stands out for me even today. Mrs. C was coming for me at 7:30 in the morning. I woke up before 6:00 and lay in bed. Suddenly a man in a black robe appeared to me at the foot of the bed and said in a manly, stern voice: "To do My Father's will, detach from creatures." Then He was gone. Those words were not said aloud; they just flashed into my mind. It happened so quickly that I couldn't get a good look at His face. But the image and the words "To do My Father's will, detach from creatures" are printed in my memory. Although what happened startled me, I felt peaceful. I lay still in bed pondering His words. The word "detach" puzzled me.

I figured out that the man was Jesus, but I never told anyone that He appeared to me, except to Mrs. C that morning (and my spiritual son many years later). I didn't let this vision affect what I did every day or wondered what would happen. I just let Jesus lead me as though I were a puppy following its master.

When Mrs. C came to pick me up for the retreat, I told her exactly what had happened. I asked her the meaning of what I had heard, especially the word "detach." She explained detachment clearly enough for me to understand its meaning.

From time to time the "inner voice" reminded me of these words: "To do My Father's will, detach from creatures." At first I thought I had to be away from my friends, relatives and neighbors. But I never thought I had to be away from my husband, children and grandchildren. Those words became real as God led me step-by-step to a high degree of detachment.

[*Catholic spiritual writers have used the term "attachment" to denote undue preoccupation with a person, activity, or thing to the detriment of one's spiritual progress and union with God. The goal of "detachment" is to put God above all creatures and to focus on pleasing Him rather than on one's own satisfaction. Florence used to say, "Jesus, detach me from creatures that I may be attached to You 100 percent."*]

At the retreat, the preacher was a young priest. In his first conference he said, "We should try to see Christ in everyone." Because I thought I was in class, I raised my right hand. Surprised, the priest stopped talking, looked at me and nodded. He probably expected me to ask to be excused to use the bathroom.

"Yes, what is it?"

"But Father, sometimes I can't see Christ in people. I see more of the devil in them. How can I see Christ in everyone?" I was speaking from my experience of being mistreated by others.

The young priest didn't know what to say; his face turned red. The room with 83 women was completely quiet and still. The priest didn't answer me. He continued talking.

After the conference Mrs. C told me softly, "Florence, if I had orchids, I would give them to you because you were brave enough to speak the truth." But the ladies in charge of the retreat told Mrs. C to keep me quiet during the other conferences.

In a kindly way, Mrs. C said, "Florence, the ladies in charge said you shouldn't raise your hand. It's not a classroom. Just let the priest talk without asking any questions."

I really wanted to know how I could see Christ in everyone. I was hoping the priest could teach me how to do that.

To make up to the priest, after the retreat I thanked him for the retreat and said, "I'll remember what you said about being content. Every time I get angry, I'll think of the picture of the contented cow on the can of evaporated milk to remind myself to be content like a contented cow." He and the ladies around him smiled. I think he realized that I had little schooling.

Several weeks after our retreat, Mrs. C told me to see Father McMonagle at Star of the Sea Church. She said he would help me in my spiritual life, and made an appointment for me to see him. When I kept my appointment with him, he asked me a few questions. I don't remember what I said to him, but I usually talked about Jesus.

That evening Mrs. C telephoned me and repeated what Father McMonagle had said about me: "I have never come across such a beautiful soul." I was puzzled. How he could see my soul?

Now I understand the meaning of his words. What a person says and how one says it can reveal one's soul to a spiritual person. Shortly after my baptism, I told God I wanted my soul to be like a shining star to give Him glory or like a burning candle to grace His altar.

After my baptism, I began to dress conservatively. My sister Gertrude told me, "You dress so conservative now. You used to be so stylish. You've changed." I wanted to imitate Blessed Mother in being modest. She was the model I imitated because I wanted to be like her. I think Mary was ordinary only in appearance; it was her soul that was so beautiful. The state of my soul worried me much more than my physical appearance did. I was content to dress neatly, simply and modestly. If my soul was truly beautiful, it was because God made my soul special to be the dwelling place for the soul of a saint.

*Many people care only about their physical appearance: their face, hair, body, weight, clothes. What about their souls? Physical appearance matters little to God. What matters to God is the state of one's soul: how just, pure and loving.*

At a day of recollection Mrs. S, the president of the Guild, treated me badly at the retreat. At breakfast and lunch she sat at the head of a long table and made me sit at her left. At both meals she humiliated me in front of the other women at our table. As I began buttering a slice of bread, she said, "That's not the way to do it, Florence. Break your bread into smaller pieces before buttering each piece like this. Put your butter knife over here like this."

During breakfast, she corrected me as though she were training a small child. While she was humiliating me before the other women at our table, the "inner voice" told me, "Listen humbly and do as you're told, like a good child of God." I obeyed, and accepted the public humiliation for love of Jesus. To accept the humiliation willingly and calmly, I kept repeating during both meals, "All for Jesus; all for Jesus; all for Jesus." She should have shared her knowledge with me in private and with kindness, not in public with strictness.

*Corrections should be made in private. I never corrected my husband or my children in public. I did it at home, and I never corrected my children when I was angry, but waited a day or two before making the correction.*

When Mrs. S received a platter full of food, without helping herself to the food she passed it to the person on her right. By the time the platter came to me, very little scrambled eggs was left. Out of consideration for her, I took a little so Mrs. S could have a regular serving. The "inner voice" was teaching me the important lesson of being considerate toward others.

*Thoughtfulness and consideration are a big part of charity. Without it, no one can enter heaven. True charity includes being understanding and kind toward the uneducated and the less fortunate.*

I don't know whether Mrs. S treated me the way she did because I lacked education or because I was Chinese. People who are better off should be careful about how they treat the lowly: the minorities, the uneducated, the poor. What they do to the lowly, they do to God Himself. I gained many graces from the retreat through obedience and the humiliations I suffered.

God sees the heart and the real motive. The best motive for a retreat is being with Jesus and getting closer to Him under the guidance of the Holy Spirit. Months after the retreat Mrs. S telephoned me to ask, "Florence, please pray for my son Joseph."

I was surprised by her asking for my prayers. She had never done that before. I asked, "Is he sick?"

"No, but he's 12 years old and he's retarded."

"Sure, I'll pray for Joseph."

I kept my word and prayed for him. *I have never refused to pray for someone when asked. One of the main duties of being a Christian is to pray for others. Joseph's condition touched me.*

Although I made every retreat seriously, I was always myself. At one retreat that Mrs. C and I made together, I was in the ladies' room, which had four toilet stalls. I was alone and in the first stall when a lady walked in. I could see below the door of the stall, and I recognized Mrs. C's shoes. I said, "In my Father's house there are many mansions; take your pick." Mrs. C laughed out loud. After the retreat she said, "Florence, you're the only one who makes me laugh. All my other friends are so serious."

At another retreat, after breakfast and lunch, no one took the garbage out to the dump site away from the building, so I did it without being asked. I thought of St. Bernadette's father, who had to haul contaminated waste from the hospital to the dump site away from the village. Following his example, I wanted to take the lowliest job for love of Jesus. So I hauled all the garbage to the dump site. I did it to become like Jesus and Blessed Mother.

When a rainstorm flooded the kitchen with an inch of water, I volunteered to mop up the floor. I did it for Jesus, and because I was the only lady there who didn't wear stockings. I went in barefooted to mop up the floor. I didn't mind doing it for Jesus.

At another retreat the next president of the Guild asked me to taste the cream to see whether it was sour. The cream was curdling in the coffee. She expected me to drink some of it to see whether it was sour.

But the "inner voice" told me to get a cup of coffee and pour some cream in it to taste. I obeyed. It tasted all right. Since I consulted Jesus on everything, I asked, "What's wrong with the cream, Jesus? Everybody says the cream is curdling in the coffee." The thought came at once: "The coffee is so hot that it's cooking the cream." I went into the kitchen to tell that to the ladies. Some giggled; one smiled and said, "Of course." The president didn't say a word. She just stared at me.

The ladies were relieved, because breakfast was about to begin and someone wouldn't have to go to the store to buy some cream for the coffee. Common sense should have told them to smell the cream to see whether it was sour. I felt good in solving the problem for them. God helped me and used me to share the knowledge with the ladies. He can speak to us in many ways, even through a lowly, uneducated person.

At one retreat Mass, Mrs. S sat next to me in the pew. When Mass began, she kept showing me the Latin responses to the Mass and saying them louder than usual. She expected me to say the Latin responses along with her all through the Mass. She was trying to be helpful. The Latin was too hard for me, but I tried my best and didn't rebel.

Mrs. S meant well, but during the Mass was not the time or place to help me with the Latin responses. She distracted me and stopped me from taking part in the Mass with my usual attention and fervor. But I used the incident as a test to practice obedience and humility before the Blessed Sacrament. What irritated me was not the humiliation of being treated like a child in the chapel before the other retreatants, but not having the chance to prepare for Mass.

*I always prepared for every Mass 10 to 15 minutes before it began. I knew it took time and effort to prepare for being a guest at a big, special party. Yet the Mass is the greatest banquet of all and the most sacred. So I prepared spiritually for the Mass because I wanted to be a deserving, worthy guest of Christ.*

I began preparing by naming my intentions: besides family members, grandchildren, relatives and friends, acquaintances and those who asked for my prayers, I also named certain needs of the Church and of the world. Then I offered myself as a little victim soul of the Sacred Heart of Jesus in union with Christ, the victim of all the Masses being offered throughout the world. I also used the private time before Mass to recollect myself (calm my mind and heart) and to have a heart-to-heart talk with Jesus. I wanted to be attentive and a good listener at Mass.

"Jesus, help me be a listener of Your word, a keeper of Your word, and a doer of Your word. I believe You are the Son of the Living God, and You are true God and true man. There is no God but You. I adore You, I worship You, I believe and trust in You. Jesus, I believe it is Your body and blood, soul and divinity, that I receive in Holy Communion."

Then I greet Mary of the Blessed Sacrament. I believe that wherever Jesus is, His mother is also there spiritually. Their two hearts are forever united, so she is always with her son Jesus wherever He is, including being with Him spiritually in the Blessed Sacrament. The thought came of how much it would please Jesus to come into the heart of His mother. So before receiving Communion, I prayed: "Blessed Mother, lend us your Immaculate Heart for receiving your son Jesus, and fill our hearts with your love for Him."

Although I didn't understand the Latin at Mass, God read my desire to worship and praise Him. Years later Jesus used me and the Saint in my soul to change the Mass from Latin to English. Since I used to spend an hour or two with Jesus in church after the weekday Mass every morning, the pastor of St. Augustine Church in Waikiki, asked me to take care of the visiting priests who wanted to say Mass there. Vacationing priests came at different times to say Mass at St. Augustine. I set up the altar, put things away after Mass, and locked up the chalice.

Each visiting priest asked me whether I could give the Latin responses at Mass. When I said no, each priest dismissed me. I had to stay and wait till the Mass was over anyway, so I stayed for the Mass in the front pew. After months of this, I asked Jesus, "What's wrong with English, Jesus? Why does the Mass have to be in Latin? Why don't You change the Latin Mass to English?" Years later Jesus did.

As soon as the daily Missal came out in English, I bought one. No one taught me how to use it. I struggled to learn how to use the daily Missal, and the Holy Spirit helped me because he saw how great my desire was to learn the Mass and to worship God more fervently. The Holy Spirit will never deny help to anyone with a great desire to learn about God and the spiritual life.

Besides changing the Mass from Latin to English, Jesus also made other changes in the Catholic Church in 1963. With the priest's back to the people during Mass, it was difficult to hear the priest. Sometimes I wondered why the priest couldn't face the people as he offered Mass. Then the Church changed this custom and had the priest face the people while offering Mass. This was much better because it was easier to hear the priest, and it showed the Mass as a sharing kind of community worship. Besides, Christ Himself is offering the Mass through the priest, and He would never turn His back to the people.

Another change dealt with the fast before receiving Holy Communion. This fast was a spiritual preparation and a reminder of how special it is to receive Jesus in Communion. The fast allowed no food or drink from midnight until Communion time. Then the pope changed the rule to no food or drink three hours before Communion.

On the Feast of the Assumption of Mary, August 15, I went to the morning Mass, but I didn't receive Communion because I wanted to receive with my son Stephen at the 7:00 evening Mass. Before going to Mass, while cutting some celery I tasted a piece without thinking. Then I realized I wouldn't be able to receive Jesus in Communion. I felt terrible. I complained to Jesus, "What's wrong with celery? Why is the Church so strict about receiving Communion?"

One weekday morning as I was rinsing my mouth after brushing my teeth, I swallowed a bit of water. Again I felt terrible because I wouldn't be receiving Jesus in Communion. Again I complained, "What's wrong with water, Jesus? Water is clean; it washes us. There's nothing wrong with water." Months later the pope changed the Communion fast to our present rule: no food or drink an hour before receiving Communion, but water is allowed at any time. Jesus made these changes for all the people.

I cannot take any credit for these changes. Jesus said, "Ask and you shall receive." So the Saint in my soul used me as her instrument to pray for those changes. In her first lifetime, St. Therese of Lisieux said that from age three on she never refused Jesus anything He asked of her. Because of that and her great love for Him, He has never refused her anything she asked of Him, even granting her desire, "To spend my heaven on earth in doing good."

## Gift from a Saint

Whenever I spent time with Jesus in St. Margaret Mary Chapel at Sacred Hearts Academy, I looked at the words of Jesus to her which were painted over the sanctuary: "Behold this heart which has so loved man, and yet has received so little love in return." I pondered over those words a lot. Later I told Jesus, "I want to love You as You have never been loved before. When I learned about His Blessed Mother, I said, "Jesus, I know no one will ever love You as much as Your Blessed Mother loves You. But I want to challenge everybody else in loving You. I want to love You even more than the Little Flower loved You."

On the Feast of St. Margaret Mary, October 17, I went there for a special High Mass in her honor. The altar was decorated with many large red anthuriums, which resembled hearts. There were no roses. I told St. Margaret Mary I would offer up each bead of the rosary I prayed as a rose for her, so that after five decades of the rosary she would have bouquets of multicolored roses. After the High Mass, a Sister and her helpers brought in one bouquet of roses after another, of all colors. The bouquets were placed on the floor around the altar. They were sent by the alumnae and friends of the Sisters, but they didn't arrive in time for the Mass. The roses brought me special joy, because they were the answer to the rosary I offered to St. Margaret Mary for her feast day. God made my prayers come real.

After Mass I walked a block and a half to Mr. Hickey's home, where he sold religious items. I gave him a pack of cigarettes as I usually did, and then looked at the things in his parlor. The "inner voice" told me to go to the next room and look in the closet. I obeyed. When I opened the closet door, I saw something on the floor with a bed sheet over it. I removed the sheet and saw a statue of the infant Jesus standing and pointing to His exposed heart with the index finger of His left hand, while His right hand was raised to give a blessing. It was a 21-inch statue.

I felt as though I had found Jesus, and I really wanted to take Him home with me. I pictured myself carrying Him home with me.

"Mr. Hickey. Mr. Hickey."

He entered the room.

"You shouldn't keep the statue of Jesus on the floor and covered with a sheet. You should set Him on a table somewhere. I found it and I want to buy it."

"It's not for sale."

"I just came from the High Mass at St. Margaret Mary Chapel for her feast day. I think she wants me to have this statue of Jesus."

"It's not for sale, Florence."

"I want it. You should sell it to me."

"I told you it's not for sale."

Then his niece from Kailua came in to visit him. He introduced her to me as Margaret.

"Happy feast day, Margaret. Today is the feast day of your patron saint."

"I forgot about it."

"Mr. Hickey, sell me that statue of Baby Jesus. I'll pay you whatever you ask. I think St. Margaret Mary wants me to have it."

"I keep telling you it's not for sale."

"Oh, sell it to her, Uncle."

"All right, but I'll sell it to you without the sheet and without any wrapping for $20."

That was a lot of money and he knew I couldn't afford it.

"Can't you make it cheaper?"

"Let her have it for $16, Uncle."

"All right, but you have to carry it home unwrapped. I dare you to carry it home like that."

"I will, I will. I'll give you all the money I have now, and I'll bring you the rest next week."

"Okay."

"Thanks, Mr. Hickey. Thanks, Margaret."

I carried the statue of Baby Jesus in my arms as if I were carrying a baby. When I got on the bus, the driver and the other passengers stared at me as I went to the back and sat down. Perhaps some of them thought I was a religious fanatic, or crazy.

At one of the stops my daughter Audrey got on with some of her high school classmates. I called out to her, but she wouldn't look at me. I told her to come to the back where I was, but she ignored me. She was ashamed to be seen with me.

When we got off near our home she asked, "Mom, why did you carry that statue like that? Why didn't you have it wrapped?"

"Mr. Hickey wouldn't sell it to me unless I carried it home like that. He dared me to do it, so I did it."

At home I dusted the statue and then wiped it with a damp cloth in our bathtub. Then I put the statue of Baby Jesus on the bedstand in my bedroom. The next day I bought a bunch of small dark-red chrysanthemums to put in front of the statue. I asked Baby Jesus to make the flowers last because I couldn't afford to buy more. He answered my prayers – they stayed nice and fresh for more than four weeks. My friends and neighbors came to look at the statue and flowers. Several asked me the title of the statue, but I didn't know it. More people came to look at the flowers that stayed nice and fresh for so long. Then the "inner voice" told me to throw out the flowers, to stop people from coming to look at them out of curiosity. So I threw them out even though they were still good.

I went to pay Mr. Hickey the rest of the $16 I owed him for the statue. I brought him a whole carton of cigarettes to show my gratitude, and I asked him what the title of the statue was, but he didn't know.

Since my friends asked about the statue's title, every day I asked Baby Jesus what it was. Then in the mail I received a leaflet with a prayer that I said every day in front of the statue. While saying that prayer one day, I read the words "O Sacred Heart of the Holy Infant Jesus." That was the title of the statue! I was happy and excited. I said, "So that's your title, Jesus." I was happy because I realized that He had answered me through that leaflet.

I bought a special round stand of hardwood just for the statue. That statue meant so much to me because Jesus was so real to me. I prayed to Baby Jesus often, and He answered all my prayers.

When I visited the home of Mrs. Anna Muraki, my godmother, I saw the same statue in her living room. I told her I had one just like that in my home.

St. Margaret Mary was the saint who had spread devotion to the Sacred Heart of Jesus throughout the Catholic world. I think she gave me the "Sacred Heart of the Holy Infant Jesus" for three reasons. First, I had the Enthronement of the Sacred Heart of Jesus in our home. Second, I had a great devotion to the Sacred Heart of Jesus, especially after Our Lady of Sorrows showed me the beating heart of her son Jesus. Third, I offered my five decades of the rosary as roses for her on her feast day.

Many years later my daughter, Audrey, gave me a book full of pictures of St. Therese of Lisieux and of her convent. In the book is a picture of that same statue in her convent.

Even today I cherish this statue, which stands in my bedroom as a gift from a saint. Even 30 years later while watching a basketball game or football game on TV, I turn to Baby Jesus and ask, "Help them win by one point, or make them turn over the ball." And Jesus answers my prayer. Jesus turns my prayer into reality because I pray from my heart and mean it. I like to play games with Jesus. Now at 83 I'm still a child of God, and I talk to Him like I'm a little girl. So just be yourself and talk to God the Father as a child would.

Every morning as I get up, I face the statue to say, "Good morning, Jesus." My prayers and talks with Jesus are so real to me because Jesus is so real to me. Every statue of Christ should be a reminder to pray or to talk to Him.

For me Jesus is truly present in the Blessed Sacrament. Throughout these past 48 years, I have spent a lot of time with Jesus before the Blessed Sacrament whenever I had the chance. This practice of mine began shortly after my baptism. After daily Mass, I spent about two hours in church or in chapel before the Blessed Sacrament. I just wanted to be with Jesus. Sometimes I was reluctant to leave, so I asked Him to leave my soul with Him in the church or chapel while my body went home to do the chores.

One day, after spending time before the Blessed Sacrament, I left the Chapel of St. Margaret Mary. I was outside the chapel on Sixth Avenue when the "inner voice" told me, "There's no happiness for you in this world." I remember the exact place where I heard those words.

Looking back on my life of 83 years, I see the truth of those words. My life has been full of suffering. But at the time of the suffering I just accepted everything and kept going. Yet God has blessed me with deep peace and many spiritual consolations throughout my life. I have lived a sad life, but I have not been a sad person. People who know me and who meet me know how cheerful I am. Most of my sufferings have been so hidden that only God knows of them.

Because I spent so much time in church or in chapel, some people thought I was either troubled or lonely. I wasn't. I just wanted to be with Jesus. *I don't believe in praying or in going to church only when I'm troubled or when I need help from God. We should pray not only in times of trouble, but also in times of peace.* I didn't want to take Jesus for granted, so I told Him, "Jesus, please don't let me take You for granted, especially in the Blessed Sacrament." Then, as now, I talked to Jesus as I talk to any friend. We don't have to be so formal with God. He's our Father. For Christians, Jesus can be a best friend.

The only difficulty I had in spending about two hours in church or in chapel was having a toilet I could use, or having friends wanting me to go to breakfast with them. Those friends took up hours of my time with idle chats, and I had chores to do at home or volunteer work to do elsewhere. Once I accepted an invitation from one, I had to accept the invitations from others so I wouldn't hurt anyone's feelings.

## My First Job for God

God gave me my first big job for Him in the spring of 1952. I read the obituary section of the Honolulu Star Bulletin every day, so I could pray for any friend who passed away, and then attend the wake and funeral to pray for the deceased and to console the family. I read about the death of Mrs. Victoria Young and the family members who survived her. One of her children was Brother John Young, a young religious on the mainland who couldn't attend her funeral Mass. Although I didn't know Mrs. Young and her family, I told Jesus I would represent Brother John Young at his mother's funeral.

Before the funeral Mass began in the cathedral, I went up to the casket and spoke to the soul of Mrs. Young: "I know your son John loves you and wants to be here but can't because he's a religious. So I'm here to represent your son Brother John." The "inner voice" told me to offer up the death of Mrs. Young in union with the death of Jesus on the Cross for conversions and for the return of fallen-away Catholics. I did that right away.

Then I introduced myself to the family and told them I was there to represent Brother John. After Mass I remained in church to pray for his family. His youngest brother, Tony, came to ask me, "Florence, would you go with us to accompany the casket back to Keanae, Maui, for the burial there?"

"I would, but I don't have the money for the plane fare."

"Don't worry about that. We'll pay for the plane fare."

"I'll ask my husband when he gets home from work, and then I'll let you know what he says."

"I'll call you this evening for your answer."

When I asked Thomas about my going with the Young family, he thought I should go. Tony came to pick me up at 6:00 the next morning, a Friday. That was my first trip to another island, and I didn't have a suitcase, so I carried my dresses, petticoat, underwear, toothbrush and toothpaste in a brown grocery bag. The Youngs had 10 children and many grandchildren, so the family chartered a small plane for everybody. After everyone was seated, the casket was tied down in the aisle beside our seats. During the flight Tony asked me to lead the rosary. Tony's relatives met us at the airport and drove us to the village of Keanae along the winding Hana Road.

Before the wake began in the church hall, individuals and groups came to me one after another to question me about religion and about being a good Catholic, or to ask me to teach them how to pray the rosary. Then some came seeking help for going to confession, since they hadn't gone for years. I felt uneasy as each made an open confession to me in private so I could instruct and then direct the person to the pastor for confession. Only priests, who represent Christ, receive His power and authority to forgive sins through the Sacrament of Confession. Actually, it is Christ Himself Who forgives sins in confession; the priest is only His human instrument.

My first encounter with the devil happened that night. During the wake in the church hall, Tony stood up, walked to his mother's casket, started yelling nonsense, pushed the casket with both hands and almost knocked it off its stand. Several men rushed forward to hold the casket and to center it again. Two other men held Tony back. I sensed the presence of the devil. It was scary. Tony's face was black and he seemed to be in a trance. I sprinkled Tony with holy water and the Saint in me said sternly, "Tony, listen to me! Look at me! Keep quiet and calm down." He went limp. I told the two men holding him to take him back to his sister's house. I was driven there in another car.

That was my first encounter with the devil, and it was the scariest experience of my life. If it weren't for the Saint in my soul casting the devil out of Tony at the church hall, I don't know what we would have done.

When I arrived at Dora's house where Tony and I were staying, I found Tony in the basement ready for bed. I decided to stay on the cot near the open entrance to watch over him. Tony didn't even know what had happened to him at the hall. I told him to get a good rest after our long, tiring day. I blessed him with holy water.

I put my holy water and my lighted blessed candle on the nightstand next to Tony's bed. Then I stayed up all night holding a crucifix and praying the rosary. I was too frightened to sleep because I felt the scary presence of the devil. I had goosebumps and chills from fear. I think the devil was after Tony because he had applied to become a religious Brother and was accepted.

The best defenses against the devil are having a crucifix, some holy water, a blessed candle, and praying the rosary. I learned this while doing volunteer work at St. Francis Hospital. The chaplain, Father P, taught me this with the following story:

*There was a holy hermit living on an island across a river. From time to time someone wanted to see him and to ask for his prayers and blessing. At the river's edge was a man with a boat who offered to take anyone across the river. But soon after rowing away from the shore, the man – actually the devil in disguise – would push the person out of the boat into the river.*

*A young man thinking of becoming a priest wanted the advice and prayers of the holy hermit. But he had heard about what the devil was doing to those trying to visit the hermit. So he asked a priest how he could get across the river safely. The priest told him to bring a crucifix, some holy water and a blessed candle, and to pray the rosary. The young man obeyed the priest. As the devil rowed him across the river, he prayed the rosary. When the devil stood up to throw him into the river, he took out his crucifix and blessed candle and sprinkled the devil with the holy water. The devil lost his balance and fell into the river. The young man then rowed himself to the island to seek the advice of the holy hermit.*

Ever since I heard that story, I always wear a crucifix and carry a rosary. I carried holy water in my purse whenever I visited someone's home. If I knew I might have to deal with the devil, I also brought along a blessed candle. These blessed religious objects also helped me in my other encounters with the devil.

After the funeral Mass the next morning, all of Keanae gathered at the gravesite. The pastor began the burial service. Suddenly he started to sob and then hurried away. The visiting priest from Wailuku had to continue and complete the burial service.

Afterward I asked Tony, "What happened to the priest?"

"He does this at every burial. That's why there's always another priest there, because everybody knows he'll break down and can't continue the service. Ever since his mother died, he breaks down at burials because he never made it back to Belgium for his mother's funeral."

After visiting with Tony's relatives at his sister's home, I went from house to house to visit with the people of Keanae.

I felt sorry for the pastor. The "inner voice" told me to visit him at the rectory. After my supper of raw watercress and some cooked vegetables, I went to console him.

"Father, don't feel bad about missing your mother's funeral. She knows how much you love her and why you couldn't be there. She knows how much you prayed for her. Be thankful to God she's in heaven and no longer has to suffer on earth. We all have to learn acceptance and to practice detachment from loved ones. Here's a stipend for you to offer a Mass for yourself."

Father listened but said nothing. So I said, "Good night, Father," and left.

My shower was a cold one because all the hot water was used up. I spent another sleepless night on the cot in the basement while Tony slept. I could still sense the presence of something evil at the entrance. It was just as scary as the night before.

The next morning after Sunday Mass, Tony and his family went to visit relatives and friends. They left me behind. Jesus planned it that way to let me rest and to give me some peace.

I was filled with sadness and compassion for the people of Keanae, because they were such good people hungering for the things of God, and yet were so neglected by their pastor. They had not received any religious instructions, and some had not gone to church for years. Most were baptized Catholics when they were infants. Some of the adults weren't even confirmed. I felt only love and compassion for them.

When I explained the meaning of the Enthronement to a group, Tony's sister Dora wanted the Enthronement done in her home. So I promised her I would return to help her with it. She could be the first person in Keanae to have it, and then help to spread it to other homes.

I was concentrating so much on helping Tony's family and the people of Keanae that I forgot about my hunger. At every meal, Tony's family served sour poi, which I didn't eat because sour poi made me want to throw up. It was the same with raw fish. The only things I ate were some raw watercress and other vegetables. They never cooked any rice, and I never asked for it. I just offered up my hunger as my secret sacrifice to God. Because of my love for Jesus, I never asked for rice or complained.

The evening before leaving Keanae, I heard the family discussing the cost of the chartered flight from Honolulu. When someone mentioned that I should pay my $20 like everyone else, Tony said he would pay the $20 for me. He knew I couldn't afford the $20, especially after seeing the few simple things I had carried in the brown grocery bag. The next morning Tony drove me to the airport for my trip back to

Honolulu. Even though I was hungry and tired out by three sleepless nights, I enjoyed deep, peaceful satisfaction at completing my first big job for God.

In Keanae I saw the miracle chapel and heard how God supplied the material for it. After the Protestants built a church nearby, the Catholics wanted a church of their own, but they didn't have the money to build one. Lumber and other materials were expensive because they were shipped from the mainland to Honolulu, then shipped to Maui, and then trucked to Keanae along the Hana Road. So all the Catholics kept praying to God for help. They prayed with the fervor of simple faith.

During the night a big storm threw chunks of white coral along the beach. The next morning people saw the coral lying on the coarse black sand. They knew God had sent the coral because the sea around Keanae never had coral. They gathered the coral and carried it to the village. They needed sand for mortar, so they prayed for sand.

Several days later, another strong storm washed up a blanket of fine white sand over the coarse black sand of their beach. Keanae had never seen white sand on the beach before, because the sand had always been coarse and black. People sifted the fine white sand from the coarse black sand to use for the mortar.

The people raised the money to buy cement for mortar, and then volunteers built a tiny chapel with the coral and sand God had sent them. Several men finished the walls with a smooth coat of stucco on both the inside and the outside of the chapel.

The people named it the Chapel of Our Lady of Fatima. Every first Saturday of the month, many gathered in the chapel to pray the rosary. Years later, with donated funds, the Catholics of Keanae built a small wooden church next to that miracle chapel. Father Schoofs, the pastor of the cathedral in Honolulu, wrote the story of the miracle chapel at Keanae in the *Hawaii Catholic Herald*.

The miracle chapel is still there in Keanae. If you visit Maui and drive the road to Hana and the Seven Sacred Pools, stop in Keanae to visit this miracle chapel. No matter what religion you belong to, pray and praise God in that chapel. He will bless you for praying there.

Then it was time for me to return to Keanae to help Dora with the Enthronement. Tony bought the plane ticket for me, but I supplied the two large pictures and pamphlets. Tony lent me an old leather suitcase that smelled musty. It embarrassed me at the airport when it popped open to let my dresses and underwear fall out for everybody to see. I had to tie that old suitcase shut with a cord.

I hand-carried the pamphlets for the ceremony and two framed pictures: one of the Sacred Heart of Jesus and one of the Immaculate Heart of Mary. The two bamboo frames came from my pictures of flowers, the pictures I had bought with the $5 I had won from my bet with Fred.

When I arrived in Keanae that Saturday, I went to ask the pastor about performing the ceremony of Enthronement. Even though he was a Sacred Hearts priest, he didn't know how to perform it. So I briefed him on the ceremony and gave him a pamphlet on it. We scheduled the ceremony for 3:00 in the afternoon, but Father was late in arriving. Dora and her family celebrated the Enthronement with a luau (Hawaiian feast) for a large crowd of people. Relatives and friends came from all over the island of Maui

While I was serving food at the luau, Father said loudly, "Florence, there's no room for you here in Keanae."

"Father, I don't need a house or a room. I would be satisfied sleeping under somebody's house or even in a doghouse. I would be happy there as long as I know I'm serving God and He's with me.

When the people around us heard this, they clapped.

After the luau, a group of ladies told me, "Father said you're crazy, and not to listen to you."

"If I'm crazy, how come I taught people how to pray the rosary? If I'm crazy, I wouldn't talk about God and help people the way I do."

As I prayed the rosary in the miracle chapel, a Hawaiian lady came and said, "When you were getting off the plane, I saw a bright glow around your head. The light was so bright it was blinding. I just wanted you to know." I told her not to tell anyone what she had seen. God let that lady see the glow around my head as a sign of the Saint in my soul. That was the first sign from God that revealed the Saint in my soul to another person.

The next morning, as I was walking to church for the Sunday Mass, barefooted people began coming out of their homes to follow me to church. It was like a procession. (I thought of the people who followed St. Bernadette to the grotto at Lourdes where Blessed Mother had appeared to her.) Some of them had not been to Mass for years. The church was so full that some stood outside the entrance. During his sermon, Father scolded the people: "Where were you the other Sundays? Where were you all these years?"

The pastor had been there for 10 years. Yet many of the adults were never confirmed and never went to church. The people and their children received little or no religious instruction. Before leaving Keanae, I urged the people to love God by attending Sunday Mass and practicing their religion.

The people of Keanae touched my heart with their respect, simple faith and goodness of heart. As I was leaving Keanae on Monday morning, people gave me vegetables from their gardens, papayas, bananas, multicolored ti leaf plants and a big box of white gardenias, my favorite flower. They all waved good-bye to me.

After my return to Honolulu, I told Mrs. C on the phone about my two trips to Keanae and the miracle chapel, but not about the help I had given Tony, his family and the people there. She said, "Florence, what do you have that I don't have?" I didn't understand her question. I took it only in a physical way. So I answered, "I'm a woman just like you. You have everything I have." After that I never revealed my work for God to her or to anyone.

My two trips to Keanae, especially the people there, stand out as my first big jobs for God. I never revealed my work for God to my family. I wanted only God to know what I did for Him. But I did tell my family the story of the miracle chapel. They all wanted to see it for themselves, so we planned a trip to Keanae for that summer.

At the Maui airport Thomas rented a car to drive us to Keanae. First we made a visit to the Blessed Sacrament in the wooden church. Then we examined the inside and the outside of the miracle chapel. We also went to see the pastor. When he opened the door of the rectory, I introduced my family to him, and we gave him an aloha shirt as a gift. He greeted us, accepted our gift and thanked us, but he didn't invite us in. Then we paid a short visit to Dora, Tony Young's sister, before leaving Keanae. The miracle chapel impressed my family and made the trip worthwhile for them. I learned important lessons from my first big job for God.

*The "inner voice" taught me to offer Mrs. Young's death in union with Christ's death on the Cross, so people would return to the practice of their religion. Many did. Ever since then, I have always offered a person's death in union with Christ's death on the Cross for conversions to Christ and for the return of fallen-away Christians. I recommend this practice to all Christians.*

The following summer, the pastor returned to Belgium for a visit. He had never seen his mother's grave. His brother, also a priest, met him at the airport to drive him to their home town. They never arrived. A highway accident killed them both.

My first big job for Jesus was among the poor. My love for them was greater than my love for the rich and famous. God loves everybody, but He has a special love for the poor, lowly and uneducated, because they believe with a simple, sincere faith. God favors some of the uneducated because they usually seek his help and are docile to the Holy Spirit, while some of the educated have a mind of their own and a will of their own.

Jesus told His priests to feed His sheep and lambs. So priests should take good care of the entire flock. Like Jesus the Good Shepherd who went after the lost sheep, they should work to bring back to church those who have fallen away.

I later learned that Dora never spread the Enthronement to other homes according to our agreement and plan. Through the years I've learned that many people perform religious acts to gain respect and praise for themselves instead of doing them to honor and praise God. When you take part in religious ceremonies, be sure to do so to give due thanks, honor and glory to God, and not for selfish reasons.

*Many of us don't share our spiritual blessings with others. A true Christian life is a life of sharing, so we shouldn't keep good things just for ourselves. I tried to share the many blessings of the Enthronement with others because it was one of the greatest blessings I received from God. Having it in our home deepened our faith and reliance on God. If we welcome God into our homes and hearts with love and gratitude, we will experience His presence and love in a special way through many special blessings.*

## A Bond Severed

God gave me a special sign that He would be leading me along a different path in my future. Although my marriage to Thomas was stable, it was full of difficulties. Divorcing him never entered my mind, because I had made a lifelong commitment to him. This is how God gave me a hint of what was to come.

At Tommy's graduation from St. Louis High School in 1952, I asked my husband to give our seats, reserved for parents of the graduates, to his parents. So they were close to the stage and had a clear view of their first grandson receiving his diploma. Then we made them our guests of honor at a Chinese restaurant for a nine-course dinner that lasted more than two hours. My in-laws even ordered an extra bowl of bird's-nest soup for themselves.

After we dropped off Thomas' parents at their home on Punchbowl, we were returning home on Prospect Street near the top of Punchbowl when it happened: Something came out of the sky to sting the tip of my ring finger. Something hit my fingertip like a dart hitting the target. I cried out from the sudden, sharp pain. Thomas pulled over and stopped the car.

"What happened?"

"Something stung my finger."

"Was it a bee?"

"No, it wasn't."

The children remained quiet in the back as Thomas checked my finger. Even with the pain I felt a special joy, so I said, "I'm okay now, let's go home."

The next morning, the entire ring finger was black and blue and so swollen that it almost covered my wedding band. I went to the doctor that afternoon. After Dr. C examined my finger, he gave me an injection. But he couldn't explain what made it so swollen. He sent me home and said he would come by that evening about 7:00 to check on it. When he came, the swelling was still the same. Because he thought I might lose my finger, he told Thomas to cut the ring off.

As Thomas was cutting my wedding band in the bedroom, the "inner voice" told me that Jesus was severing my marriage bond to my husband. That mysterious event (something coming out of the sky to sting my finger and the cutting of my wedding band) was the first step leading to my private religious vows to God. I later made temporary vows to God; then perpetual vows.

When I made my perpetual vows to God with the full consent of

Thomas, he told me he had a hunch that God was taking me back from him when he was cutting off my wedding band.

The Enthronement of Jesus in our home brought me many special graces. Looking back 48 years later, I now realize it was a Saint guiding and helping me who obtained those graces for me.

*You must truly care from your heart*
*and not just with words.*

# 5

# WORKING FOR GOD

G od gave me a loving heart when he made me, and He
deepened my love through baptism and Holy Communion. My
past suffering also deepened my compassion and desire to help people
with problems.

One day I saw a picture of the smiling Jesus at the Cathedral Gift
Shop across from the cathedral. All the pictures of Jesus I saw showed
Him as serious or sorrowful. I wanted to buy that picture of the smiling Jesus, but I didn't have the $6 for it. When I had the money, it was
gone. I never saw such a picture of Jesus again.

Ever since I saw that picture of the smiling Jesus (not laughing, but
smiling), I told Jesus I wanted to turn His holy (sorrowful) face into a
smiling face by my acts of love and service to others.

## Volunteer Work

After my baptism I did more than 17 years of volunteer service to
hospital patients, couples with marital problems, Catholics who had

fallen-away, teenagers with family problems and others. Helping people in any way I could brought me much joy from the beginning of my Catholic life.

On my own, I began visiting the sick at St. Francis Hospital. I asked the patients whether there was anything I could do for them. I tried to cheer them up, and sometimes I brought a rose for some of the lady patients. For love of Jesus, I tried to help the sick and the dying and to visit the religious in the hospital.

At first I visited both male and female patients. Then one day a male patient reached out to grab me. I pulled away and left the room. From then on I visited only female patients. When Father P, the hospital chaplain, saw and heard what I was doing, he asked me to visit some of the patients to comfort the dying, to console families, to teach someone how to pray the rosary, or to say the prayers for a dying person. When people heard about the volunteer work I was doing at the hospital, some asked me to visit a relative, friend or religious who was there as a patient.

Before Mother's Day, I went to Catholic friends to ask for a dollar stipend for a Mass on Mother's Day to honor our Blessed Mother. Some gave more. I usually collected between $35 and $40, which I gave to a priest to offer that Mass. (I stopped this practice after two years when my spiritual director told me that I shouldn't do that.)

Henry Lum, an alumnus of St. Louis High School, sold my husband a life insurance policy. Afterward I decided to ask Henry for the dollar offering and to invite him and his wife to the Mass on Mother's Day. I didn't know they were fallen-away Catholics then. At their big home on Center Street in Kaimuki behind the Bank of Hawaii I met his wife Beatrice. We recognized and remembered each other, even though we hadn't seen each other for more than 18 years. They made the dollar offering and accepted my invitation. That Mass was the first step in their return to the practice of their Catholic faith.

After I had invited the Lums to the Mother's Day Mass in honor of Blessed Mother, I wanted to bring Henry a cake for Father's Day and to visit with them. I went to a bakery in Kaimuki the afternoon of Father's Day. All the chocolate cakes were gone; only angel food cakes remained. At the counter the man beside me said, "I saw you at the St. Louis graduation; my son graduated with your son Tommy. Did Tommy get a job yet?"

"No, he's still looking for one."

"My son just got two job offers: a part-time job at KGMB radio station and another full-time job. He's taking the full-time job. Why don't you have Tommy apply for the part-time job at KGMB? I'll call them up and put his name in for it. Have Tommy go down to KGMB tomorrow morning."

"Thanks, I will. God bless you."

When I brought the cake to Henry Lum and wished him a happy Father's Day, the house seemed empty. During my visit, I learned she and her husband were fallen-away Catholics, and they wouldn't see or talk to their only daughter because she had married a *haole* (Caucasian). They asked me to pray for her. I said I would, and I comforted them about their daughter.

I said, *"If you love your daughter, you have to love the person she loves. Not accepting your daughter's husband is hurting her and hurting you. What really matters is that she loves him and that he's a good husband to her."*

They listened to me, and then decided to reconcile with their only daughter.

The next morning Tommy went to KGMB to apply for the job. That part-time job became a full-time job after a month. He received $250 a month as a bookkeeper. With his first paycheck, Tommy bought me our first TV set for $250 so I could watch a cooking class that was being taught by a Hawaiian lady. With another paycheck he bought me a fancy family Bible for $50, a lot of money for us then.

I told Tommy if he wanted to go to the University of Hawaii, I would pay his tuition by cleaning apartments. Tommy said he didn't want to go to college, so I respected his decision and never pressured him to go to college.

I give God the credit for everything: the Lums' return to church, their reconciliation with their daughter and Tommy's first job. In the spiritual life there are no coincidences. All the credit for good results should go to God. We are only His instruments when we help others.

*It's not hard being God's instrument to help others. He doesn't ask anything big of us. Just show others real concern and sincere kindness along with the secret prayers you offer for them. Be yourself without pretending and be kind and good from the inside. God will do the rest.*

While I was doing volunteer work at St. Francis Hospital, Mrs. Kam approached me on the third floor outside her husband's room. She said, "My husband is dying in there and he's so afraid at nights. Could you visit him and talk to him?"

I knocked and entered Mr. Kam's room. He was rich and only in his forties.

"Hello, I'm Florence. I'm a volunteer here. Is there anything I can do for you?"

"I'm so scared at night. I don't understand. A strong fear just comes over me."

"Death is not so scary because your soul never dies. Don't let the devil put fear in you. Mr. Kam, do you believe in God?"

"Yes, I believe in God. But it's because I'm dying. During my life I never went to church. I was interested only in making money."

"Pray to God; He'll help you. Trust in God. It doesn't matter whether you're a Christian or a Buddhist. Pray to God."

"I don't go to church at all."

"It doesn't matter. I'm going to pray real hard for you." I gave him a rosary, and then I blessed him with holy water. I traced a cross on his forehead with holy water and then made the sign of the cross with holy water from his forehead to his chest to his shoulders.

"I feel better now, refreshed. I feel at peace. Thank you."

Those about to die have a special kind of fear. Maybe it's a sign for them to prepare for death. One fear they have is of dying alone. Before dying, my mother had told me that she heard footsteps even though no one was walking around. That happened to her several times.

Every day I went to the chapel to pray the rosary for Mr. Kam. I also visited him every day. When his wife visited him, he told her how much I had helped him. She was pleased that I had set him at peace.

Several days later, on the way to his hospital room, I learned that he had asked for baptism and was baptized a Catholic by the chaplain before he died.

Even though I didn't know his family, I attended his funeral and comforted his family. During the funeral I offered up his death in union with Christ's death on the Cross for his family and for sinners to return to God. *I always made sure to complete a job for God. When I helped the dying in the hospital, I always attended the funeral, whether the person was a Christian or of another faith. In my volunteer work, the sorrows of others became my sorrows and their joys became my joys.*

I didn't do anything big for God. God simply used my sincere kindness and words to touch the hearts of others. You can comfort anyone, even a stranger. Your concern and gentleness can bring peace. Your love can help a person conquer fear. But good deeds are not enough. You also have to pray for that person, so God can put the finishing touches the way an artist puts the finishing touches to his painting.

I never neglected my family or put my volunteer work before my duties to my family. If I was delayed at the hospital, I always telephoned my children to tell them. I didn't use my volunteer work to run away from my family duties or from my problems. I really did it all for love of God. So I experienced a lot of joy through my volunteer work, which also took my mind off our financial problems.

My volunteer work brought rewards years later, even though I didn't expect rewards and I never looked back at what I did for others. I did it all for God. I did what Jesus said: "What your right hand does, don't let your left hand know."

During one of the retreats I made, the Catholic Women's Guild asked for volunteers. So I volunteered to help out at St. Francis Hospital by directing visitors to the patients they came to visit. I did this besides my own work of visiting the patients.

*The Honolulu Advertiser* reported a car accident that killed two teenagers. Michael, 17, and a Catholic, was a senior at St. Louis High School. His friend was a Protestant boy who attended a public school. I felt compassion for the mothers, as though my own son had been killed. The "inner voice" told me to write each mother a consoling letter and then helped me with each letter. I signed each letter "Florence" without giving a return address.

The two mothers wondered who wrote them such consoling letters. They asked people and checked around. Finally one mother asked Father Adrian at St. Augustine Church, "Does a lady named Florence come to church here?"

"Yes, there's a Florence who comes to our daily morning Mass. Come after the eight o'clock Mass and you'll see her."

Next morning a lady introduced herself to me after Mass. She thanked me for my letter and asked if she could drive me to the other mother, Mrs. Green, who wouldn't listen to her. Mrs. Green, a nurse, divorced and alone, couldn't get over her son's death. Michael was her only child. Mrs. Green spent most of the day in bed and wouldn't leave the house and wouldn't eat. I left with the lady right away.

She drove me to Mrs. Green's home overlooking the ocean near Diamond Head and led me into her bedroom. Mrs. Green was sitting up in bed, crying. I sat at her bedside. When I tried to console her, she said to me: "What do you know about suffering? Leave me alone."

"I'm not leaving."

"I want you to leave."

"I said I'm not leaving."

I told her about the abuse I had received from my in-laws, my unfaithful and irresponsible husband, my attempt at suicide, and my worries over my only daughter in New York because a few months earlier in Honolulu the doctor had poked a long needle through her throat to get a piece of her gland to examine it for cancer. My sorrows surprised Mrs. Green out of her grief.

"Florence, would you get me that box of Kleenex on the dresser."

I walked over to get it for her. "Wow! These are big Kleenex. I never saw such man-size Kleenex before."

Mrs. Green smiled. "You know, Florence, I was surprised to see how young you are. After reading the letter you wrote me, my friend and I thought you were in your sixties. I sent the letter to my sister who's a nun in New York City. She was so impressed with its wisdom that she showed it to some of her friends."

I said, "I know Michael's death will spare him the temptations and trials young people face today. There are so many difficulties and hardships in life. Life on earth always brings suffering. Even though his death is hard on you, Michael is now in God's hands and at peace. You have to let go of him so he can be at peace. I'll be praying for you and Michael every day."

Then I ordered her sternly, "You get out of bed to eat something. You need the strength for the rosary tonight. Your friend is in the kitchen making some coffee. I just came from Mass, so I haven't eaten either."

I helped Mrs. Green with her robe and took her arm as we went to the kitchen.

She asked, "What do you want for breakfast, Florence?"

"I just want some coffee and a piece of toast."

Her friend said, "Have some eggs. I'm going to scramble some."

"No, thanks. I just want a piece of toast." I ordered Mrs. Green to eat some scrambled eggs and toast, and she did.

I told her, "I'm going to accompany you to Michael's wake tomorrow, and even squat on the floor with you. (I was thinking of the Chinese custom of relatives kneeling or squatting on the floor during wakes.) Then I'll accompany you to Michael's funeral Mass and burial. Will you be receiving Communion at the Mass?"

"I'm a fallen-away Catholic, Florence. In fact, St. Augustine Church is my parish. But I'll go to confession so I can receive Communion at the funeral Mass. My friend is a Protestant and she goes to her church every Sunday."

After our visit, her friend dropped me off at my bus stop.

I accompanied Mrs. Green to Michael's wake, and also to his funeral Mass and burial. I taught her to unite Michael's death to Christ's death on the Cross and then offer it to God for special graces for family and friends.

A few days later she telephoned me to ask, "What's your favorite charity, Florence? I want to make a donation to it in your name from Michael's insurance money."

"Make a donation to Chaminade College."

Mrs. Green followed my request and made a generous donation to Chaminade College in my name for the help I gave her. Her donation made the papers.The compassion I felt for those two mothers was real. God used that compassion to move me to write each of them a consoling letter. Through those letters, God used me as an instrument to help Mrs. Green overcome her grief and depression, and return to the practice of her Catholic faith.

*Whenever God moves you to console someone in sorrow or to help someone in need of kindness or encouragement, go through with it. God is using you as His instrument to bring His peace and blessing to that person. Don't let the opportunity pass. The outcome may be greater than you think.*

God also used me to help Sadie L. Because of marital problems, she suffered severe depression and talked of suicide. Her family took her to the hospital for treatment. In the hospital Sadie continued to talk of ending her life. I was the godmother of her daughters, Linda and Kathleen.

I had just gotten home and had put some soup on the stove when

Linda telephoned from the hospital. She said her mother was on the balcony of her room and was threatening to jump off. Her mother had locked the door and wouldn't let her or anyone into the room.

My daughter Audrey was entertaining a classmate of hers from the mainland. I told her I had to go to the hospital for an emergency and to take care of the soup being warmed on the stove. Then I took the bus to the hospital.

When I knocked on her door, Sadie wouldn't let me in. I talked to her through the locked door. Finally I said, "Sadie, open the door, quick. I have to use the toilet. Come on, open the door quick. You don't want me to make wee-wee in my pantie, do you?"

My trick worked. Sadie opened the door and locked it again after I entered. We sat on the two chairs and I talked to her. I knew about marital problems, depression and suicide from my own attempt at suicide. Sadie could sense how understanding, sincere and compassionate I was.

I told her, "No man is worth dying for. If I were you, I would challenge his mistress. Check out of this hospital tomorrow, go to the beauty shop to have your hair done, and then charge some nice clothes. Give your husband the silent treatment. He has all that money and yet you've been so thrifty trying to save him money. Run him broke by buying and charging things for yourself. Your behavior will shock the hell out of him, and it's going to bug him."

We both laughed.

"Why die? You want his mistress to get all his property? Put up with him and see who wins. Challenge her."

Sadie began to smile. I made her eat the next meal by refusing to leave until she ate.

Sadie did exactly as I suggested. She checked out of the hospital the next day, had her hair done and shopped for expensive clothing. She later told me her husband was completely confused by her surprising behavior, but he didn't do anything to stop her.

In gratitude and appreciation for Sadie's recovery, her husband, Henry, said, "Florence, pick a place anywhere in the world and I'll send you and Sadie there with all expenses paid."

"No, thanks. I don't want to go anywhere."

I helped Sadie with love and real concern. *I have never helped someone with the idea of getting a reward.* Looking back at Henry L's offer, I know that if I had asked to go to New York City or to the Holy Land, he would have sent Sadie and me there with all expenses paid.

Henry, an excellent cook of Chinese food, kept inviting me to dinner at his home. Because of my secret fast and abstinence for God, I kept refusing his invitations.

Linda and Kathleen respected me and showed their regard for me by remembering me with a gift every Christmas, Easter and Mother's Day.

Sadie and Henry stayed married. When he passed away, Sadie inherited their large home, all his money and real estate.

Jesus, our Savior, had given me a little taste of being the savior of a person. I take no credit for helping Sadie. The Holy Spirit was my teacher and guide. God used me as His instrument to help her. I just used my past experiences and my common sense to talk her out of trying to kill herself.

God also used me to help Margie and Jimmy W, who were divorcing. Early one morning Margie was waiting for me as I returned from Mass. She needed my help because the court hearing for her divorce was set for 10:00 that morning. I went with her right away. First I took Jimmy into the bedroom to talk to him in private. Then I took his mother into the bedroom to tell her not to meddle. Finally I took Margie into the bedroom to speak to her.

I never took sides when I helped couples or families. I never scolded anyone. I just pointed out the faults of each person and encouraged each one to make improvements.

The divorce hearing came and went while I was talking to them. So the divorce case was dropped, and Margie and Jimmy stayed happily married until his death years later.

When Jimmy died of cancer, his family kept his death from his mother, because she had a heart condition and they thought the news might cause her to have a heart attack. On the day of Jimmy's funeral and burial, they asked me to keep his mother company and to break the news to her gently while they attended the services. I was scared and I prayed for God's help because I didn't want to cause her to die of a heart attack. If she died of a heart attack while I was telling her about Jimmy's death, I would be alone with her dead body. But what would have been worse is that I would blame myself for causing her death.

While Margie and Jimmy's family were at his funeral and burial, I visited with his mother in her room. She was crying because she knew Jimmy had died. I comforted her and began telling her about my trip to China.We exchanged stories about our childhood in China. She knew all along that Jimmy had died and that the family was at his funeral and burial. After the burial, the family came into the house very quietly to listen to Jimmy's mother and me in her room. They expected to hear her crying and mourning. Instead they heard her laughing loudly as I told her how in China I was constipated in the middle of the room with all the village neighbors watching me.

When the family entered the room and saw us laughing, I said, "She knew about Jimmy's death and how you were hiding it from her. Because you tried to fool her about it, she turned around and fooled you instead. We had a good laugh over that."

Looking back on my own marriage with an unfaithful husband, I now realize that I had followed the same advice I had given to Sadie. I stuck it out for the sake of my children and didn't take the easy way out through divorce; and I ended up being the sole beneficiary of my husband's estate. My patience won it for me.

I ask God to sanctify all the marriages in the world, and to grant peace and harmony to every family in every home.

God used me to save a lady who tried to commit suicide by swallowing Lysol, and later to save the life of her unborn child. She was lying on the abortion table when something told her to get up and go see Florence. She got up and came to see me right away. That's what she told me when she arrived at my home. I comforted her and reassured her that her baby was going to be all right. I told her I would pray for her every day. She believed me, and months later gave birth to a normal, healthy baby.

The Saint in my soul also used me to guide and help young men and women to answer God's call to the religious life.

Paul Nomi, a student at Chaminade College, was Stephen's friend, and visited us often. He brought along a classmate to play cards with Stephen and me some Saturday evenings.

Paul and I got to know each other well. He thought about serving Christ as a Marianist Brother. But when he sought guidance from Father

M, the president of the college, Father told Paul he didn't have a religious vocation. He said Paul lacked the conviction to become a religious. Discouraged and depressed, Paul told me about his disappointment on the phone. I could see the fine qualities of his soul, so I encouraged his desire to become a Brother.

I told him to come over so I could talk to him. "Don't listen to Father M, Paul. If you have the desire to serve God as a Brother, don't let anyone kill that desire. Just keep praying for God's guidance. I'll join you in praying for God's will for you. You have nothing to lose if you join to try it out. If you don't like it, you can leave. If you like it, you can stay."

I talked to him with honesty as a truthful mother would. I continued to encourage and counsel Paul during his frequent visits to our home. His mother expressed her appreciation to me on the phone for the help I was giving him. Later Paul did join the Marianists and became a Brother with perpetual vows. Today Paul is still a faithful Brother.

Father M was wrong to discourage Paul from joining the Marianists. He should have encouraged Paul to give it a try. If the religious way of life didn't suit him, then he could leave on his own. I think he misunderstood Paul because he was Japanese and reserved as most Japanese were in those days.

Paul Nomi brought his classmate Judy Benz to meet me, and I invited her to come for lunch the following week. I served her tuna sandwiches and milk. She told me her parents did not approve of her conversion to the Catholic Church. Later she confided in me about her desire to serve God as a nun. I listened and then encouraged her. Her respect and trust in me made it easy to guide her. I prayed often throughout the day for God to guide and protect her from the devil. Her soul was precious to God.

When she decided to become a nun, her father, a medical doctor, was against her decision. Judy visited me often. I continued to pray for her and to encourage her. That summer she entered the Benedictine Convent of Perpetual Adoration in Clyde, Missouri. Before leaving Hawaii to enter the convent, Judy asked me to keep some of her belongings for her. I told her I didn't have the space with three children at home. Years later, as a Benedictine nun, Judy Benz wrote to thank me for my prayers and help.

She also sent me the following prayer to the Holy Spirit that I want to share with you:

## *Come, Holy Spirit*

Replace the tension within us
    with a holy relaxation
Replace the turbulence within us
    with a sacred calm.
Replace the anxiety within us
    with a quiet confidence.
Replace the fear within us
    with a strong faith.
Replace the bitterness within us
    with the sweetness of grace.
Replace the darkness within us
    with a gentle light.
Replace the coldness within us
    with a loving warmth.
Replace the night within us
    with Your day.
Replace the winter within us
    with Your spring.

Straighten our crookedness,
    Fill our emptiness.
Dull the edge of our pride,
    Smooth the flow of our humbleness.
Illumine the light of our love,
    Quench the flames of our lust.
Let us see ourselves
    as You see us,
That we may see You
    as You have promised,
And be fortunate
    according to Your word:
"Blessed are the pure of heart,
    for they shall see God."

At Saint Francis Hospital, as a young lady in a hospital uniform walked toward me in the hallway, the "inner voice" told me she had a vocation to the religious life. So I greeted her, "Good afternoon. What happened to Father Victorinus? I brought him some grapes."

"He was released this morning."

"I'm so disappointed. I came to bring him some grapes. By the way, have you ever thought of becoming a Sister?"

Looking surprised, she stared at me and said, "How did you know about me?"

"There's something special about you. I think God has special plans for you. I'm Florence. What's your name?"

"I'm Harriet M. I'm so confused about my vocation. I don't know what to do. Can I talk to you somewhere?"

"I have to pick up my son's watch at the jeweler this afternoon. It needed fixing. The jeweler said the watch would be ready any time after four o'clock."

"I have a car, so I can pick up the watch for you after work and then bring it to you."

"But it's out of your way."

"That's okay, I don't mind. I want to talk to you."

"All right. Here's the claim check for the watch, with the address of the jeweler. And here's my address."

That's how God used Tommy's watch to bring Harriet to my home. When she came with the watch, I learned she had been a classmate of my daughter Audrey when they were in high school. In our living room Harriet confided in me.

"I've been thinking about becoming a nun, but I just can't make up my mind. At the hospital you really shook me up when you asked me if I had ever thought of becoming a Sister and when you said God had special plans for me."

We discussed the meaning of religious life and her desires and doubts about becoming a nun. After that discussion, Harriet visited me regularly. I kept encouraging her about her religious vocation and reminding her to pray for God's guidance. I prayed for her every day. I asked God to safeguard her vocation and to reveal His will to her.

When Harriet decided to join the Franciscan Sisters, I arranged for a donation of $400 for her dowry, the most the Catholic Women's Guild ever gave. The Guild helped young women with their dowry after they had been accepted by a religious order if they couldn't afford it. As a member of the Guild, I could telephone to mention the name of a young lady who needed help. If the Guild agreed to help, then I would make an appointment with the president and take the young lady to her so the president could hand her the check for the dowry.

Barbara Shimabukuro was another young woman I encouraged to answer Christ's call to the religious life. Her parents objected to her becoming a nun. At that time they hadn't become Catholic yet. So I went to speak with her parents.

I told them: "Don't you want your daughter to be happy? Be glad that God is sparing her all the problems of married life." After my talk with them, they finally gave their consent for Barbara to enter the religious life.

When Barbara's mother was in the hospital, I spent time with her during the day while Barbara was at work. I returned in the evening to join her in watching over her mother. Barbara was told by Sister Cabrini to lie on the bed next to her mother's bed. There was another bed in the room, but Sister moved a chair next to the doorway for me. While Barbara slept, I kept watch over her mother and prayed for her recovery.

Suddenly a shape appeared at the entrance of the doorway. I saw the black shape of a shadowy person from the waist up. I was terrified. Nothing is scarier than a direct experience of the devil. I knew it was the devil because of the fear I felt and because I saw only the upper half of that being. We never see the whole being of the devil; we see him only from the waist up without a face or features, or from the waist down. The shape of the devil is always black.

I blessed myself with holy water and sprinkled the doorway with it. I asked Jesus to protect us from the devil. I told the stinking devil, "Begone, you unclean spirit; Jesus is with me." I also sprinkled Mrs. Shimabukuro with holy water. Then the "inner voice" told me she was in danger of dying. I noticed the intravenous unit of blood was empty. The "inner voice" told me to wake Barbara up so she could ring for the nurse. I woke Barbara and she rang for the nurse. The nurse came in and then rushed out to bring back a doctor. The doctor and nurse replaced the unit of blood and then left. Later outside the room, I heard the doctor scolding the intern: "What's the matter with you? Why didn't you check on that patient? She could have died."

After that I wanted to go to the chapel to thank God for helping us save the life of Barbara's mother and to pray for her recovery. I was still afraid because of the stinking devil. But I knew I had to be brave and strong, so I went anyway. I wasn't going to let the devil stop me from going to the chapel to thank God and to pray.

After praying in the chapel, I returned to Mrs. Shimabukuro's room. I sacrificed my sleep for her recovery by spending the night with her while praying the rosary for her.

The next morning Thomas came for me at the hospital and took me home. After I bathed and changed, he took me straight to St. Francis Convent for a day of recollection that Sunday, the Feast of Christ the King. After the day of recollection, back home I lay down on the couch for a nap because I was tired from lack of sleep. Then the phone rang. It was Dr. C.

"Florence, it's a miracle. Barbara's mother is over her crisis. We rushed her to surgery, found the cause of her bleeding and stopped it. She's going to have a full recovery."

I was so happy that I forgot about my tiredness and didn't care about eating supper. I asked Thomas to drive me to the hospital right away to see Barbara and her mother.

Mistakes and negligence happen in hospitals. During my volunteer work with patients, I saw some of those mistakes and negligence. If your loved ones are in the hospital, besides praying, be sure to check on them, especially during the night.

Mrs. Shimabukuro recovered completely and left the hospital. I continued to encourage Barbara in her desire to become a nun, and I prayed for her every day. I asked God to help her choose the right religious order. She made me so happy when she told me she had finally decided to join the Carmelites. I never suggested any religious order to her. She had decided to become a Carmelite on her own. Then I knew the Saint in my soul had a lot to do with Barbara's becoming a Carmelite.

Barbara decided to enter the Carmel of St. Joseph in Long Beach, California. She sent me a big picture of herself in a bridal gown when she made her profession of vows. She was the only religious who remembered me for helping her. She died a faithful Carmelite in 1993. Of all those who sought my guidance and prayers about their religious vocations, Barbara is the dearest. She has a special spot in my heart because she is so dear to God and to the Saint in my soul. She had been in my daily prayers, and I will never forget her.

God used me to speak to Barbara's parents on her behalf and to keep watch over her mother in the hospital. If I had fallen asleep and didn't notice the empty IV unit of blood, her mother might have died. Then Barbara might not have entered Carmel. I am sure the Little Flower had a lot to do with her vocation and her entering Carmel.

Barbara's parents gave the credit for her mother's recovery to Dr. C, and brought him presents. I never told Mrs. C what I had done for Barbara and her mother. But Barbara knew everything. Both her parents became Catholic after she entered the Carmel of St. Joseph.

Helping young men and women answer Christ's call to serve Him in the religious life brought special joys to me while dealing with my sorrows. I never pressured any of the young men and women who told me they had a desire to serve God as a religious. I respected their free will and free choice. I just prayed for them and encouraged them in their desire.

## Professor John W

My daughter Audrey was once a student at Maryknoll Grade School. When the fourth grade teacher there left in October because of yellow jaundice, the principal, a Maryknoll Sister, asked me to take over her class until she could find a replacement for her. She knew I wasn't a Catholic, and I told her that I had little schooling and didn't know how to teach. Sister told me not to worry about it; she would take care of everything.

She brought me the class work and the homework each morning. After school I turned in the work at the office. Someone corrected the work, and the next day I returned all the papers to the students. If I needed help in class, I sent a student to the office to get the principal. The students never caused me problems because they respected me and liked me. I helped out this way for the rest of the school year for free.

While substituting, I sometimes sneaked in some cookies for my students. I would teach them some Chinese words on the blackboard with some word games I knew. I gained the respect and trust of my students, even though I wasn't qualified to be a substitute teacher, because they knew my kindness was sincere. I loved to be with the children. They were so innocent and so easy to please. They never gossiped. Love and kindness mattered more to them than the subjects they were learning.

I skipped lunch and went out to help the students jump rope or play their other games during lunch period. But I was happy to do this for the students and the Sisters. If they had offered me lunch, I would have refused it anyway.

One of my students, Theresa W, was doing poorly. I spoke to her after school and found out her father was a professor at the University of Hawaii. That surprised me. I expected the daughter of a professor to do well in school. One evening I went to her home to speak to her father.

When Professor W answered the door, I told him I was Theresa's teacher. He looked down at me, dressed casually in a "sloppy Joe" sweater and in loafers without stockings. With hands on his hips he said, "You? Theresa's teacher?" His words, tone and face showed surprise and contempt.

"Yes, I'm the substitute teacher. The regular teacher is sick, so I'm taking her place. Theresa is doing poorly in school, so you should help her with her school work."

He said he would. He didn't invite me in, so I left.

Professor John W was a "big shot" in Honolulu. He had become a Catholic in China and then translated a lot of the Bible into Chinese. He was later appointed as the ambassador to the Vatican from the Republic of China before the Communists took over. The author of several books, he taught a class on religion as a visiting professor at the University of Hawaii. He wore the traditional Chinese gown, walked with a cane and acted like a scholar. But his appearance and title didn't impress me at all.

After I became a Catholic and met Mrs. C, she told Professor W about me. Then he recalled how casually dressed I was when he looked me over from hair to shoes. He may have criticized my appearance and ridiculed me, because Mrs. C told me what she said to him: "You know, Jesus can come in disguise, too."

One day he waited for me after Mass to invite me to his home for breakfast. The "inner voice" told me Professor W was waiting for me at the back of the church. Deliberately I prayed the rosary and some other prayers slowly to keep him waiting to humble him, because he had been so arrogant with me when we first met.

At his home I met his wife, who spoke only Mandarin. Since I spoke Cantonese, his wife and I conversed with gestures and facial expressions. Professor W had three-minute eggs with tea and I had toast with coffee. His wife remained in the kitchen while Professor W and I ate in the dining room. His table manners shocked me, because he sipped his tea from the spout of a little teapot the way it was done in some parts of old China.

When I saw the shelves of books from floor to ceiling, I said, "Professor W, you have so many books it would take a lifetime to read them all. Did you read all these books?"

He laughed. "No, Florence, I didn't."

I told him Theresa did improve in her school work, and left for home after I shared some of my thoughts on the spiritual life. Days later he told Mrs. C, "You can teach Florence knowledge, but she can teach you how to love."

Mrs. C couldn't teach me knowledge of the spiritual life. My only teacher in the spiritual life has been the Holy Spirit. Looking back on my relationship with Professor W and Mrs. C, I think of her words, "You know, Jesus can come in disguise, too." Both gave credit for their conversion to St. Therese and claimed to have great devotion to her. Yet St. Therese did come to them in disguise, but they didn't recognize her.

Professor W came to the Enthronement ceremony in our home. After the ceremony I served *chow mein* to the guests seated around our living room. Audrey served Father J first because he represented Christ. Everyone expected me to serve the Sisters next. But I surprised everyone by serving Mr. Vilada next and then Mrs. Vilada, because I knew the other guests looked down on him as an uneducated Filipino. I said, "Papa Vilada, I'm serving you first because you are the oldest. That's our Chinese custom." The Sisters laughed. I served the Viladas first because of their sincere goodness of heart.

Mama Vilada was Chinese and related to Dr. Wah Kai Chang. But because she had married a Filipino, her family excluded her from family events because of prejudice against him. Because of all the prejudice the Viladas experienced, I touched them deeply with the honor and respect I gave them in front of all the guests.

I met Mr. and Mrs. Vilada after enrolling Audrey at Maryknoll

School. I had to buy uniforms for her, so I was sent to Mrs. Vilada, who sewed uniforms for students. Knowing I was poor, she gave me a discount. Out of respect, I called them Mama and Papa Vilada.

The Holy Spirit moved Mama Vilada to teach me two ancient prayers that I have been saying these past 48 years. When I see a crucifix, I usually say, "Thy image, crucified Savior, is my supreme consolation to believe, love and hope." The other prayer is "Glory, honor and thanks be to the Father Who has created us; glory, honor and thanks be to the Son Who has redeemed us; glory, honor and thanks be to the Holy Spirit Who has sanctified us; blessed be the Holy and Undivided Trinity now and forever, amen."

Professor W was served by Thomas after the Sisters and Brother Edward Strauss were served by Mrs. C and Audrey. Because I was so talkative, Professor W said, "Thomas is just like St. Joseph, the silent one." Like others, he was fooled by Thomas' quiet manner and soft-spoken ways.

Before Sunday Mass in Sacred Heart Church one summer, I was in the middle of the church. The church was full. Professor W was at the front. He stood and turned to look around the church to be seen and recognized. He began staring at me. I felt someone staring at me, and looked up and saw Professor W. I sensed that he was staring at my face but saw someone else. Something strange was happening between Professor W and my soul. I knew he was looking at me and yet he was seeing a nun, so I ducked behind the people in front of me so he couldn't see me.

Days later Mrs. C told me what Professor W had experienced in church. He saw me and yet he was looking at a nun with a brown habit. He wondered whether that nun could have been the Little Flower. I didn't tell Mrs. C that I had felt someone staring at me and that I had ducked behind the people in front of me.

God revealed to me that the Saint in my soul was being active. Even then I knew a saint had an abiding influence of my soul. I never revealed that secret to anyone, but I used to hint about it by telling people, "The Little Flower has a lot to do with my life." No one ever caught on to my secret, not even Father Francis, my spiritual son, who stayed with me for more than 30 years. He learned about this secret only when the "inner voice" told me to reveal the secret to him on Christmas Day 1993 in Jerusalem. Professor W gave St. Therese the credit for his conversion to the Catholic Church after reading her autobiography. He and Mrs. C had a deep devotion to her. Because of their deep devotion to her, she gave them the opportunity to meet her in my soul.

Professor W had a beautiful bronze statue of St. Therese, which he treasured. Before he left Honolulu for his new position at Seton Hall University in New Jersey, I went to his home to say good-bye. He told me to wait while he went upstairs. I thought he had gone up to get a copy of his book *Beyond East and West*. I expected him to sign it and then give it to me. Instead, he brought his beautiful bronze statue of St. Therese to present to me.

Several years later, I was home ironing. The "inner voice" directed me to write a letter to Professor W. I stopped ironing and knelt on the floor with the note pad on my bed to write him. The "inner voice" told me what to write. I don't remember most of what I wrote in that letter. The only thing I do remember is: "Friendship binds souls together the way the links of a rosary bind the beads together in a circle."

When Mrs. C visited Professor W in New Jersey, he told her he struggled to end the book he was writing, because he had so many friends to thank and he didn't want to leave anyone out. After her return to Hawaii, she told me how Professor W quoted that sentence from my letter to end his book *The Interior Carmel*.

When Mrs. C told me that Professor W didn't say the conclusion was from Florence but "from a mutual friend," I told her I didn't care.

Writing the letter with that sentence to Professor W was not my doing. I didn't know he was struggling to end his book, and I didn't know he would use those words for the ending. It was all the work of the Holy Spirit, who moved me to write that letter and who inspired me with those words.

The following summer Professor W returned to Honolulu for a visit. Before the noonday Mass began in the cathedral, he saw me at the back of the church and came toward me. I stood up and walked toward him. We greeted each other in the center aisle. He thanked me for helping him with the ending of his book. I told him that all the ideas in that letter really came from the Holy Spirit, and to thank the Holy Spirit. Then he kissed the back of my hand and went back to his pew. That was our last meeting.

God used the lowly to confound the haughty. Professor W looked down on me with contempt when I introduced myself as his daughter's substitute teacher. He was so proud that he didn't even say his conclusion was from Florence. Instead, he wrote "from a mutual friend." Yet God used me, uneducated and lowly, to help him end his book. Remember that God can use any instrument to help us.

## Lessons from the Holy Land

Mrs. Jeanette Bolles suffered a broken leg in an auto accident and was recuperating at home. Her sister Dorothy Ring was with her when I paid her a visit one day. Both of them had heard Professor W speak about religion. They asked me, "Who would you like to follow as your model, Professor W?"

"No – Jesus. I want to follow His footsteps, and no one else."

My answer surprised them. They were quiet. The two sisters looked at each other and then back at me. When I told Mrs. C what Mrs. Bolles and Mrs. Ring had asked me and what I told them, her eyes got big. She didn't say anything, either

I meant it. I wouldn't follow anyone else but Jesus. I knew they were talking about this in a spiritual sense. But many years later, I did follow the footsteps of Jesus in a physical way, too. When I visited the Holy Land, I followed the footsteps of Jesus at Nazareth, at Capernaum, at the Sea of Galilee at Tabgha, on Mount Tabor, on the Mount of the Beatitudes, in the Cenacle where he celebrated the Last Supper and where the Holy Spirit descended at Pentecost on his disciples, in the Garden of Gethsemane, along the Way of the Cross in the Old City of Jerusalem and on Calvary. I also stood in his "footprints" left behind on the Mount of Olives after his Ascension. I even have a photograph of me standing in those "footprints" to prove it. Jesus made my words come real. I have another photograph of me standing on the "rock of St. Peter" at the Sea of Galilee, where Jesus told him to feed His lambs and His sheep.

The first time Jesus appeared to me, I knew He was not a white man. When I saw the people of Israel on my first trip to the Holy Land, the "inner voice" told me, "Jesus had olive skin like these people."

Sometimes while praying the third decade of the rosary (the Crowning of Jesus with Thorns) I had wondered what kind of thorns had been used. While riding in a taxi coming down the Mount of

Olives, the "inner voice" told me to look out the window to the left. Over the low stone wall I saw the upper part of a tree with branches full of thorns 1 to 2 inches long. The "inner voice" said, "That's the kind of thorns that were used to crown Jesus." Back home after the trip, I found a picture of the same kind of thorny tree in the book *In The Footsteps Of Jesus,* which I bought in Israel.

A new church was being built at Capernaum near the home of St. Peter. When I returned a few trips later, the church was finally finished. Its outline resembled the shape of a fishing boat. I wanted to make a visit to the Blessed Sacrament with the hope that Father Francis would have the privilege of offering Mass in that new church. But the gate was locked. I asked the young man who collected the tickets to the sacred site whether we could visit the church. He came out of his booth and jumped over the locked gate to talk to the Franciscan Brother in charge of the church. Brother opened the gate and allowed Father the privilege of offering Mass in the new church. God granted even my unspoken thoughts and secret desires.

I believe that Christians who can afford it should visit the Holy Land once in their lifetime, if it's safe to do so. Muslims all try to make a pilgrimage to Mecca once in their lifetime. The Holy Land is the homeland of Jesus, and should be the spiritual homeland of every Christian. There I felt the spirit of Jesus present in a powerful way, especially where the Blessed Sacrament is kept in the small side chapel of the church at Tabgha. That tiny chapel with the Blessed Sacrament is my favorite place in the Holy Land. The Saint in my soul never visited the Holy Land herself. But her soul inside mine traveled all over the Holy Land during my seven trips there. At some sacred places, I felt how deeply moved her soul was by the presence of Christ's spirit.

About two years after Mrs. Bolles was injured in the auto accident, she asked me to pray for her sister Dorothy Ring, who had injured her back and was in bed for a month. I told her I would go and see her.

Dorothy needed surgery, but refused to have it because she was afraid. I told her, "I'm going to pray really hard for you. Your doctor is the best neurosurgeon in Hawaii. Trust in God. Jesus will guide the surgeon and help you get well. I'll stay at the hospital to pray for you all during the surgery, and I'll stay with you after the surgery. Trust in Jesus and everything's going to turn out all right. Believe me."

Dorothy believed me. During her surgery, I prayed and made the

Way of the Cross for her in the hospital chapel. When it was time, I helped her to stand and to take her first steps as she leaned on me for support. I spent many hours with her in the hospital.

To thank me for my prayers and daily help, Dorothy and Jeannette gave me a white satin bathrobe full of pink embroidered roses. I gave that beautiful bathrobe to my daughter Audrey.

Their appreciation for my prayers and help were so deep that they offered to pay Audrey's hospital bill when she was there because of a serious illness. I thanked them for their offer and told them it wasn't necessary, because Audrey was a nurse and would get a big discount on the bill.

## Another Encounter with the Devil

Mr. and Mrs. Y and I were friends for many years. On the way to town I often stopped in their grocery store and butcher shop to chat with them. When I visited them at their home, Mr. Y made the best coffee I ever tasted. I asked him several times how he made his coffee, but he wouldn't share his secret with me. He told me I had to go there for his coffee. I only knew that he made it in a saucepan and used egg-shells in some way. I wondered whether he died with his secret. The Christian life should be a life of sharing. Christians should share their knowledge and recipes with others instead of being buried with them.

When I became a Catholic, the Ys treated me coldly. One afternoon Mrs. Y called me from their car in front of our home on McCully Street. She wouldn't even get out of the car to walk to the gate of our yard. I went out to their car to invite her and her husband in for a visit. Because I had become a Catholic, she made an excuse for refusing. They just wanted some leaves from the Chinese grapefruit tree in our front yard. I plucked a handful of leaves and brought them to their car. They thanked me and left. Many Chinese Buddhists put those leaves in a pan of clean water, then wash (purify) their faces and hands with the leaves to ward off evil spirits after a funeral or for the new year.

Several months after the Ys asked for the grapefruit leaves, Mr. Y returned to our home. I invited him into our living room, where he began crying and telling me about his problem. Every night, between 11:00 and midnight, Mrs. Y felt blows on her body but saw nothing and heard nothing. The blows were hard enough to leave black-and-blue marks on her body. She struggled to ward off the blows, but she couldn't because she couldn't see anything. While sleeping on the couch in the living room because she was afraid to sleep in the bedroom, she was pushed off the couch and fell to the floor. At midnight, the sight and sound of gravel thrown against their picture window terrified the whole family. They didn't see anything outside the window. Both scary incidents happened every night for over a month.

After the first three nights of those terrible incidents, Mr. Y called Father Albert, the pastor of St. Patrick Church, for help. He blessed the whole house with holy water and special prayers, but the horrors continued. The prayers and blessings of a Protestant minister didn't work; nor did those of a Portuguese-Hawaiian lady, known as a *kahuna* (priestess). The prayers and blessings of a Chinese Taoist priest didn't help; nor did those of a Japanese Shinto priest. The horrors continued.

In desperation, Mr. Y sought my help. He said his wife told him to seek my help because I went to church every day, so maybe I could help them. Mr. Y told me everything that had happened and how every person they had called on to help them had failed. With tears on his face, he begged me to help them in any way I could. I told him to stop crying.

I told the children to eat their dinner, do their homework and then go to bed. My three children obeyed and never gave me problems. Then I left with Mr. Y without eating. Guided by the "inner voice," I brought a crucifix and rosary, and I asked him to drive me to Sacred Heart Church so I could get a bottle of holy water and two blessed candles for protection against the devil.

As Mr. Y drove into the garage, the fear I felt gave me goosebumps on my arms and sent shivers down my spine. I felt the same strong fear every night that I helped them. But I never let fear stop me from helping someone in need. (When you're being influenced by a spirit, check whether the spirit is evil or good. An evil spirit sends fear to discourage a person from doing good; a good spirit sends peace to encourage a person to do good.)

I followed him into the house. Mrs. Y and the children greeted me with looks of relief because the crucifix, rosary, holy water and candles brought them some security. I asked them to be silent while I set up a table as an altar and lit the blessed candles. They all knelt beside me as I led them in praying the rosary. I ended the rosary with this prayer:

"Heavenly Father, in the name of Jesus, please restore peace and good health to this family. If these horrible experiences come from the devil, I pray to you, Father, in the name of Jesus, to overpower the works of the devil and prevent him from disturbing this family. And please grant eternal rest to all the suffering souls in purgatory."

I repeated this prayer as I sprinkled holy water from room to room. Then I sprinkled each person with holy water and traced a cross with my thumb on each forehead.

The first night, Mrs. Y wasn't beaten, but I heard the gravel being thrown at their window. I told the family nothing would happen to us because God was watching over us. For five nights I prepared dinner for the children and then left with Mr. Y without having dinner. When God uses a human instrument to cast out the devil, that person must fast and make sacrifices. Every night I lit the blessed candles, led the family in praying the rosary, blessed each room with holy water and then blessed each person with holy water and the sign of the cross. Every night I stayed with the Y family until 1:00 in the morning.

From the second night on, nothing happened. At the end of the fifth night, the "inner voice" told me to tell the Ys that everything would be all right. But every evening the parents should lead the children in praying the rosary and then bless each room and each person with holy water. Every member of the family thanked me. Nothing scary ever happened again.

The devil and haunted houses cannot cause us serious physical harm. God would not permit it. If the restless soul of a dead person is haunting a place, that soul needs prayers. Many Chinese believers bring food to the grave or elsewhere for the spirits of the dead. The souls of the dead don't need food; they need prayers. All souls must be purified of the sins they committed on earth before entering heaven, and sincere prayers can help them.

*Learn to pray for the souls of the dead; not only for your deceased relatives and friends, but also for people you don't know. God will hear your prayers and alleviate their suffering. I also pray for the sick and dying every day. If you do this, when it's your turn to die, God will then inspire the souls you prayed for to pray for you. Since I prayed for so many dying persons and for all the souls in purgatory every day, I know I have an army of souls praying for me in return.*

Mrs. Y telephoned two days later to thank me again, and told me everything was back to normal again. She said her two daughters had seen me sprinkling holy water in the kitchen and as I walked up the stairs of their home. She told them I wasn't there, but they insisted they saw me there and argued with her. Her two daughters felt reassured by seeing my spirit, and they even showed her the holy water that was still wet on the carpet.

I think God somehow left my spirit there for awhile. I used to tell Jesus to leave my spirit with Him in the church or chapel when I had to leave because of chores to do at home. Whenever I helped others, I went the extra mile to make sure everything was all right with the people I helped.

God also drew good from what the Y family went through. Winston and Garritt Y wanted to become Catholic and asked me to be their godmother for their baptism.

Thomas had quit his job in June to withdraw $4,000 from his retirement fund, so he could pay some bills and send Audrey to a mainland college. I never told the children that Thomas had quit his job, because I didn't want to worry or burden them. I just told them he was out of work. But the six months after Thomas quit his job were difficult ones for me. It would have been easier to accept the worry and struggle if Thomas had been laid off from work instead of quitting his good-paying job at Pearl Harbor.

In December I asked Tommy to let us have his paycheck of $250 to pay the mortgage and other bills, and to buy a Christmas tree, some presents for the children and a carton of cigarettes for Thomas. He did, but begrudgingly, and we were so grateful. Without that paycheck, Christmas would have been a sad time for us. I wanted my family to celebrate Jesus' birthday in a special way. So the week before Christmas, every evening after our family rosary and during our evening prayer, I prayed out loud: "It's Your birthday, Jesus. Please help us celebrate your birthday by sending us a fresh chicken, dried Chinese mushrooms and a ham." That prayer made the children laugh on the first three evenings.

That Christmas eve, Mrs. Y telephoned me. Her son Winston had a gift for Stephen, and she wanted me to come by for it. On the way to her apartment, Thomas and I stopped at the Japanese florist for a dozen roses for our altar to honor Jesus on his birthday and to honor Mary for giving birth to Him. Thomas had only 50 cents to give me.

I bought flowers regularly from that florist for special religious days, so I asked for some roses for 50 cents.

He yelled, "Where can you find roses this time of the year for 50 cents? A dozen roses cost $1.75."

"I have only 50 cents, and I need the roses for our home altar for Christmas. But that's okay. Merry Christmas."

Walking back to our car, I heard a man calling out in Japanese, "Lady! Lady!" I stopped and turned. The florist waved at me to return.

"Here, I'll let you have these roses for 50 cents."

"Thanks. God will bless you in a big way for your charity and kindness. I'll be praying for you. Merry Christmas."

In the car I remembered Mrs. Y's birthday was December 25. I told Thomas, "Tomorrow is Mrs. Y's birthday. It would be nice to give her these roses for her birthday. I am going to give the roses to her."

"What! I gave you the 50 cents to buy roses for our altar for Christmas, not for Mrs. Y's birthday."

When we arrived at her apartment, I begged Thomas to go in with me to wish the Ys "Merry Christmas" and to present the roses to Mrs. Y. He gave me a dirty look and refused. He said harshly, "You can give her the roses if you want, but then we won't have any for our altar for Christmas."

I went in and wished Mrs. Y a happy birthday with the roses. The birthday wish and roses touched Mrs. Y because most people think of December 25 as Christmas, a time for exchanging gifts. I told the Ys to excuse Thomas for not coming in, and that he had been out of work for six months. Then they told me their grocery store had gone bankrupt because a supermarket had opened two blocks away. They lost their home because Mr. Y had been out of work for a year. Their struggles saddened me. I saw no Christmas tree there, so I knew it would be a sad Christmas for the Ys. I was glad that God had moved me to bring Mrs. Y the roses to give her some cheer.

I asked Winston to bring out his 10-inch statue of Blessed Mother from his room. I placed the statue on a small table. Then I arranged the roses in a tall drinking glass before the statue of Blessed Mother. I had bought the roses to honor Jesus on His birthday and to honor His Mother, but I knew in my heart that Jesus and Blessed Mother had already accepted those roses as coming from me.

I asked Mr. and Mrs. Y to join me in kneeling before the statue of

Mary and in praying to God to help him find a job for the sake of the children.

Then Mr. and Mrs. Y gave me Winston's gift to Stephen, the usual necktie, and they walked me to the car. When they greeted Thomas in the car, he was curt to them. I was hurt by his bad behavior and his heartlessness.

On the way home I told Thomas about their losing the grocery store and their home, and Mr. Y being out of work for a year. Their trials were bigger than ours. Thomas was without work only 6 months, and we still had our home. We also had our Catholic faith to lean on.

When we arrived home, Audrey and Stephen rushed to tell us all the things our friends had brought us: a fresh chicken, a pound of dried Chinese mushrooms and nine hams (fresh, smoked and canned). None of those friends knew about Thomas' being out of work, and none knew what I had prayed for. Immediately I knelt before our altar to thank Jesus for answering my prayers and for the extra eight hams. (I later shared a ham with the Q family, one with the Hs and one with the Lees.)

As I prepared dinner, the doorbell rang. When Audrey opened the door, a delivery boy asked for me. There he was, holding two fancy green bowls, each with a dozen red roses. I told him I hadn't ordered any roses. He said to read the card, which was signed, "From Mr. and Mrs. T." Leila had sent the roses.

Before her marriage, Leila S spent a lot of time with me, often dropping in during her lunch hour to visit with me. She helped herself to the little food we had, such as rice and fried eggs, or a tuna sandwich. During our lunches I encouraged or comforted her whenever she was troubled.

She had tried to instruct me by reading to me from the New Testament. She stopped when I told her I just didn't understand what she was reading. I didn't hear from her for three years.

The two dozen roses were a belated gift of thanks and appreciation from Leila. I placed the two bowls of roses on our altar and knelt to thank God with tears of joy. Even Thomas had tears of shame and regret for being angry at me for giving Mrs. Y the roses and for his curt behavior toward the Ys. Only God could have arranged for my receiving two dozen long-stemmed roses beautifully arranged in two fancy bowls after I had given Mrs. Y the roses for our altar. God's goodness brought me tears of joy. Who else but God could arrange such a joyous surprise for Christmas? He went way beyond answering my prayers. He has always gone beyond granting me what I needed. I realized early in my Catholic life that my giving with a sincere heart made me rich in God's graces.

A month later Mr. Y was put in charge of the produce section at Foodland in Kapahulu. In February Thomas got a job with Holmes and Narver, a heavy-construction firm, to work on Eniwetok in the Marshall Islands.

My love for the Ys and their sufferings in the past year made that Christmas Eve a real sad one for me. I never mentioned my own sufferings to them or to anyone. But God had seen everything and had come to my rescue by giving me two dozen roses arranged in two fancy bowls and much more food than I had asked for. God also answered my prayers for Mr. Y to get a job for the sake of his family.

*Giving your last dollar to a friend who is down and out is something like laying down one's life for a friend.* I never asked any of the Ys to become Catholic. Yet Winston and Garritt asked to become Catholic on their own, and I became their godmother. Years after Mrs. Y died of cancer, Mr. Y was baptized a Catholic on his deathbed. God used my sincere compassion and kindness to lead the Ys into the Church. *We win souls for God not by preaching or talking, but by good example and sincere kindness.*

## A Difficult Case

Sometimes the person we help the most will hurt us the worst.

I stood in a crowded bus to attend the noonday Mass at the cathedral on Fort Street. A hefty Japanese lady standing near me was angry because she was standing and was being jerked about by the bus. She bragged loudly to people near her about how rich she was, about her wonderful husband and four loving children, about her nice big house, and about their new car and a second good one. She said this was her first time on a bus because her car was being serviced.

After the noonday Mass I went to The Fair department store nearby to buy a skein of crochet cord, because a friend had asked me to crochet her a beanie cap for use in church. As I talked to the salesgirl, that same Japanese lady I had heard boasting on the bus came by. Her name was Mrs. G. When the salesgirl brought out a box of crochet cord, I told her I needed only one skein.

Mrs. G: "I need a whole box of 12 skeins to crochet a handbag. Do you have any more?"

Salesgirl: "No, but she was here first, so I'm letting her have the skein she needs. You can have the other 11."

Mrs. G: "But I want the whole box."

She expected the salesgirl to sell her the whole box. The salesgirl didn't know what to do, because I was a regular customer who often bought crochet thread there.

I told the salesgirl, "That's okay, let her have the whole box. I can look for a skein somewhere else." As I turned to leave, Mrs. G told her to let me have a skein. So I bought one for a dollar and hurried away because I didn't like to associate with rude boastful people.

Mrs. G: "Hey, lady!"

I turned to face her. She was rushing toward me.

"I'm Eleanor G. Why didn't you fight for your skein?"

"I didn't think it was worth the trouble to argue over something so trivial as a skein of crochet cord. Besides, I felt sorry for that poor sales-girl who has to put up with customers during her work day."

"Where are you going?"

"I'm going to the florist to buy six roses for 50 cents to give my six patients at the hospital. I work there as a volunteer in the afternoons."

"My husband is a patient at Queen's Hospital. He had a heart at-tack. Will you visit him? He's the butcher at the Piggly Wiggly market right across the street from the hospital. "

"I visit only lady patients, and only at St. Francis Hospital." (I have always been careful about my moral reputation.) But I promised to visit her husband in the hospital if she would be there with him, because I didn't know him. I picked a day when I would be free to visit with her and her husband in the hospital.

At Queen's Hospital the nurse directed me to Mr. G's room. Mrs. G was waiting for me and she introduced me to her husband, Bill. He was so pleasant that he put me at ease. I told him I was a Catholic and that I visited the sick at St. Francis Hospital. I also told him I would pray for him.

One day I heard a car clunking toward the front of our home. I looked out and saw an old car ready for the junk yard. Out came Mrs. G. Then I recalled how she had bragged about their new car and their second good car. She came with a large bag holding the skeins of crochet cord. After I welcomed her in she asked, "How do you make the 'popcorn' stitch?"

"Sit down; I'll teach you how."

As I taught her the stitch, the phone rang. As I went to answer it, she said loudly, "I haven't gone to church for 19 years."

Her words surprised me. I felt Jesus had sent her to me so I could help her return to church. I cut the phone call short.

While I taught her the stitch, she told me about herself. She was taught by the nuns, but she had stopped going to church 19 years ago when she married. God used the "popcorn" stitch to lead her and her family to church.

She said. "My husband was released from the hospital, and he wants to become a Catholic. We want our four children to become Catholic, too."

I replied, "I can make arrangements for him and the children to receive instructions from Father McMonagle, the pastor of Star of the Sea Church in Kaimuki."

Every Monday evening after dinner, Mr. and Mrs. G and their children came by in their old car to take me with them to Star of the Sea Church in Kaimuki. After we prayed the weekly novena prayers, Father McMonagle instructed Mr. G and his children while Mrs. G and I listened.

I enjoyed being with them at the weekly novena and instruction. Yet I dreaded it because we came so close to accidents: The car stalled in the middle of a busy intersection; a car almost rammed us on my side of the car. God was protecting us.

One day Mrs. G drove me to her home for a visit. They lived in a rented cottage toward the end of Kalihi Street. When I got out of the car, I saw an old cottage in need of paint and repair. The cracks on the kitchen wall and bathroom wall were so wide that I could see through them to the inside. Again I recalled how she had bragged about her nice big house. When I learned how they struggled financially, I gave them a canned ham or some other food whenever I could.

Finally, with me as their godmother, Mr. G and his four children were baptized at Star of the Sea Church on Christmas Eve.

Then the entire family received Holy Communion together at the glorious Christmas Mass the next day.

One evening I received a telephone call from Mrs. G. The two previous nights the whole family had been terrified by something moving in the dark outside their house. Then they felt something scary moving inside the house, but they couldn't see anything. So she asked me for help.

I told her I would come as soon as I could. Thomas refused to drive me to their home after dinner when I asked him, because he was too scared. I was more frightened than he was, and I dreaded going alone in the dark. But I have never denied help to a friend because of fear. So I caught the bus, bringing with me a crucifix, a bottle of holy water and a blessed candle. I remembered how those blessed sacred objects helped me at Keanae and with the Ys.

When I arrived at their house, I was so scared that I got goosebumps and cold shivers. I could sense the presence of a scary spirit.

After entering their home, I blessed each of them with holy water. Then I lit the blessed candle and sprinkled the whole house with holy water. I told them to stay in the house and pray for me while I went outside with Bill G, who held the blessed candle. Even though I was scared, I carried the crucifix in my left hand and used my right hand to sprinkle the house and grounds with holy water as we walked around the house. I asked God to chase the devil away and to protect the family and set them at peace again.

When I reentered the house I said, "Everything's going to be all right. Trust in God. I'm going home now, but you stay inside the house and lock the door. Don't go outside with me. Make some hot chocolate for everybody and then go to bed."

The next day Mrs. G telephoned to thank me because they had seen nothing and felt nothing, and everything was peaceful again.

I remember seeing several programs on TV about cases of evil spirits haunting a house or a place. I think that in most cases the spirits of dead persons were restless and needed help in the form of sincere prayers from the heart and soul of a person with deep faith and trust in God. In such cases, pray for the spirits of the deceased and have some Masses offered for the repose of their souls.

With the Gs, I think the devil was trying to destroy their gift of faith. Bill and the four children had just been baptized, and Eleanor had just returned to the sacraments. Since I was the godmother of Bill and the children, it was my duty to help them. And since I was their godmother, my motherly heart wanted to protect them from the devil. Only God can cast out the devil. Jesus did it when He was on earth, and He can still do it. But Jesus can also use a human instrument to cast out the devil and to protect others from him. That was the third time that God used me as His instrument to cast out the devil.

*I fear no evil spirit because I have God with me all the time. The only one I fear is God, and the only thing I fear is offending Him. Because of God in me and because of the Saint in my soul, I am the devil's worst enemy after Blessed Mother. Because of my prayer life and how I helped others, I also became the devil's worst enemy.*

## Duffy

The G family wanted to give me a Christmas gift. Knowing their financial situation, I told them it wasn't necessary. But they insisted that I select a puppy from their newborn litter of cocker spaniels. I wanted a male that was blond in color. They had only one male, and it was the only blond in the litter. The puppy was a week old when the Gs brought him to me on Christmas Day. At that time I was afraid of animals, but I was also happy because it was the first puppy I had ever had. After they left, the puppy went to our statue of Mary and started whimpering in front of it.

"That's only a statue. Come here." I picked him up and lost my fear of dogs from then on. Audrey was also afraid of animals, but he would sleep in her room at the foot of her bed. Then Audrey also lost her fear of dogs. She named him "Duffy."

I gave Duffy the best of care. I took him to the vet for all his shots. From time to time I saved part of my small allowance to buy him a piece of meat. I boiled it, cut it up and fed it to him by hand. He would poke his nose through the venetian blinds to watch for my return from daily Mass. How he wagged his tail and jumped about to greet me when I returned from Mass every morning! Whenever I was praying or meditating, he lay still near me.

One day I gave Duffy a bone to chew on. Later I noticed it had no meat on it. So I got another bone with meat on it. I reached out to remove the bone, and he snapped at me and bit my hand. Then, whimpering, he went to the kitchen corner. He wouldn't leave that corner and he wouldn't take the bone I offered him. He vomited later that day and during the night. He wouldn't eat the next day and he wouldn't come near me. He seemed sick, so I carried him to the vet. When the doctor examined Duffy and found nothing wrong with him, he asked me what had happened. After I explained, he said Duffy had behaved like that because he had bitten me. His regret for biting me was so strong that it made him sick. The next day Duffy was fine.

I had trained Duffy not to play or move during our family rosary. Several months earlier he started to jump around and to jump on me and on the others when we knelt to pray the rosary. I stood up, took a roll of newspaper and hit him on the rump, and then locked him outside the screen door. He scratched at the screen door and whined while we finished praying the rosary. After that, whenever we knelt to pray the rosary he lay still beside me.

When I led the family rosary, I knelt at the Enthronement altar while the family knelt behind me. Duffy lay still beside me. Then one evening Duffy surprised all of us by sitting up with his front paws in the air, wagging his tail, during the entire rosary. He did this on his own without any training from anyone. He did not change from that praying position until he heard the final loud "Amen." Only then did he move about happily. It took a week before my children stopped giggling during the rosary because of Duffy's praying posture and wagging tail.

Whenever the G family visited us, they played with Duffy and noticed how well-trained he was. They came after dinner one evening and joined us in our family rosary.

When the G family saw how Duffy behaved during the rosary, they were amazed. They joined us for the family rosary more often, just to watch Duffy's posture for prayer, and then stayed to visit awhile. Thomas and the children never complained to me about our loss of privacy, but I could sense what they were thinking and feeling.

After seeing how lovable Duffy was, the G children wanted him back. One evening the family came and asked me to return Duffy to them. Duffy was my constant companion at home. He was like my own child. Cocker spaniels are very affectionate, and I was very attached to him.

Reluctantly I let them have Duffy back right away. I returned him to stop that family from coming so often because their frequent visits bothered my husband and children, even though they didn't complain about it. After the Gs left with Duffy, I cried because I had become so attached to him.

The day after the Gs took Duffy back with them, he was left alone at home. He chewed up slippers. Then he went to the closet and chewed up Mrs. G's shoes and ripped her dresses before running away. Mrs. G telephoned to tell me what he had done.

Duffy ran away to St. Anthony Church. The pastor found him and telephoned me. "I found a cocker spaniel here at the church. The Gs told me it's your dog. Do you want it back?"

"The Gs gave him to me and took him back after 6 months, so I don't want him back."

I missed Duffy so much that I cried every day in church for a whole month. I never let my family know how much I missed him. Several people came up to me in church and asked, "What's the matter, Florence?"

I answered, "Nothing; nobody can help me."

***It's wrong to ask for a gift back after giving it, because that goes against justice and charity. After you give someone a gift, for the sake of justice and charity do not ask for it back.***

In his kindness, Jesus consoled me by telling me to spell "dog" backward for my best friend, and to be attached to Him.

Duffy taught me a big lesson on detachment then, and my experiences these past 48 years have shown me the importance of detachment from creatures for a closer union with God and for greater peace of mind, peace of heart and peace of soul.

There is no true love in this world. Only God's love is true. I forgave the Gs long ago for taking Duffy back, and now I thank them again for helping me learn the important lesson of detachment from creatures. Above everything else, God's love and wisdom are the only things I have wanted.

Despite all I did to help Mrs. G and her family, she lied to her pastor about me. He became so angry at me that he ordered me to see him across town immediately. After I arrived at his rectory by bus, he began scolding me with anger.

He told me that Mrs. G came to tell him with tears that I was having an affair with her husband. He accused me of committing adultery, of trying to break up their marriage and family, and of other wrongdoing. He went on and on, talking fast. He kept accusing me.

I kept silent and let him talk. At first I was shocked by the false accusations. Then they began to cut deeply because they were so untrue, so unjust. I sat in silence, recalling how Jesus remained silent before his accusers. While silent, I practiced control of my emotions and words. I knew what he was saying was not true, so I wasn't afraid any more. I had been afraid that I had offended God.

With calmness and composure I said, "Father, are you through? May I say something? I'm not saying things just to defend myself. I must tell the truth to guard my reputation for the sake of my husband and three children. I usually keep everything confidential when a person confides in me. Your rash judgment and false accusations force me to reveal something I don't want to reveal."

I told him all that I had done for Mrs. G and her family, and that she was the one who was having an affair. I ended by saying, "Remember, Father, there are two sides to every story. Be careful. Rash judgment and false accusations can cause a lot of suffering to an innocent soul. Just be careful."

My words brought tears to his eyes. As I stood to leave and walked out, he followed me to the gate. There he asked to bless me.

*In all matters, especially serious ones, get all the facts before making a judgment against someone. If you don't know both sides of a case, don't condemn one of the persons.*

Besides the lesson on detachment I learned from Duffy the dog, I also learned that there is often a payment for doing good, because the devil will go after us to get even. But we have to be strong and courageous no matter what others do to us. With God helping us, the devil can't win out.

## *Sister David Ann*

Winifred L, who was born in China, lived across from our McCully Street home. She had three children, as I did, and we became friends. At that time I was cleaning apartments for $2 an hour around the area of Ala Wai Boulevard. I worked hard to earn between $16 and $20 on some days. If I was working late, I telephoned Winifred: "Please open a can of soup and warm it up for my kids; I have to work late."

Then Winifred and her husband bought a home in Kalihi. After they moved away, I seldom saw her. She invited me to visit her, but I was too busy. One evening she knocked at my door. I saw her standing and crying at our door and I invited her in.

"Florence, I don't know what to do. Something told me three times to see you."

I found out she was so troubled that she had gotten on the bus without the bus fare and told the bus driver to let her off at McCully Street. The bus driver saw how troubled she was, so he let her on without paying and let her off as she asked.

I said, "The children and your husband are going to worry about you. Come; telephone and tell them that you're with me and you'll be staying with me tonight. Tell them to go to bed."

Winifred told Betty, her oldest daughter, who was eleven, "Put the two kids to bed and then go to bed yourself. I'm staying with Florence tonight, but I'll be home tomorrow morning."

We sat in the living room, where she poured out her problems to me. I made her a cup of hot tea to calm her. Suddenly she stood up and came at me. She began sniffing at me: my head, body and hands. "It's so sweet. What kind of perfume is it?"

I was embarrassed. "I don't use perfume." I knew it was the Little Flower. She sometimes gave out a sweet scent to win souls for God.

(This happened to me several other times. Once my son Tommy smelled that fragrance and asked me what perfume I was wearing. He didn't believe me when I told him I wasn't wearing any perfume. Another time a friend whom everybody called "Buck Jones" said my home had the smell of the sweetest perfume. My neighbor Rose told me, "Your house smells so sweet, Florence." Brother Strauss also told me that.)

The next morning after Mass, I accompanied Winifred on the bus back to her home. She surprised me by asking to become a Catholic. She didn't belong to any religion, and I had never said anything about her joining the Catholic Church. First I helped her to reconcile with her husband. Then I introduced her to Father McMonagle for her baptismal instructions. When she and her three children were baptized Catholic at St. Theresa Church, I became their godmother.

*When a troubled person comes to you for help, make her a cup of hot tea to calm her and help her regain her composure. Control your tone of voice. A gentle voice and tone will help the person confide her problems and innermost thoughts to you. Be a good listener with compassion and understanding. You must truly care and help from your heart and not* gentle kindness, Winifred joined my Church without being asked. *The example of sincere love will win souls for God much better than the fanciest words can.*

After the baptism, Winifred enrolled her children in St. Theresa School. Her daughter Betty was in Sister David Ann's class, and Winifred told Sister all about me. Then Sister David Ann was transferred to St. Joseph School in Waipahu.

Winifred showed her appreciation for my help in two ways. When I gave a nine-course dinner for Tommy's graduation from high school at a Chinese restaurant, Winifred was a waitress there. Without saying a word, she paid the bill of over $50 for the dinner. When Audrey graduated from high school, Winifred gave her a piece of jade as a graduation gift.

One day Sister David Ann telephoned to ask me to pray for one of her Sisters who was about to leave the religious life. I asked to speak with that Sister in person. So Sister David Ann invited me to meet her and all the Sisters at St. Joseph Convent in Waipahu.

I asked my friend Sinnie to drive me there. The day before my visit with the Sisters, Sinnie drove me to Waipahu for a practice trip. She took the wrong turn onto the freeway. Our car was moving toward the one-way traffic heading toward us. The drivers were tooting their horns and pointing in the direction they were heading. Sinnie panicked. I prayed. Sinnie pulled over to the side and stopped. Then a man pulled over and parked in front of us. He got out and told Sinnie to back up slowly while he directed the oncoming cars away from our lane. Sinnie finally backed out of the freeway. I thanked God for protecting us, and I asked God to bless and reward that brave man for us. I felt the devil was trying to stop us from going to the Sisters. But we did find the convent.

The next afternoon we made it to the convent safely and on time. Sister David Ann welcomed us into the convent. I asked to make a visit to Jesus in their chapel. Then Sister served us apple pie before introducing us to her community of Sisters.

I never figure out or plan what I'm going to say to a person or to a group. I rely on the Holy Spirit to guide me. I ask the Holy Spirit to help me say what I should say and to stop me from saying anything I shouldn't. The Sisters were seated in a large circle along the walls of their community room. I spoke to them for more than an hour. I forgot most of what I said, but I do remember how hot my face felt while speaking to them. It felt like I had a high fever. The Holy Spirit was inspiring me with His ideas and words. The Sisters listened attentively. I did not take sides with the superior or with the nuns. I recall that I told the Sisters to obey Sister Superior because she represented Blessed Mother. To obey their superior was to obey God. Even if they make a mistake by obeying the superior, God would not hold it against them. In fact, God would straighten things out for them because of their obedience. Then I said the superior should not misuse her authority and power. She should respect and show concern for each Sister. She must be firm, but she must also deal with each Sister with patience and gentleness.

Because of that visit with the Sisters, I missed a housewarming party given by Tommy and his wife, Carol. It was also a party to welcome Thomas home from working overseas. I thought that trying to save a religious vocation came first, so I gave up that dinner as a sacrifice to God. I didn't tell Tommy and Carol what I had done, because I never told my family about the volunteer work I did for God. I just let Tommy and Carol judge me as they liked.

Sinnie sat at my left and heard everything I said. She was my witness. Sinnie and I returned to her home at 6:00 that evening. I thanked Sinnie for driving me and then walked home, because my home was only a block away.

*Especially for priests and religious, saving a soul or a religious vocation should come before a family gathering or other socials. Nothing is more important than saving a soul or a religious vocation; not even an audience with the Pope. For me, God's will came first. Because I put doing His will first, the best of parties meant nothing to me. My love for Jesus made me want to work hard for Him and for souls.*

Months later Sister David Ann told me the good news that the Sister who was thinking of leaving had decided to remain a Sister in their religious order.

I thanked God for the good news and for using me as His instrument to help the Sisters. I also thanked Sister David Ann for her respect and her trust in me. She was humble enough to trust and confide in me about the Sister who was about to leave her order and to ask for my prayers. Sister even asked me to speak to her community. I kept all confidences and honored every trust. The proud never seek help from others because they think they can handle things themselves.

When I'm inspired by the Holy Spirit I can't remember what I say, because the ideas are directed to the person or people I'm talking to. I never plan what to say ahead of time. I believe in the words of Jesus: "Do not worry about what you are to say. When the time comes, the Holy Spirit will provide what you are to say." While I'm talking, my mind is blocked from knowing what I'm saying. That's how I served God as a messenger of His love and instrument of His love.

God helped me to grow in my spiritual life to show His appreciation for my helping and praying for others. God even worked some small miracles for me, and the big miracle of helping me to sell our home and buying another home at a bargain price all within 24 hours. As I kept working for God, He kept guiding me and helping me with my spiritual growth.

*God did not make different classes of people.*
*People are people,*
*and all are children of God and deserve respect.*

# 6

# SPIRITUAL GROWTH

Our family had serious financial problems the first three years of my Catholic life. Thomas worked at Pearl Harbor, but I never saw his paycheck. Every payday on Friday he went with his buddies to a bar for several rounds of beer. They took turns paying. He gave me an allowance of $2 a week for my bus fare to daily Mass. Since I made lunch for my husband and three children every weekday, I counted slices of bread and slices of luncheon meat to make sure I had enough for the week.

## Small Miracles

I washed, starched and ironed Dr. C's white shirts for 20 cents each so my children would have their daily lunch and bus fare for school. I had to iron his starched shirts carefully because they scorched easily.

One Friday I waited for Mrs. C to pick up the shirts because I needed the $2, but she never came. I had no money and there was no food in the refrigerator. I asked Audrey to cook a pot of rice, and she asked me to iron the red dress I had washed that morning, because she needed it for a meeting of the Junior Chinese Catholic Club that evening.

I gave Audrey that red dress with small black checks, a white collar, white cuffs and two big pockets, because it fit her so well. If there had been anything in the pockets, I would have noticed it when I checked the pockets before washing the dress by hand, or when I hung it upside down with the pockets out. While ironing the dress, I felt a lump in one of the pockets. I stuck my hand in and pulled out the damp lump. When I unraveled it, I saw three one-dollar bills bunched together in a ball.

I yelled for the children. The three children ran out of their rooms to see what I wanted. I showed them the three damp dollar bills I was pressing to dry.

I asked Audrey, "Sis, did you put the money in the pocket?"

"No, Mom. I didn't have any money."

I asked the children to kneel with me to thank God for giving us the money for our supper, so Tommy and Audrey wouldn't be hungry at their meeting. Then I ironed the three bills smooth and dry. I sent Audrey to the corner store to buy a piece of round steak and some Chinese cabbage. I taught her about picking a steak with a small bone.

Even today I still can't figure out how those three bills got into the pocket of that dress. I can still picture that red dress with small black checks. I can still feel the joy of seeing those dollar bills that somehow came from God.

As I ironed the shirts, I was hoping Mrs. C would come for them because I really needed the $2. If she had come by to pick up the shirts and paid me the $2, I'm sure that small miracle wouldn't have happened. I give God the credit for that miracle.

I recall another small miracle. I had to take my husband to the doctor because he was sick. We didn't have enough money for the taxi fare. At the early morning Mass I asked God to help Thomas get well and to help us through our trials. I took the bus home as soon as Mass ended. It was raining so hard that I missed my stop. I got off at the next one. As I stepped off the bus, I saw some dollar bills in a pool of water beside the curb. I picked up the bills, wet and bunched together: three $1 bills. I held up the bills to ask the people at the bus stop whether anyone had dropped them. Someone said they had been there at the bus stop for a while and no one had seen the money. One lady saw the rosary in my left hand and said, "You must have come from church. Since you found the money, it's yours to keep." Right then and there I thanked God silently for the money.

Taxi fares were cheap in those days. I went into the bakery near the bus stop and bought some doughnuts for Thomas. When I got home and showed him the wet bills I had found, he didn't believe my story. He said I had borrowed the money from a friend.

My favorite number is three because it represents the Holy Trinity: the Father, the Son and the Holy Spirit.

*As we keep doing God's will, God will provide for our needs, small and big.*

## The Third Order

I remember several years earlier, I brought Mrs. C a dozen roses for her birthday. I asked her for a vase, removed all the thorns and arranged the roses for her. As I walked through her living room to leave, I saw a booklet, *The Secret Of Mary*, on a table. Mrs. C snatched the booklet from the table and said, "Oh, I wasn't supposed to let you see the booklet or tell you about it."

"That's all right."

"And I didn't even offer you a cup of tea or a glass of water."

"That's all right."

Mrs. C made the booklet a big secret, but I didn't mind.

As a recent convert, I was eager to learn about God, Jesus and Mary. I was confused about Mary's many different titles, such as the Immaculate Conception, Our Lady of Lourdes, the Rosary, Perpetual Help, Fatima and so on.

One evening Mrs. C gave a dinner party and invited Father Joseph R of Star of the Sea Church, Father P of St. Francis Hospital, Professor W and six other persons. The main reason for the dinner was to choose 12 persons (like the 12 Apostles) to form the first group of Third Order Marists in Hawaii. The people there began discussing who should be in that first group. After 10:00 that evening, Mrs. C telephoned to tell me that the first group of Third Order of Marists had been chosen. She said, "When your name came up, someone said that you're much too boastful to be a member of that group. So you weren't chosen."

Those stabbing words made me cry loudly after I hung up, because I was not a boastful person and because I was so eager to learn about my spiritual mother. Was it boasting when I always gave the credit to Jesus and Blessed Mother? When someone praised me, I said the inspiration came from the Holy Spirit. I didn't pretend. I didn't lie. I told the truth.

Thomas and the children were asleep. But my crying woke Thomas, and he came out to ask me what was the matter. I told him what Mrs. C had said. Thomas put his arm around my shoulder to comfort me. A true friend would not have told me at that late hour what Father R had said about me unless it was something good. *A good friend shouldn't repeat bad things to hurt a friend. A true friend would defend her absent friend instead of repeating cruel gossip to hurt her.* We all have feelings. Besides, the discussion should have been confidential.

I later learned from Mary Jefferson of the first group that she had put in my name for the first group, and that Mrs. C had put in her husband's name. Mary told me, "Of all people, you should have been in that first group, Florence." Later, when the first group discussed the names for a second group, Mary Jefferson brought up my name again. The following year I was included in the second group.

The first group was received as Third Order Marists on August 15, the Feast of the Assumption of Mary. The reception of our second group was set for November 1, the Feast of All Saints. I believe that date was chosen because of the Saint in my soul.

I needed a patron saint by November 1 for the ceremony. The other members wanted to know which saint I would choose. They asked me for weeks. One suggested St. Bernadette, another St. Catherine of Siena. At our weekly Monday meeting, Father asked me, "Well, Florence, have you chosen a name yet?" I told them I didn't know yet.

There was an annual novena at St. Theresa Church in honor of the Little Flower for her feast day. I decided to make that novena to help me choose a name, even though I had to transfer to three buses to get there. Every day for nine days I kept asking St. Therese, "Who's your pal, Little Flower?" On the ninth day, as I was leaving the church, a pamphlet fell off the rack near the entrance and landed at my feet. I picked up the pamphlet. It was about St. Margaret Mary. I thought, "So she's your pal."

St. Margaret Mary was the source of spreading devotion to the Sacred Heart of Jesus in the Catholic Church throughout the world. She also helped me to get the statue of The Sacred Heart of the Holy Infant Jesus on her feast day.

The admission ceremony was set for November 1, the Feast of All Saints. In a dream the night before, I saw an endless procession of saints in white robes, waving palm branches. In my much-worn dress with small black and white checks and with its dainty white collar and white-trimmed sleeves, I marched with those saints at the end of the line, but without a palm branch. Every time I heard the song "When The Saints Go Marching In," I recalled that dream of my marching with the saints.

I understood that dream to mean that I belonged with that procession of saints because of the Saint in my soul. I realized soon after my baptism and confirmation that a saint had taken possession of my soul. But I kept it a secret between me and God.

Just before the ceremony the next day, Father R asked me what patron saint and name I had chosen. The others turned to look at me and waited for my reply.

"I picked St. Margaret Mary."

Father R said, "So you'll be Sister Mary Margaret Mary."

I answered, "Just like a sandwich."

The group laughed. I was tickled because I had such a fancy name: Sister Mary Margaret Mary.

Wearing the same dress with small black and white checks as I had dreamed the night before, I became a Third Order Marist on the Feast of All Saints. Holding my lighted candle, I stood at the center of the Communion rail. Instead of beginning at the end of the row, Father R came to me first. I recited the formula after him and became the first of our group to become a Third Order member.

I found out gradually that our elite group was not really very elite. At the end of our weekly meetings Father R would ask, "Who's going to give Florence a ride home tonight?" Two or three hands would go up, and Father would choose someone. After I moved up to St. Louis Heights, Dr. and Mrs. C offered to drive me home several times. But once they dropped me off at the bottom of St. Louis Heights instead of driving me home. Mrs. C said, "Dick has an early surgery tomorrow, so we'll let you off here."

My problem was that the last bus had already left. The gas station was closed. I had to use the pay phone to call a taxi to take me home. It would have taken them only another ten minutes up and ten minutes down to drive me home. I was afraid of the dark, and being alone at night after 9:30 was scary. But God protected me.

Leila S did that to me, too. They were not obligated to drive me home. Others were willing to do it. The Cs and Leila S offered to drive me home to make a good impression on Father and the others, instead of doing it for Jesus or from the goodness of their hearts. I wondered how many people said things or did things just to impress a priest, minister, rabbi or others without really meaning what they said, without doing deeds for the love of God.

Joseph Lee, however, always drove me all the way to my home, even though he lived in the opposite direction, up Kaimuki. He even walked me to my door.

The kindest of the group was Mary Jefferson, not because she fought to include me in the first and second group of 12, but because of her kindness and goodness of heart. A longtime widow, Mary needed a wise confessor because of a personal problem. I took her to Father Victorinus for confession. I went to confession first to tell Father that Mary Jefferson needed guidance and was coming in next.

Afterward, Mary was so relieved and so appreciative that she wanted to thank me in a special way. As we walked past McInerny's clothing shop at Fort and King streets, she urged me to go in with her so she could buy me a dress. I refused, but she kept insisting.

I told her, "Mary, when I help someone, I don't want any reward or favor."

"Please let me do this for you, Florence. I really want to get you a new dress."

"No, I don't want you to buy me a dress."

Mary was upset at my refusal, but she didn't hold it against me.

One evening I came to a Third Order meeting straight from the airport after seeing someone off. I was shivering from being cold, because I had given away my sweater at the airport to a young lady who was leaving for the mainland to become a nun. When Mary saw me shivering, she excused herself from the meeting, returned to her home in Kahala and came back with a full-length coat. By waving at me, she called me out to the porch of the hall and offered me the coat. I didn't want to put it on, but I did it to show my appreciation to Mary for going all the way home to get it.

I was 5' tall and thin, while Mary was 5'8". She helped me with the coat, and I let her do it, as a child would. She rolled up the sleeves for me. While walking to the front of the hall, I lifted the coat to keep it from dragging on the floor. I could hear giggles and suppressed laughter. Even Father R had a strange smile. I felt like a little child. The "inner voice" told me I was a spectacle and a lesson in humility, for my act of humility showed that I was not proud and boastful.

I was was so cold at that meeting because earlier I had been at the airport to see Magdalene K off. She was leaving for the mainland to become a nun. She was without a sweater at the airport, so I gave her my best sweater, a white cable-knit cardigan that had cost $10. I had been counseling and encouraging her about her religious vocation.

Since Magdalene's mother was not Catholic and opposed her daughter's becoming a nun, I went to explain the meaning of a religious vocation to her. They lived in a shack in the middle of a taro patch outside of town. Her mother welcomed me into their spotless home and served me lunch with green tea. I can still picture the cracked, bare wooden floor, worn smooth from daily scrubbing. I have never felt more welcomed and more at ease than I did in that shack. Her mother had changed it into a spotless home. *I have been in beautiful houses that were empty and cold. A spiritual person with love for God can sense the coldness of a house without love and peace. Such a house is like a beautiful rose without any fragrance. A house needs peace and love to be a home.*

I told Magdalene's mother, "If your daughter marries a man, she will have difficulties and problems. Her husband may drink or gamble or neglect her. Every man has faults. No man is perfect. But Jesus is perfect because He has no faults. If Magdalene becomes a Sister, it's like marrying Jesus. Jesus will be real good to her and take good care of her."

She nodded to show me that she understood what I was telling her. Then she gave her consent.

When I learned that Magdalene lacked the dowry needed for becoming a Sister, I obtained it for her from the Catholic Women's Guild, which gave dowries to needy young women entering religious life. She was to pick me up at the cathedral after the noonday Mass so we could get the check from the Guild's president, who lived in Manoa. Magdalene was late, keeping me waiting for more than an hour. When she arrived, she said, "Hi, let's go." She never excused herself or apologized for being so late. I wasn't upset because God taught me patience while waiting for her by moving me to say several rosaries for her.

*(I practiced being prompt for appointments by reminding myself that Jesus can disguised as any person at any time. For example, whenever the doorbell rang, I stopped what I was doing to answer the door right away because I pictured Jesus at the door, and I didn't want to keep Him waiting.)*

God also taught me patience while helping Hazel M when she took advantage of my kindness. She asked me to stay with her elderly mother for two hours while she shopped on Saturday mornings. She paid me $2 for this service. The two hours stretched to three. Then she asked me to sweep the stairs and do some dusting – for the same $2. She added chores each Saturday. She even asked me to wash her underwear by hand in the basement and to help make lunch – all for $2. I did everything out of charity, and I never told anyone how she took advantage of me. Her mother slipped me a dollar several times. Hazel did let me join them for lunch after I made the sandwiches for them. I stopped helping her after five Saturdays.

*When you ask someone for a favor, keep your word. Don't take advantage of that person's kindness by adding things to the favor. If you say two hours, make it two hours. Be sincere and honest in dealing with others. Treat everyone with honesty and fairness.*

Hazel donated to charity to be seen and praised by others while hiding her true character. She was not being true to herself. She thought no one saw how she treated me, but God saw everything. He sees how we treat everybody.

Hazel's mother enjoyed my company and appreciated my help. She left me a Lalique crystal statue when she died. I treasured that 10-inch statue of Blessed Mother from Mrs. M. Yet I made the sacrifice of giving it to my sister.

When I found out that Hazel, Mrs. C and several other ladies got together several times to learn how to pray the breviary, I wished they had invited me to join them. I had a strong desire to learn because I thought the breviary was the highest form of prayer. I wanted to pray along with the priests and Jesus as they prayed the breviary.

The Sisters I asked to help me said it was too complicated. Brother Yap told me he didn't know how because he didn't have the duty of praying it. Only priests and contemplative monks and nuns had that duty.

Later I found a simpler form of the breviary that I prayed every day. *I knew that Jesus accepted my prayers from that shorter version because I did it with love. But later I learned from the "inner voice" that the highest form of prayer is sincere heart-to-heart talks with God done with love and meaning. Many people pray but don't really mean what they pray. Some priests and religious pray the breviary (now called the Liturgy of the Hours) in a routine way without devotion and love.*

## A Miracle Home

A second mortgage Thomas made almost cost us our home on McCully Street. We wanted to sell it quickly because we were behind on both mortgage payments. We also had to find another house to live in. I prayed to God for help.

I went to Father Timothy J with a Mass stipend.

"Father, would you please offer a Mass to ask Jesus to help us sell our home, and at the same time to help us buy another home right away so we can have a place to move into."

His eyes got big and his mouth opened. He scratched his head and looked at me as if I was crazy. No one had ever asked God for such a miracle before. Then he asked, "Florence, why do you want to sell your home?"

I didn't answer, because I didn't want to shame my husband and embarrass my children by letting others know we were three months behind in our mortgage payments.

He shook his head from side to side as he walked away.

The next day Mrs. C telephoned me to repeat what Father Timothy had told her on the phone: "Is there something the matter with your friend Florence? She's strange. Is she crazy? With her $1 stipend she wants me to offer a Mass so she can sell her home and buy another home on the same day." (The usual Mass stipend was $2, and $1 for those who couldn't afford the $2.)

I told her, "I don't care what he thinks as long as he offers the Mass for my intention." I believed with my whole heart that God could do it for me.

Mrs. C wondered why I wanted to sell our home, because it was so convenient for people to visit me there. She asked, "Do you have another place to move into?"

"No, I want to sell our house and use that money to buy another house."

"That's quite hard to do, Florence."

"But I have full confidence in God."

The next Sunday at the end of my day of recollection at St. Francis Convent, the "inner voice" told me there was a home for me and to go immediately that Sunday afternoon to a house for sale up St. Louis Heights. When Thomas came to pick me up, I told him there was a house for us on St. Louis Heights.

He said, "Do you know the address? There are so many houses for sale there."

"No, just go and we'll look for a house with a 'For Sale' sign."

So he drove me to St. Louis Heights. (Thomas had such faith in me that he told people I was an ardent Catholic.) We didn't see any "For Sale" signs until we reached upper St. Louis Drive.

We found a beautiful house for sale. I went in to ask the price, but it was too expensive for us because the "inner voice" had told me to pay $17,000 for the house, no more, no less. Just around the bend we saw another "For Sale" sign at the entrance of a hundred-foot drive-way off Noah Street. The sign read, "House for sale by owner."

We knocked and were invited in. As we entered, I asked, "Is this house for sale?"

Mr. Saffrey, the owner, answered yes, and introduced us to his wife. She said, "I would like to show you the house, but I can't show you one of the bedrooms because my two girls have the flu."

I said, "I don't know what faith you belong to, but I'm a Catholic. May I bless the girls with holy water and say a prayer for them? I also have a religious medal for each of them."

They said I could. So I went into the bedroom of their two small girls to bless them with holy water and to pray aloud for their recovery. Then I left a Miraculous Medal of Mary at the bed of each child.

Through the picture window in the living room I had a clear view of Diamond Head and Waikiki on the left all the way to the distant view of Pearl Harbor on the right. The lawn was weedless and landscaped like a Hollywood home, with three terraces.

Mr. Saffrey said, "We had this house built and we landscaped it ourselves. But we can't afford to keep it because my wife has cancer."

"I'm so sorry. I'll pray for all of you. Maybe God sent me here not to buy your house but to pray for you. How much are you asking for house?"

"This three-bedroom house has one-and-a-half bathrooms and is only a year and a half old, so we're asking $19,500 for it. We already have a cash offer of that amount from another lady."

"That's too much for us. We can't afford it. We can afford only $17,000." (The "inner voice" had told me to pay $17,000, no more, no less.) "Please sell the house to her. You need the money. God can get us another house. Get as much as you can for this house. No matter what, I'll be praying every day for you and your two children." The Saffreys sensed that I really cared more about their welfare than about buying their home.

As Thomas and I walked to our car, Mrs. Saffrey asked us to wait. She went into her hothouse to cut a bunch of red and pink anthuriums for me. She said, "Since you'll be praying for us, this is for your altar."

"Thanks for the anthuriums. They're one of my favorites. I'll place them on our altar in front of Jesus' picture. They'll remind me to pray for you every day. Be sure you sell your house for that cash offer."

My understanding and compassion touched their hearts.

That evening at 7:00, our real estate agent brought Mrs. Nakamura, a widow, to look at our home on McCully Street. She liked the house, especially the convenient location. She offered us $19,500 for it in cash. We signed the papers right away.

As soon as the agent and Mrs. Nakamura left, I hurried to kneel at our altar to thank God for the quick sale and the big cash offer. God had saved our home.

About 7:00 the next morning, Monday, the phone rang.

"Hello, is this Florence?"

"Yes, it is."

"This is Mrs. Saffrey."

"Oh, good morning. How are the children?"

"They're much better. Their fever broke during the night; they no longer have a fever. After you left, my husband and I kept talking about your kindness and sincerity. Last night we talked it over and decided to let you have our home for $17,000."

"Won't you be needing the extra money? Why didn't you sell it for the cash offer of $19,500? That's a lot of money."

"My husband's father is a minister, and my husband and I value your prayers more than the extra money. We want you to have our home, because we did so much work on the house and the yard by ourselves."

Her words touched my heart. I cried as I spoke to her. "I don't know how to thank you. I'm so grateful to you and your husband. I'll never forget you. I'll always pray for you. I rely on God to bless you and reward your goodness of heart for me."

"My husband is on his way to work. He'll drop off the keys and the deed to you on the way. He'll be by in about 20 minutes."

"Thank you again."

"I cleaned the house and even washed the windows for you. I know you'll enjoy our home. Good-bye."

I hurried to our altar to kneel and thank God for this big miracle. As Mr. Saffrey entered our home to deliver the keys and the deed, he was pleased to see the bouquet of anthuriums on the altar. I thanked him again for his generosity of heart. Later that morning after returning from Mass, I telephoned Thomas at work to tell him the miracle. The miracle of selling our home and buying another one within 24 hours was a big one. Only God could have planned and worked such a big miracle.

That afternoon the realty agent took me to the bank and transferred $19,500 into our account. That evening Thomas and I took a check for $17,000 to the Saffreys. We used the extra $2,500 to clear our debts. My gratitude to Jesus was so great that I wanted to offer a Mass of thanksgiving to him.

The next day I telephoned Father Timothy.

"Father, please offer a Mass of thanksgiving for our miracle."

"What miracle?"

"Sunday night around seven a Japanese lady bought our home on McCully Street with cash, and yesterday morning around seven we received the keys and the deed to our new home up on St. Louis Heights."

"What? Let me hear you again."

"We did sell our home. And I want to thank God for this big miracle." I told him the whole story.

"Florence, I just don't know what to say. I'll say the Mass for you."

I pictured Father shaking his head from side to side.

Father Timothy doubted that God would work that big miracle for me, but God did. Father even thought I was crazy. But I believed without a doubt that God could do it if He wanted to. Jesus said that if our faith is deep and strong enough, we could move mountains.

My compassion and sincerity of heart touched the Saffreys. Because of their goodness of heart and lack of greed, God used them as His instruments to work that miracle to confound Father Timothy and Mrs. C. Even then my faith and trust in God were so deep that I relied on God to come through with a miracle.

Ever since that miracle, Father Timothy began asking me to pray for his intentions. Thomas and the children never gave it a thought. They didn't realize what a big miracle it was.

I telephoned Mrs. C to tell her about the big miracle Jesus had worked for me. Her first words were: "Is your new home bigger than ours?"

"No, it's a simple home with three bedrooms and one-and-a-half baths."

God used that miracle to teach a lesson to Father Timothy and Mrs. C. That miracle can also teach you readers a lesson. *The lesson is to believe and trust in God all the time for everything. My faith and trust in Him brought me the biggest blessings. This story shows the kind of miracle He can work. So have faith and trust in God. It is more profitable and reassuring to trust in God than to trust in human beings.*

Everything was packed for moving on August 25, 1953, the Feast of St. Louis. I telephoned the Kam Express Moving Company to send a truck. The driver and his helper filled the truck with a load. Audrey rode with them to our new home to begin the unpacking. When the movers returned and loaded the second, final load, the driver said, "Lady, you have to pay the $40 now, because we'll go straight to another job from the other place. It's $20 a load."

"I can pay you only $20 now. I'll pay the rest on Friday when my husband gets paid."

"I can't do that, lady. I have to call my boss about that. Can I use your phone? Where is it?"

He explained the situation to his boss. Then he said, "Here, lady, my boss wants to talk to you."

"Hello, is this the boss?"

"Yes, it is."

"I have only $20 now. But I'll be sure to pay you the rest on Friday when my husband gets paid. He works at Pearl Harbor."

She recognized my voice and said, "Are you the lady who visited my husband in the hospital before he died and who spoke to us at his funeral? He said a volunteer lady really helped him. He told me all about it."

"You mean Mr. Kam?"

"Yes, he was my husband."

"Yes I was the lady who visited him in the hospital and who spoke to you at his funeral. How are you?"

"I'm doing okay. I'm trying to run his business as best as I can. I thought I recognized your voice. You comforted us at his funeral. Why didn't you tell me it was you?"

"I didn't know he owned this company. Even if I did, I wouldn't take advantage of you."

"I really appreciate what you did for him. Please put the driver back on the phone."

After speaking with Mrs. Kam, the driver said, "Lady, my boss says to forget it; you don't have to pay for anything."

"Thanks. You want a cold soda?"

"No, we have to be going."

Then I telephoned Mrs. Kam to thank her for her kindness and generosity.

I have always helped others without expecting any favor in return. If I do something good in a place, I never return for special treatment.

Moving from McCully Street to Noah Street was a turning point in my life. When I lived on McCully Street, many people asked me for help and I never refused a call for help. My location there made it easy for many to drop by for a visit. But my home on Noah Street was out of the way and difficult to get to because of the two steep roads leading to it.

God gave me the miracle home on Noah Street to lead me to a contemplative life. I wasn't a Carmelite, but I did live a very strict life. I needed solitude and silence so God could teach me and guide me. I asked Jesus to govern my every thought, word and action. I asked Him to direct my actions the way a pilot directs a plane. I told Jesus He was my Good Shepherd, and that I wanted to follow Him and to go along with Him. At Noah Street I wanted to obey and follow Jesus the way an obedient puppy obeys and follows his master.

Besides giving us a miracle home, I felt more blessed because the bus route changed so I could attend daily Mass more easily at St. Patrick Church, my new parish. The week before we moved in, the transit system extended the bus route to Noah Street and set the last bus stop across from our driveway. Otherwise all of us except Thomas would have had to catch the bus by walking down the hill to the last bus stop. But the bus system moved the last stop just across our driveway, to our great advantage. Every weekday Tommy, Audrey, Stephen and I took the bus: Tommy to work, Audrey and Stephen to school, and I to church.

My doing God's will and my relying on Him brought our family many advantages. Jesus paved the way and provided the means to make my life easier, because I sought to do His will and to please Him. I never questioned Jesus about His plans for me. I just accepted whatever He planned for me. The miracle home God gave me was part of His plan for my future way of life. He led me from an active life of volunteer work to a quiet and more prayerful life.

I never told my family about my volunteer work or about my prayer life. My family just expected me to clean the house and do the laundry and the cooking. I still did volunteer work while living at Noah Street. *I never refused a call for help. When someone telephoned to ask for help, I just picked up my purse and went. While going by bus to help, I prayed for the person and asked Jesus to help me to help the person.*

God used me to prevent several suicides and several divorces. I also helped some parents who had problems with their teenagers, and some married persons with unfaithful spouses. I kept everything confidential.

*My volunteer work was my way of serving God. Because of my love for Jesus, I did everything I could to help others. I never took credit for helping. All the credit went to Jesus for helping me and guiding me.*

In St. Patrick Church, the life-size statue of St. Therese, the Little Flower, held a bouquet of roses, which often symbolized this saint. She predicted that after her death, blessings from God "will be like a shower of roses." At the ceremony of her canonization into sainthood, a shower of roses fell in front of the pope in St. Peter's Basilica. Many saw the roses fall, even though no roses had been strung up to decorate the basilica.

I knew St. Therese's scattering of roses after death meant her spirit would scatter spiritual graces to people. One day after daily Mass at St. Patrick Church, as I did from time to time, I went to her statue at the side altar to tell her, "I will gladly be your handymaid to carry your basket of roses while you scatter them." She needed my consent to be her handymaid. At the Annunciation, Mary said, "Behold the handmaid of the Lord." I said "handymaid" because I was lowlier than a handmaid.

Even after I moved to the mainland in 1969, I told St. Therese from time to time that I would gladly be her handymaid with a willing heart. I asked her, "St. Therese, help me be a true instrument of God's love and a good messenger of His love." Being a true instrument of God meant letting the love of God in me go out to others in the form of kindness, service and prayers. Being a good messenger of His love meant bringing God into my conversations with everybody.

With a willing and loving heart on my part, how could the Little Flower not use me as her handymaid for doing good and for winning souls for God? I called it a partnership for winning souls for heaven. My part was nothing big. I just led a prayerful life by praying for everybody. My faith and reliance on God were so deep that I knew He answered my prayers for everyone I prayed for. God answers the prayers of a faithful soul who makes the problems of others her own.

By taking the bus to church every day, I became friendly with all the bus drivers. Jimmy, a Japanese driver, had to work on Thanksgiving Day. I knew his bus schedule and I knew when it was time for his meal break. At our Thanksgiving dinner, I filled a plate with turkey, dressing, gravy, yams and cranberry sauce. I brought the dinner and a piece of pumpkin pie to Jimmy at the bus terminal.

Jimmy was touched. Weeks later he told me that my act of kindness had touched him more than the delicious Thanksgiving dinner itself. He had this incident printed in the *Star-Bulletin*, our daily newspaper. He asked me whether I had read it, and I told him I never saw the article.

While down with the flu several months later, I heard the doorbell.

Jimmy and his wife were at the door. After introducing his wife, he handed me a cake. He hadn't seen me on the bus, so he came by to see whether I was all right. I told him that I had the flu but I would be going to church again in a day or two. I learned that he and his wife were cared for by the Salvation Army when they were children. That's how they met.

One day after Mass, I bought a loaf of bread, a pound of sliced luncheon meat and a head of lettuce for the five sandwiches for the next day's lunches. I spent about $2, all the money I had. As I left the market, I realized that I didn't have bus fare. I thought about returning the head of lettuce. But the people at the market knew I went to daily Mass, and I didn't want anyone to mock my God with "You go to church every day; how come your God doesn't help you out?"

I thought about walking home. I once walked up the steep roads to my home from the bottom of St. Louis Heights as a sacrifice for a seminarian. But the walk from Kaimuki to Noah Street was too long.

Then the bus for St. Louis Heights stopped in front of me, and the bus for Kalihi-Kaimuki pulled up behind it. Out came Jimmy, the driver of the second bus. He called me over, shoved a transfer into my hand and said, "Hurry up and catch your bus in front." Otherwise I would have to wait another hour for the next bus. I thanked him and hurried to my bus. Jimmy didn't know my situation. He just wanted to save me the bus fare.

Only God knew I didn't have the bus fare, so he timed the buses and moved Jimmy to give me the transfer. God knew beforehand that I didn't want anyone to mock him, so he arranged to have Jimmy transferred to the Kahili route before this incident happened. God blessed me for wanting to protect His honor.

Weeks later on Jimmy's bus, I told him how I had lacked the bus fare and how God had used him to help me. We both praised God. Then he said, "If I ever join a church, I would join your church because of you."

## Two Souls for God

When my father-in-law was punched in the chest by his wife during an argument, he suffered a heart attack and was taken to St. Francis Hospital. The "inner voice" told me he didn't have long to live.

Then I recalled how the "inner voice" had foretold his death at our last Thanksgiving dinner. The "inner voice" told me someone at that dinner wouldn't be present for the next Thanksgiving. So I said, "I think someone at this table won't be here next Thanksgiving." Everyone was silent, wondering which person it would be. After dinner, my father-in-law's request for a third piece of pie told me he was the one who wouldn't be present. As the "inner voice" had predicted, he died the following October. During my father-in-law's last week of life, I visited him at the hospital every day. I spent the entire day with him from 8:00 in the morning to 4:00 in the afternoon, when I had to return home to prepare dinner for my family. After dinner and a shower, Stephen drove me back to the hospital so I could spend the night with my father-in-law. I sat on a chair beside his bed. His wife and family didn't think his illness was serious, so they never visited him. I spent five days and nights with him.

In his hospital room, my father-in-law told me that his brother had asked for baptism on his deathbed in a Hong Kong hospital. Then I recalled that I had given his brother a Miraculous Medal and had prayed for him during his visit to Hawaii.

Every day I blessed my father-in-law with holy water, comforted him and prayed the rosary for him in his room. He said that if he ever joined a church, he would join mine. In the middle of one night, I saw a white figure on my left while I was sitting in the chair. I wasn't scared at all because I felt that it was Blessed Mother watching over us.

One morning my father-in-law asked for baptism. I went to the hospital chaplain to ask him to baptize my father-in-law because he had asked for it. Father P didn't believe me. He thought I wanted him baptized just because he was my father-in-law.

When Mrs. C saw me at the hospital one morning, she said, "You look terrible, Florence. You go home and rest." I told her my father-in-law had asked for baptism, but the chaplain wouldn't baptize him. While I was home resting, Mrs. C asked Father to baptize him that afternoon, and Father did. Then Mrs. C telephoned to tell me, "Florence, we baptized your father-in-law this afternoon. I was his sponsor and I gave him the name 'Francis.'" I was happy that he had been baptized, although I did not attend.

On the day of his death, I was at the morning Mass at the hospital chapel, as I usually was before going to my father-in-law's room. The "inner voice" told me to receive Communion and then go straight to his room. When I arrived at his room, he told me in Chinese, "I'm going home now." I replied, "But the doctor won't let you go home yet."

Then his head slumped to the side. I knew he had died. I rang for the nurse. I had to borrow a dime from the nurse to telephone my mother-in-law to inform her of his death.

I was with my father when he died, I was with my mother when she died, and I was with my father-in-law when he died.

I made all the funeral arrangements for my father-in-law. His son Henry returned from overseas two days after his father's death. We were making funeral arrangements at my mother-in-law's home when Henry yelled at me, "Why didn't you let me know my father was dying?" Henry threatened to punch me, his right fist raised. Tommy stood up and took off his glasses to fight and defend me. Thomas did nothing to defend me, but he separated the two of them.

I told Henry, "I was going to inform you, but your mother stopped me. She didn't think your father's illness was serious enough, and she was afraid that if you left the Army she wouldn't get any more free treatment at Tripler Hospital."

His mother was smoking a cigarette and sticking her head out of the doorway of the kitchen to listen to us. I asked her to confirm my words, but she kept silent and pulled her head back away from the doorway.

I continued, "When I knew your father's illness was serious, I wrote you a letter telling you about his illness. You and that letter must have crossed each other. When you return you'll find that letter waiting for you."

He left angry because he didn't believe me. As I was leaving my mother-in-law's home, I said, "I'll never set foot in this house again." God made those words come true.

I led the rosary at my father-in-law's wake, and I united his death to Christ's death on the Cross for the conversion of sinners. I asked my father-in-law to beg Jesus to grant the gift of faith to his Chinese friends and especially to Jimmy A, whom I had chosen as a pallbearer. I wasn't able to attend his funeral Mass and burial because I was sick in bed.

I was the godmother of Jimmy's wife, Harriet, and their children. I had reminded Harriet not to nag Jimmy about becoming a Catholic, but to help convert him by setting a good example and by being patient with him.

After the burial of my father-in-law, Jimmy drove from the cemetery straight to church to ask the pastor for instructions for becoming a Catholic. When he got home, he telephoned to tell me the good news after he informed his wife about it.

After Jimmy's phone call, I went straight to our altar to kneel and thank Jesus for Jimmy's conversion and to thank my father-in-law for his intercession.

In his will my father-in-law left Thomas only $10; maybe because Thomas had embezzled more than $2,000 from City Mill. My father-in-law left me nothing, but he did leave Tommy and Stephen about $4,000 each.

On my father-in-law's birthday, in the middle of the night I woke up. Half-awake, I saw the spirit of my father-in-law at the foot of my bed. He wore the same suit that he was buried in. I was terrified. I thought, "Don't come near me; you're dead." He didn't move. He looked sad and regretful. Then I knew that he had come back to thank me for his conversion and his baptism. I wasn't afraid anymore. I told him to remember our Chinese people and to pray for their conversion. Then he disappeared. His soul finally knew how much I had respected him, loved him.

Then my mother-in-law sent her son Fred to ask Tommy and Stephen to let their grandmother have the money left them by their grandfather. Tommy and Stephen didn't think the money was worth fighting over, so they both agreed to let their grandmother have the money.

Many Chinese believe in *Hui Yong* – forty days after death, the spirit of the dead person returns in the evening to pay a final visit to the family. The family gathers in the evening with an offering of food and drink to wait for the spirit of the dead relative. When it returns, that spirit somehow shows its presence.

I recalled how my grandmother and my two aunts had joined my family 40 days after my father died, to wait for the return of his spirit. We were in the living room with food and a small cup of whiskey placed on a table. We felt a sudden chill. Some of us had goosebumps. Then Grandma noticed that the small cup of whiskey was almost empty. We all looked. My father's spirit showed it had returned for a final visit. He used to enjoy his whiskey.

Forty days after Popo died, we gathered in the parlor of my mother's place to wait for the return of Popo's spirit. About 7:00 in the evening a sharp metal sound from the kitchen scared us. We all ran into the kitchen to check on the sound. Even though the stove was off, the heavy lid of the cast aluminum pot had flipped over on its own. We all saw it for ourselves. Popo had given us the sign that she had come for a last visit.

I think that Popo's spirit flipped the lid of the rice pot because she loved her rice. I knew that Popo didn't have enough rice to eat while staying with her daughter Ah Gnan, who cooked a small pot of rice and limited Popo to only a single serving in a small bowl. Ah Gnan ate fast so she would beat everyone to the final helping of rice in the small pot. So Popo never had enough rice to eat while staying with her.

My mother-in-law wanted Thomas, the children and I to join her for the *Hui Yong* of my father-in-law. She wanted company that evening. Thomas, being a coward, didn't want to go, and the children wouldn't go without him. I had planned to go to church for novena prayers that evening.

Before I dressed for church, the "inner voice" told me to stay home. I obeyed. At 7:00 that evening all the lights in our home went out. Frightened, the children in their rooms called out for me. I told them to join me in the living room, where I calmed them and reassured them that everything was going to be all right. Then the lights came back on. I knew the spirit of my father-in-law had returned for his final visit to our family.

I later learned from my neighbors that only our lights had gone out. Nothing had happened to the neighbors' houses. When I told my mother-in-law what had happened, she complained that her husband's spirit didn't pay her a visit that evening, because nothing happened at her place.

For me, the return of the spirit of a dead relative for a final visit was proof that the soul never dies. This Chinese belief in *Hui Yong* also helped me to believe in the Holy Spirit and to understand Pentecost. The Holy Spirit is the Spirit of Jesus. Fifty days after His death, His Spirit came down to be with His mother and His disciples. The big difference is that the Holy Spirit is God, Who remained with them to teach and guide them. When we are baptized and confirmed, the Holy Spirit comes into our souls and remains with us to teach and guide us.

## My Fast and Abstinence

Before the Lenten season of 1954, the Marian Year, the "inner voice" asked me to abstain from meat and poultry and to fast as sacrifices to God. At first I ignored this request. I didn't think that abstaining and fasting were good for my health because I was an active wife and mother with a family that needed me. My mother had died of tuberculosis, and a touch of it kept me from working for a year. I'm sure that God understood my lack of trust in Him, since I was a recent convert.

But I checked about this sacrifice with Father Colloton, my spiritual director. He asked about my health and told me I should check with my doctor. My doctor gave his okay. So for love of Jesus I obeyed the "inner voice" and began my Lenten fast and abstinence.

Soon after I began my fast and abstinence, the solid food I ate came back up through my mouth and nose. Yet I wasn't sick; nothing was wrong with me.

When I told Father Colloton about this, he said, "Florence, man does not live by bread alone." He taught me to replace the meat in my meals with milk, eggs, cheese or fish. He told me to drink a mixture of water, molasses and some kind of powdered milk. Father used to be a Trappist monk, with a special diet for his health because of their strict fast and abstinence. He had to transfer to the Sacred Hearts Order in Hawaii for health reasons.

God led me step by step. He did not give me the full picture of my fasting and abstaining for the rest of my life. After the Lenten season the "inner voice" told me to continue my fast and abstinence.

During Advent of that year, I was reading *The Imitation Of Christ* under the holly tree in our front yard. The "inner voice" told me to offer my fast and abstinence for the recovery of Pope Pius XII, who was very sick. I loved him because he was so prayerful and holy. I told myself that if he died I would never visit Rome, because seeing him would be my only reason for going there. He did recover, and lived another four years. I was cooking in the kitchen when the "inner voice" told me the pope had just died. Later that evening there was a special report on the news that he had just died. I cried because he was such a holy and good pope. I've never visited Rome.

My spiritual director, Father Colloton, told me to check with my confessor, Father Victorinus, about continuing my fast and abstinence. I went to see him at the cathedral. From his place in the third pew he led me into the sacristy, where he heard the confessions of the bishop and other priests.

"What is it, Florence?"

"The 'inner voice' told me to fast and abstain for God, and Father Colloton told me to check with you if it's okay. He and my doctor said I could."

"Do you like beef, pork and chicken?"

"I love to eat all kinds of meat."

"When God asks for a sacrifice, it's never something we don't like. Otherwise it wouldn't be a sacrifice."

I smiled. "I would do anything Jesus asks of me, because He loved me enough to die on the Cross to save me."

He squeezed my arm: "Florence, you have lots of fat to give Jesus."

We both laughed.

I fasted and abstained from meat and poultry every day except Sundays. My fast consisted of a cup of coffee and a slice of toast for breakfast, a glass of milk and a sandwich for lunch, and a meatless dinner with my family in the evening. The Catholic custom of fasting was a lenient one: The two lighter meals should not exceed or equal the amont of the large main meal. Catholics have the freedom to choose a stricter fast by eating less than what the directive allows.

It was a difficult sacrifice to cook meat, pork or chicken for the family and yet not have any – not even a taste while cooking. When I was tempted to eat something that would break my fast or abstinence, I simply recalled that I was making a sacrifice to show my love for God, and then I wasn't tempted by the food any more.

From 1954 to 1987 my fast and abstinence never made me sick or weak. When we make a sacrifice to God according to His will, He sustains us. Fasting has become such a lasting habit for me that today at 83 I'm still fasting.

Father Victorinus was almost 80 when I went to him for confession the last time. That same Saturday the "inner voice" told me Father would die suddenly. Father confirmed it by what he said in the confessional: "Florence, promise me that when you're seriously ill, you'll obey your doctor and forget about your fast and abstinence." He surprised me with that request. I promised him I would, and then continued with my confession. He ended the confession by asking me to remember him in my prayers.

The following Tuesday I received word of Father Victorinus' death. I missed him. He was a kind and holy priest. Through his death I learned the important lesson of detachment from human persons for attachment to Jesus, Who never leaves. I gradually learned to rely more on Jesus for spiritual guidance and help than on human persons.

## Baby-sitting for a Neighbor

Larry and Yoshie H lived next door to us. They both worked, so I baby-sat their two adopted children: John, 6 months, and Patty, after she came home from the first grade. Yoshie brought John over after I returned from daily Mass. She paid me $45 a month for caring for them. After several years of caring for them, I grew to love them. They became so attached to me that they began calling me "mama." Yoshie got jealous, so I told them to call me *Amu* (Chinese for "lady").

Yoshie took Patty and John to shop for a gift for me on Mother's Day. The drugstore had a Mother's Day drawing for a gift. With their mother's permission, Patty and John put in my name for the drawing. The next day I received a phone call from the drugstore telling me I had won a prize because of Patty and John H, and I could pick up the electric can opener any time. I thanked them for putting in my name and for the prize.

Yoshie had only a brother and always wanted a sister. She told me, "Florence, you're like a sister to me. You're so kind and good-hearted. Don't let anyone take advantage of your kindness, now."

Yoshie and her friend took me to the zoo so I would watch Patty and John while they visited with each other. Then her friend invited us to her home on Kapahulu Street for ice cream and soft drinks.

On entering the parlor after washing the bowls and glasses, I heard her friend asking Yoshie, "Did you tell Florence yet?" I saw Yoshie shake her head from side to side and put her index finger to her lips. I quickly went back into the kitchen because I sensed something wasn't right and I didn't want to embarrass her.

A few days later, the day before Yoshie brought home adopted newborn twins, she asked me whether I would care for the twins along with Patty and John. She would pay me $75 a month instead of the $45 I was getting. I told her I would check with Thomas about it. I knew the responsibility of caring for the newborn twins, plus John and Patty would be too much for me.

Two frightening experiences while caring for John came to mind. I had to use the bathroom, so I told him to stay in the parlor. When I returned several minutes later, John had disappeared. He was only three. He was out wandering on the road somewhere. I was sick with worry because of the cars coming downhill on those roads. I knelt before the altar and asked Jesus, "Help me find John before something happens to him." As I rushed out the door to look for him, I thought, "If John is dead, I'll kill myself."

I asked my two neighbors to help me find John. Rose went up St. Louis Drive, Ad went down it and I went along St. Peter Street. I found John in the middle of the road. He was trying to get to his grandmother's house. I ran to get him. I cried with relief and joy.

Later, when I reflected on this terrifying experience of searching for John, it reminded me of Mary and Joseph searching for the boy Jesus when He remained behind in Jerusalem. I was given a small taste of the fear and worry they had felt as they searched for Him.

The second incident happened when I was caring for John at his home. Again I had to use the bathroom. When I came out, John was on the kitchen floor eating cockroach poison. I took it out of his mouth and telephoned the doctor. He told me to rush him to his office. I telephoned for a taxi to rush us there. After checking him, the doctor said he was fine. I had gotten to him in time and he hadn't swallowed any of the poison. When I told Yoshie what had happened, she got really angry at me and scolded me.

Those two incidents made me realize that the responsibility of caring for two small children and twin babies would be too much for me.

The next morning I went to Yoshie's home to give her my decision. I told her that the responsibility was too great and that my husband and children thought it would be too much for me. I refused her politely, and I offered to help out from time to time for free. Then I left.

She never spoke to me again. I didn't mind the silent treatment. What hurt me was her not allowing Patty and John to visit me, not even to speak to me. I missed them, and I knew they missed me, too. I thought of how they wrote my name for the Mother's Day drawing. Yoshie behaved as though I had wronged her. But she was the one who was unfair to me by not preparing me about the twins and by trying to pull a fast one on me. She thought I would agree to care for the twins because of my kindness and for the extra $30 a month. But even for $1,000 a month I would not have taken on that great responsibility.

One day when Yoshie wasn't home, Patty and John came over secretly. They said, "Mama told us not come over any more and not to call you *Amu*."

I said, "That's okay. I'm still *Amu*."

They laughed.

Yoshie quit her job to take care of the twins and John. But the children were just too much for her. Two months later, Larry had a heart attack and spent two weeks in the hospital. Two weeks after he came home from the hospital, when the twins were three months old, Yoshie was so fed up that she just took off on a tour of Europe.

Yoshie's elderly mother had to come every day to help Larry take care of Patty, John and the twins. Larry was still recovering from his heart attack, so several times a week I warmed some canned soup to bring over for their lunch and then left. I felt it was my duty as a neighbor to help out. To thank me for my help, Yoshie's mother made some pot holders for me and left them on my porch. I've always enjoyed helping my neighbors.

## The Emblem

When Audrey wanted to attend St. Louis University in St. Louis, Missouri, to study nursing, Thomas and Mrs. C sided with her and encouraged her. I thought she should go to the University of Hawaii. Mrs. C said, "Florence, just because you didn't have schooling doesn't mean others don't need schooling." I knew that schooling and education were important. I just didn't want to shame Thomas and Audrey by revealing that we couldn't afford the high tuition, the room and board and the plane fares. The tuition at the University of Hawaii was low, and Audrey could live at home. I also foresaw that studying on the mainland would not be best for my daughter.

Thomas was too proud and also too cowardly to tell Audrey that he couldn't afford to send her to a mainland university. He also wanted to brag that she goes to a mainland university. To get the money for her expenses, Thomas quit his job at Pearl Harbor in June to draw out $4,000 from his retirement fund. He also needed the money to pay the back mortgage payments and some other bills. Deciding and doing this on his own really angered me.

His being out of work for 6 months brought worry and hardship because of all our bills. The whole family suffers when the father is without a job. Audrey, Tommy and Stephen didn't have a complete picture of our financial hardship. I bore most of the burdens and the worries in silence to spare them from worry. I never told the children Thomas had quit his job. I just told them he was out of work. Thomas didn't get a job until 8 months later, in February, when he went to work on Eniwetok in the South Pacific.

*Education is good and valuable, but it should be used properly. Some educated people tend to look down on the uneducated, the poor and the lowly. The Chinese have a saying: "The higher you are, the lower you should be." This means the higher your wealth, fame or position, the more humble you should be. This is true and even more important for Christians and believers. Because of the example of Jesus Christ, the God of Christians is a God of humility. God did not make different classes of people. People are people, and all are children of God and deserve respect.*

Lacking education, I learned mainly from the School of Christ. I learned everything the hard way: being disappointed, ridiculed, hurt, betrayed. For all the lessons I learned from the School of Christ I paid the price of suffering. All the lessons in this book are from my own experiences and practices, not from ideas in books. Like an expert chef who tests every recipe before using it, I have practiced every recipe for many years before putting it in this book. My recipes are for the art of living for God and with God, and for living with peace of mind, heart and soul.

God gave me a miracle home in St. Louis Heights for my spiritual growth. At our McCully Street home, my growing children took up much of my time. There people dropped in almost every day. Sometimes they stayed more than an hour or two. But our Noah Street home was out of the way for everybody.

When Thomas worked overseas, and Tommy married and moved out, and Audrey was on the mainland for college and then for work, and Stephen was at the University of Hawaii and then at work, I was alone most of the time. When Stephen married and moved out, I lived in solitude and silence except when Thomas came home for vacation or when Audrey came home some summers. I did less volunteer work and devoted more time to prayer and meditation. God also used this life of solitude and silence to prepare me for a new way of life with private religious vows.

## An Associate of the Sacred Hearts Sisters

After attending the daily Mass at 7:00 in the morning at St. Patrick Church, I went over to St. Margaret Mary Chapel to spend time with Jesus in the Blessed Sacrament.

Sister Damien Joseph, a Sacred Hearts Sister who was a first cousin of Father Damien, the famous leper priest of Molokai, managed the religious gift shop next to the chapel. She was the one who sold me the two large pictures I used for the Enthronement of Jesus and for our Consecration to Mary. One day she surprised me with, "Don't think the Sisters are angels, Florence." I had put the Sisters on a pedestal because I thought they were like angels. She also told me, "You have a special mission, Florence." I didn't understand what she meant. She used to give me Green Scapulars of Mary to give people for their conversions, so I thought that was my special mission. Only years later did God reveal what that special mission was – being the dwelling place and handymaid of a saint who returned for a second lifetime.

Yet weeks later Sister Damien Joseph asked me, "Florence, could you mop and wax the floor of the shop for me?" The "inner voice" told me that she should ask some of the high school students to do it for her. So I said, "I don't wax floors. You have to ask my boss, Sister."

"Who's your boss?"

"Jesus." Her mouth dropped open, but she said nothing. Then she smiled. She never asked me to do that again.

Hazel M put my name in for becoming a spiritual associate of the Sacred Hearts Sisters. So the Sister in charge of the associates invited me to become one. As an associate, I was expected to pray for the

Sisters, who in turn prayed for all their associates. I was happy to be an associate of the Sisters.

The day before the ceremony for becoming an associate, I was at St. Francis Hospital doing volunteer work. I was talking to the chaplain, a Sacred Hearts priest, in his office. The chaplain, Father P, had heard how generous I was with others. He said, "Florence, if God made you a millionaire, you would give it all away. Here, I have something for you. This is an extra emblem a Sacred Hearts Sister made for me."

"Thanks, Father. I'll treasure it."

The round emblem of white wool, six inches in diameter, was embroidered with two red hearts framed by a circle of three intertwining vines of thorns. Later I had this emblem of the Sacred Hearts of Jesus and Mary framed in an octagonal frame, which I still have today.

It seemed as though God had revealed to Father P my generosity of heart. I had given my last dollar to my mother-in-law for her bus fare when she came to visit me. At the airport I had given Magdalene my best sweater. As my mother was dying of tuberculosis, I gave her my only coat.

The day after Father gave me the emblem of the Sacred Hearts of Jesus and Mary, I became a spiritual associate of the Sacred Hearts Sisters. After the ceremony, I noticed that all the Sisters wore that emblem on their white habit. Pointing to the emblem on one of the habits, I said, "I have one just like that"

"Where did you get it?"

"Father P gave it to me yesterday. He didn't even know I was becoming a Sacred Hearts associate today."

Then one Sister said, "That emblem is for our habit, which only the Sacred Hearts priests and nuns can wear."

"I'm going to frame mine and hang it on the wall."

I realized that Jesus had moved Father P to give me the emblem. I took it as a gift from the Sacred Hearts of Jesus and Mary. They accepted and welcomed me as an associate even before the actual ceremony. I treasured that emblem with the Sacred Hearts of Jesus and Mary because it came from them.

As an associate of theirs, I never refused to run any errands the Sisters asked of me. Not having a car, I walked to the post office to mail packages for them or to buy some thread or other items for them.

These Sacred Hearts Sisters were giving a farewell dinner party for their Mother General from Rome and needed someone to be in their chapel. Someone must always be present whenever there is Exposition of the Blessed Sacrament. They needed me to be in the chapel so all the Sisters could be at the farewell dinner party for Mother General.

I had told Sister Damien Joseph how I had gotten the statue of Baby Jesus and she knew I had a great devotion to the infant Jesus, so she told several Sisters, "Let's go to the chapel and ask Baby Jesus to find Florence and send her here."

I usually spent Sunday afternoons in the Brothers' chapel at St. Louis School to be with Jesus, to meditate and to pray for people. While I was in the Brothers' chapel, only a 15-minute walk from St. Margaret Mary Chapel, the "inner voice" told me to go there. I obeyed right away.

*God speaks to everyone. When you have a thought of doing something good, don't hesitate. Follow through right away. We let many thoughts of good deeds slip by because our minds are full of worldly concerns. Even if the devil tries to trick you with a thought that seems good, God will protect you.*

About 3:00 that afternoon Sister Damien Joseph heard my footsteps coming up the porch and rushed out to greet me. Being the first to see me, she pointed at me and yelled out, "There she is! There she is! It's a miracle!" Excited and happy, she and the other Sisters rushed out to greet me.

Sister Damien Joseph said, "We asked Baby Jesus to find you and send you here, and He did." She introduced me to Mother Gertrude, who asked me to be in the chapel before the Blessed Sacrament in Exposition so all the Sisters could be at the dinner party. She told me the party would end at 6:00 that evening. I told her the privilege was mine. I meant it.

First I telephoned Stephen to tell him why I would be late and to get something to eat. Because people could wander into the chapel, Mother Gertrude locked me in with the Blessed Sacrament for my protection. I enjoyed being alone with Jesus in the Sisters' chapel for the next three hours. When the dinner party ended, Mother Gertrude and Sister Damien Joseph came to thank me and to let me out.

Sister Damien Joseph had a deep respect for my prayer life and knew of my deep love for Jesus. She trusted me and trusted Jesus to find me. The Sisters asked, and they received.

Instead of wasting time in idle chats or window-shopping, I spent my time well. Every morning after the 6:00 Mass at St. Patrick Church, I spent two to three hours in the Sisters' chapel. I did this not because of being lonely or troubled, but to be with Jesus, to meditate and to pray the rosary for people.

God led me to spend time with Him in another church, and also to enjoy the beach and the zoo. Several weeks later the transit system changed the route for the St. Louis Heights bus. Instead of going east along Waialae Avenue past St. Patrick Church and up to Wilhelmina Rise and then returning, the bus went down Kapahulu Avenue to Kalakaua Avenue, and then returned around Diamond Head cemetery. The bus from my home on Noah Street stopped in front of the Waikiki Grand Hotel on Kapahulu Avenue. There I got off and walked a block on Lemon Road, which led directly to the side door of St. Augustine Church. So I began attending daily Mass at St. Augustine Church in Waikiki and remained in church to pray after Mass.

Sometimes I would spend only an hour in church and then walk to the beach or to the zoo to meditate there. *While sitting on a bench at Kuhio Park and watching the waves move in and out, the "inner voice" taught me a lesson on acceptance and a lesson on obedience: I should learn to accept the things that happen in my life the way the waves move in and out without resisting and fighting back, and to obey God the way the ocean and its tides rise and fall without rebelling or any grumbling.*

I learned how to blend colors from God, the Creator and the best artist, by looking at the different colors of the birds at the zoo. For example, seeing a gray and pink bird taught me what a beautiful combination those two colors make. I shared what I learned at the zoo by teaching young ladies how to blend colors.

On the way back from Mass, I sometimes got off at Diamond Head Cemetery to spend time there. During the day a cemetery is the most peaceful place for prayer and meditation. I had never enjoyed the peace and solitude of a Catholic cemetery before. Every Catholic cemetery is consecrated ground.

At the entrance was a big monument of Mary holding the dead body of her son Jesus next to a standing cross. I made the sign of the cross and said a prayer for all those buried in the cemetery. As I walked past each grave, I said a prayer for the person buried there. I liked that cemetery because it was so quiet and peaceful. I usually sat under the shade of a tree to pray the rosary and to talk to Jesus. The chirping of birds and the rustling of leaves were like a symphony from God to entertain me. God also made it more convenient for me to attend daily Mass and to spend time with Him.

## Vision of Purgatory

God used a Marianist Brother to teach me about purgatory. Brother Anselm worked at the switchboard near the entrance to the Brothers' residence. He directed incoming phone calls and rang for the Brothers who had visitors. Visitors didn't like Brother Anselm because he was gruff and unfriendly. They didn't know he suffered from poor health and a stomach ulcer. But I got along well with him. I always greeted him and chatted with him whenever I went to the Brothers' chapel to spend time with Jesus.

At the switchboard one day, Brother Anselm looked more downcast than usual. Usually he never smiled.

"Brother Anselm, look at the sky, look at the birds, everything is so beautiful. Smile."

He smiled.

Weeks later Father M telephoned to tell me that Brother Anselm was seriously ill in the hospital. As a volunteer there, I fed him during lunch because he was so weak. I used to feed the patients who couldn't afford a private nurse. I did everything for all the patients with love.

On one of my visits I found Brother Anselm asleep, with the blanket pushed aside and a strong breeze blowing in through the window. He was unconscious and I couldn't wake him. I rang for the nurse and told her what I had seen and done.

Brother Anselm died a few days later from pneumonia. Besides the Brothers, I was the only person to attend his funeral Mass and burial. I recalled how three weeks earlier hundreds of people had attended the funeral Mass and burial of Brother M, a part-Hawaiian local boy. Brother M did the buying for the school and the Brothers and the people respected and liked him for his friendliness.

A month after the burial of Brother Anselm, half-awake during a nap, I "saw" Blessed Mother in a white robe with a blue sash. A large gold rosary with white beads and a large crucifix dangled from her side. I couldn't see her face, but I followed her as she led me along. I tried to rush ahead of her to see her face, but I just couldn't catch up with her.

She led me through a dark gloomy place with shadowy people on different levels. I saw Brother Anselm on a higher level with shadowy people below him. He saw me and smiled at me. I asked him, "Is Brother M okay?" He didn't answer me.

After I woke up, I thought a lot about the meaning of this vision of purgatory. Blessed Mother had led me to my friend Brother Anselm and left me with him. He was in a safe place, with a smile for me. But there was no word about Brother M. I prayed for him.

Brother Anselm's smile was his way of thanking me for my prayers. I had prayed for him and had gone to his funeral and burial. I was the only lay person at his funeral, and I rode to the grave in the car behind the hearse. I felt relief for him because he no longer had to suffer from his poor health and illness. I used to think of ways to make him smile. He knew I respected him and tried to bring a small bit of cheer into his sickly life.

*Never misjudge persons because of their facial expression or grumpiness. Such persons are the most in need of our prayers and kind words. Kindly smiles are good medicine that help the sick get well or feel better.*

It seemed that Blessed Mother had given me a glimpse of what purgatory might be like: a gloomy place full of empty sadness. That place was so void that I couldn't describe or explain the suffering of the souls there, but the experience was printed in my memory. That vision taught me about the suffering souls in purgatory and encouraged me to pray more often for them. The different levels represented the different degrees of suffering based on past sinfulness.

Since that experience, I have prayed for the souls in purgatory every day. *Remember to pray for the sick, the dying and the dead every day. The souls in purgatory cannot do anything for themselves. They depend on the prayers of those on earth for relief. All of us will die someday. Then God will move the souls in heaven we prayed for to pray for us in return.*

I thank God for my meeting with Brother Anselm. From him I learned how to love a person even though I wasn't related to him by blood. That was the beginning of my universal love for all and the beginning of my praying for everybody every day. I had little schooling and little religious instruction, so Jesus and Blessed Mother taught me by showing things to the eyes of my soul.

A friend introduced me to a dignified lady from France. Because she was well-educated and in her fifties, everyone called her Madame. I invited her to lunch at our home because we needed a loan from her.

Thomas had mortgaged our home on Noah Street and we had missed the payments for 2 months because he was out of work. If we missed the mortgage payment for the third month, the bank would foreclose on our home. We couldn't borrow from anyone. So I thought of asking Madame for a loan of $125 for the mortgage payment.

People had told me that to please a husband I had to please his stomach. So I figured that to get a favor from a person, I had to please her stomach.

I asked Thomas to get a fresh chicken for me. While he went to bring Madame to our home, I cut up the chicken and marinated it in soy sauce with fresh ginger and some whiskey before frying it with large button mushrooms. Madame would smell the chicken as she entered our home. Thomas was embarrassed about asking for the loan, so he left after he brought her home.

Madame enjoyed the chicken so much that she ate three-quarters of it, and quickly. After lunch I told her about our three children and the danger of losing our home before asking for the loan.

For Madame $125 was small, but for us it was big. She agreed to lend us the money with 20 percent interest, because she wanted to donate the interest to an orphanage in France named in honor of St. Therese. I was happy that the interest was going to that orphanage. I loved France and I loved orphans. I also thought of the Little Flower. Madame didn't ask me to sign any papers. She made the loan on trust.

After repaying Madame several months later, I took her out to lunch. She saved half her lunch for her dinner. After lunch she asked me, "Where are you going from here, Florence?"

"I have to pay our water bill."

"Do you know where?"

"No, but I'll ask for directions."

"I'll take you there."

"Okay."

As we walked to the Board of Water Supply, she pointed to a building and asked, "What building is that, Florence?"

"I don't know."

"That's the main post office. What building is that?

"I don't know."

"You idiot. That's City Hall."

"What building is that?"

"I don't know."

"What an idiot you are. That's Kawaihao Church."

I accepted what she said without feeling offended. As a former school teacher, Madame was trying to teach me those important buildings. At the Board of Water Supply, she led me to the counter for paying bills. Madame was kind and helpful. She was the grand lady who helped us when we needed help. I never forgot her. I linked her with France, orphans and St. Therese whenever I thought of Madame from France.

When I told a friend on the phone how Madame had kept calling me an idiot, she laughed and laughed.

"She shouldn't call you that, Florence."

"I didn't care. It didn't bother me."

I didn't understand the meaning of "idiot," so it didn't hurt or bother me.

Next to the Catholic cemetery near Diamond Head, my miracle home on Noah Street had the most peaceful atmosphere. Everyone was away, so it was quiet and peaceful. I prayed the rosary and I prayed for people from my heart. I flipped the pages of a spiritual book at random and asked Jesus to talk to me. That was the best time of my Catholic life. The Holy Spirit was preparing me for making private religious vows. The Saint in my soul was leading me to a life vowed to God.

*My practice of living in God's presence*
*helped me to control my emotions*
*and to keep peace with everybody.*
*I could also set others at peace*
*because I was at peace.*

# 7

# A LIFE VOWED TO GOD

G od gave me a miracle home on Noah Street to draw me into
solitude and silence. He called me to a contemplative way of life
to prepare me for making private religious vows.

## Guidance from God

The "inner voice" taught me how to connect my thoughts, words
and actions to God. When a friend told me we should spiritualize everything we do, I didn't understand what she meant by "spiritualize,"
and she couldn't explain it to me. But later the "inner voice" told me I
was doing that all along. Spiritualizing everything meant connecting
everything to God, and that's what I had been doing.

Here are some examples.

Before I take my first sip of coffee in the morning, I hold up my cup
and say, "Here's to you, Jesus." When I light the candles on an altar, I
say, "Jesus, you are the light of the world; be our guiding light." Before

going anywhere I pray, "Jesus, please lead me here, there and everywhere, and please time and sanctify my presence here, there and everywhere."

When hungry or thirsty from fasting, I thought of Jesus, hungry and thirsty as He walked long distances in the heat of the Holy Land. When accused falsely or blasted with words wrongly, I kept silent as I thought of the innocent Jesus silent before His accusers. When I felt interior suffering, I thought of Mary, our sorrowful mother, as she stood looking at her son Jesus nailed to the cross. Because of her love, her sensitivity of soul and her son's suffering, no woman has ever suffered as much as Mary, Our Lady of Sorrows.

The "inner voice" also taught me to sacrifice time and preference to serve my family and friends for love of God. When a preacher in church told us we should make sacrifices to God, I didn't understand the meaning of "sacrifices." A friend later told me that I was already doing that for God without knowing they were sacrifices.

Here are some examples.

At the table I always served the better portions to others and kept the worst portions for myself. I did the same in sharing things: giving the better of two souvenirs or items to the other person. Whenever someone needed me, I gave my time and help without a thought of my own plans. I never thought I was making sacrifices; I just did it for love of God and with love for others.

As Lent drew near, Mrs. C asked, "What are you giving up for Lent, Florence?"

"Nothing; I just tell Jesus to draw whatever sacrifices He wants from me."

My answer surprised her. The two best sacrifices to God are: first, those done with love and concern without thinking or planning; second, those He chooses for us. When we choose a sacrifice, it may not be the best for us. But God knows what's best for us because He knows our spiritual needs and our limits. So we're better off accepting and dealing with the trials and problems God allows to happen to us.

I recall Mrs. C telling me that she and Father Colloton wore something that irritated and hurt their skin every time they moved. That was the penance they had chosen for Lent. But both of them had to give it up because the rash they got almost became infected.

*Sacrifices we choose for ourselves can lead to spiritual pride: "I'm making this sacrifice for God, so I'm holier than others." Sometimes we make a sacrifice for a selfish reason without knowing it; for example, sacrificing desserts for Lent when the real reason is to lose weight for the sake of vanity, and giving up cigarettes as a sacrifice but mainly for health reasons. Sacrificing what we love and practicing self-denial must be done out of love for God. Accepting and offering God a hardship or problem with a willing heart without complaining to others and without grumbling is the best sacrifice we can offer Him.*

To sacrifice means giving up something we like or love. The more we love something or someone, the greater the sacrifice. The highest sacrifice we can make to God is to give up what we love the most. Abraham is the best example. He was willing to sacrifice his only son, the person he loved most. But God has never been cruel. God only tested Abraham, who passed the test so well. Looking back these past 48 years, I see how God prepared me and led me step-by-step to give up the persons I loved the most by leaving them to live far away.

The "inner voice" taught me most of my spiritual practices before I learned what they were called. I met many priests and religious who said a lot about the spiritual life, but who practiced little of what they said. *Living one's religion is much more important than knowing and talking about it.*

Here are some examples of guidance from God.

*From my experiences I knew how deeply words can cut. Others treated me like a block of wood without feelings. We all have feelings. So I was careful with words to avoid hurting the feelings of others.* Before meeting a person who sought my help, I prayed to the Holy Spirit, "Please don't let me say anything that displeases You."

I also tried to control the use of my eyes. I didn't want to see what God didn't want me to see. A frequent prayer of mine has been "Jesus, please help me see everything through the eyes of faith," or "Let me borrow your eyes, Jesus."

*I learned from the mistakes and faults of others. When I saw a person doing something wrong, I asked God to help me avoid committing the same wrong. I tried hard not to commit the same faults that I saw others committing: being late for an appointment, lying, deceiving, being mean, breaking a promise, and so on.*

*I tried to be understanding and kind to others, but the Holy Spirit taught me that pity has no place in the spiritual life. Sometimes pity for others can lead them to pity themselves or become weaklings.* To be fair, peacemakers cannot take sides with one person out of pity against the other. True peacemakers try to bring people together in harmony, while the devil tries to drive people apart by causing dissension.

*From age five I began learning acceptance. Along with acceptance and living in God's presence, my trust in God helped me to control my emotions when something or someone stirred them up. God also trained me to put aside hurtful memories and to think of the good others did for me. God taught me to forgive by reminding me that I was not perfect myself and that no one on earth was perfect. Only God is perfect.*

## A New Spiritual Director

When Father Colloton was transferred to Maui, before leaving he said, "I know the Holy Spirit will guide you, Florence."

Then God led me to my second spiritual director. At a retreat at St. Francis Convent in 1955, the "inner voice" directed me to ask the retreat master, Father Leonard Thome, to be my spiritual director. I thought, "Him? He's not spiritual enough." So I ignored the "inner voice."

But during Father's second talk in the chapel, the "inner voice" told me sternly to do as I was told. So I asked Father after the conference whether he would be my spiritual director. He agreed to be my spiritual director and confessor, and said my weekly confession would be on Saturday afternoons at 1:00 in the chapel of St. Louis High School. Father Thome, a Marianist, was kind and well-mannered.

The priest who is both spiritual director and confessor can get to know better the people he counsels. Besides giving spiritual guidance, he also hears their confession of sins and failings.

I was serious about striving for spiritual perfection, so I was open with Father Thome. I was honest and direct because God had blessed me with simplicity. Father believed me when I told him I was guided by an "inner voice." At my confession each Saturday, Father gave me a virtue to practice for the week. For example, he told me to practice patience for the week and then report about it at the next confession. After several confessions, Father Thome gave me each of the "Five Silences" to practice. He did this without explaining what each "silence" was or how to practice it. He just said, "Florence, your practice for this week is silence of sight; then next week let me know how you practiced it." After confession, with tears I cried to Blessed Mother to teach me how to practice silence of sight.

Secretly I asked Blessed Mother to give me an example to stump Father Thome, since he had neglected to explain its practice. He was dealing with me as if I were a nun with religious training. My prayer to Blessed Mother brought a big surprise to the both of us.

On the bus to confession the next Saturday, I worried about what to say about my practice of silence of sight. I still didn't understand it and I didn't know what to tell Father Thome. As I walked past the open back entrance of the chapel toward the front entrance, Father looked up at me from his seat. Even though I was dressed properly with a petticoat under my cotton dress, I was embarrassed by Father's looking at my legs, which were outlined by the sun shining through my dress. That instant I understood the meaning of silence of sight. How kind of Blessed Mother to use the very person who assigned the practice as my example for explaining it.

I was pleased and excited as I knelt in a pew for several minutes to prepare for confession. After I made my confession, I asked Father Thome whether I was right in the example he provided me on silence of sight when I walked past the open entrance of the chapel.

"Father, maybe you should have kept your eyes on your prayer book or on the tabernacle when you heard my footsteps. Instead you looked up to see the sunlight shining through my dress. Does silence of sight mean controlling the use of our eyes? Is that the way to practice silence of sight?"

Father Thome was silent and still for several moments. Then he said "yes" softly and told me I should continue with its practice.

I found the "Five Silences" challenging because I was determined to please God. Here are the "Five Silences":

1. silence of sight = control of eyes
2. silence of words = control of words
3. silence of mind = control of thoughts
4. silence of memory and imagination = control of memories and imaginings
5. silence of emotions = control of emotions

I used these practices to prove my love for Jesus and for a closer union with God. It was like going to school, the "School of Christ."

Practicing silence of sight was the first step I took in seeing all things through the eyes of faith. I wouldn't look at a handsome man to be attracted to him. I wouldn't look at an ugly person to look down on him or to criticize him. By not looking at beautiful things in stores, I wasn't tempted to buy them. I tried to keep my eyes on Jesus Christ and on God's love for me. Silence of sight helped me to keep my eyes on God and on the path that leads directly to Him.

Through silence of sight, the Holy Spirit, my constant teacher, taught me the first step in detaching myself from people, places and things. By detaching myself from the comforts of my home, I could feel at home even in a cheap hotel or a dingy apartment. How the Holy Spirit led me step-by-step to total detachment comes later in this book.

*The tongue can be sharper than a sword. What we say to others can cut deep and hurt.* What others said to me caused me much suffering; for example, the things said to me or about me by my in-laws, Thomas, priests and friends. *Words can kill people by killing their will to live. So be careful about what you say to a person and how you say it. Words can cause harm to a person and leave scars.*

What you think about and how you think about it can affect your emotions and your decisions. Bad thoughts about people can lead to bad emotions and bad decisions against people. How you think about your behavior and about events can distort the truth and make you arrogant. *So controlling your thoughts is needed to practice charity and to see the truth about yourself, others and events.*

*We can use our memory to grow spiritually. Whenever I recall being hurt by someone, I ask God to erase that hurtful incident from my memory. If I dwelt on that sad memory, I would become bitter and start to hate the person. Some dwell so much on a past tragedy that they begin to blame God for what happened.*

Remembering every kindly deed that others did for us can teach us to love others and deepen our prayer life. I keep all my good memories and recall them to encourage me to go on doing good to others and to go on living for God.

One incident comes to mind. As I walked by a homeless man who limped with a clubfoot, I smiled at him and he tipped his cap at me. After he walked past me, I called out to him, "Sir." He kept going. I called a second time, "Sir." I had to call a third time before he stopped and turned around. When he saw me walking toward him, he took a few steps to meet me. I handed him 50 cents and said, "Have a cup of hot coffee."

He said, "Thank you, ma'am," and tipped his cap again.

I told him, "I have to run and catch my bus."

That man didn't stop and turn when I called him "sir," because no one ever called him "sir." My calling him "sir" touched him, and his calling me "ma'am" touched me. He knew I respected him and didn't look down on him when I called him "sir." I knew he was grateful and appreciative when he called me "ma'am." I have remembered to pray for that gentleman.

*Later I remembered that what we do to others we do to God, and that Jesus can come in any disguise. Remember not to look down on the homeless and on beggars. God is in them, too.*

*Cast out your bad memories to keep your mind on the things of God. Keep and recall your good memories to help you gain a loving heart. That's how controlling your mind and memory helps you to be of good heart and to do good to others. That's how it helps you to live for God.*

*Misusing the imagination can harm the soul. When we make up something ugly about a person, we distort the truth and deceive ourselves. If we imagine someone backbiting us, we might try to harm that person by ruining his reputation. Be careful about misjudging others in a bad way. Control your imagination and let God do the judging.*

*I know some persons imagine that they're making love to an actor or actress. I think it's wrong for a person making love to one's spouse to imagine that the spouse is someone else. That's not being faithful.*

Ever since my visits to the Holy Land, I imagine being back in my favorite places: the Sea of Galilee, Tabgha and the chapel there. My visits to the homeland of Jesus brought me closer to Him, so I imagine being there to keep me close to Him.

*I began learning to control my emotions when Father Colloton had me work on my temper. Those without education often have a temper out of frustration because they can't find the words to express their thoughts and feelings. What makes their frustration and anger worse is the pride of the educated who use their learning and words to stump them. I could recall the times when my husband or children got me so angry by misunderstanding me or misjudging me that I locked myself in my bedroom and wouldn't come out till I cooled down. But Father Colloton told me that was not the way to practice controlling my emotions. He told me it was better to control them while facing the person.*

*When Father Thome told me about the silence of emotions, he said to act with reason instead of acting on emotion. With reason I could figure out what was right or wrong and act with the best of intentions. A good example is pity. Acting on pity, I could side with the wrong person in a conflict.*

*Controlling our emotions makes the day go more smoothly, sets the body and mind at peace, and helps us go to bed like a child without worries. My practice of living in God's presence helped me to control my emotions and to keep peace with everybody. I could also set others at peace because I was at peace.*

Those without control of their emotions panic in times of crisis and run around like a chicken without its head. By practicing control of emotions, I was calm and collected in times of crisis and prayed, "O Lord, make haste to help me." *God respects our free will and won't interfere in our lives unless we ask for His help or allow Him to help.*

It was disgusting for me to see how politicians criticized the president or one another in Congress. When they lost control of their emotions and tried to ruin the reputation of a person, they lost their human dignity and became a disgusting sight to God. *For God, freedom of speech does not justify mean words or unjust criticism.*

*The continual practice of the "Five Silences" helps us to live in God's presence and to serve him better. Without controlling our senses and faculties, it's impossible to achieve peace of mind, peace of heart and peace of soul.*

In this "School of Christ" I must give credit where credit is due. I cannot give credit to Father Thome, because he never explained the meaning and practice of each silence. I cannot give credit to anyone for my knowledge and practice of virtues. It was the "inner voice" that taught me the meaning and practice of each silence and of each virtue. For all that I am and have, I must give full credit to God our Father and Creator, to His Son Jesus Christ our Redeemer and to the Holy Spirit, my teacher and guide.

*Although I was strict with myself, I made allowances for the faults of others. On seeing bad behavior toward myself or toward others, I*

*prayed silently to God to sanctify that soul and to help that person be-*
*come better. Making allowances for the faults of others and praying for*
*them kept me free of hatred and bitterness. This was difficult at first,*
*but with God's help and by saying lots of prayers I got good results.*

The following incident shows how the "Five Silences" helped me.
Our TV set needed fixing, so I made the sign of the cross, closed my
eyes, and asked God to guide my finger in choosing a repairman from
the Yellow Pages. I tried to seek God's guidance before doing anything.

When I dialed the number my finger pointed to at random, Mr.
Lee, a Chinese man, answered. He said he would come at noon, but he
came two hours later. He entered and went straight to the TV in the living room without returning my greeting. He took apart the TV without saying a word. Then he stood up, headed out the front door and
slammed it behind him.

His behavior shocked me. The screws and parts lay scattered on
the floor. I thought he had gone back to the shop for some parts. I
waited for his return. Finally I telephoned him to ask why he had left
so suddenly. I told him that if he couldn't fix the TV, he could at least
put all the parts and screws back in. He said he would return to put
everything back in.

When he returned, he greeted me with a "Hi." After he had put all
the parts back in, he asked to use the phone. I directed him to the
phone on the kitchen wall. After his call, he told me that the three
words "Love One Another," which I had tacked above the phone,
helped him to see things differently and that he was sorry for his bad
behavior. *(I used the sign "Love One Another" to remind myself to be*
*pleasant with everyone on the phone. I didn't want to be caught off*
*guard in a bad mood while answering the phone.)*

Because of those three words and the grace of God, he asked for
help with his marital problems and begged me to see his wife, who
was on the verge of a nervous breakdown. He was so sad and troubled
that I promised to see his wife the next day. Then he explained why he
was so upset when he first came.

He returned the next day with the proper part to fix our TV, and he
didn't even charge us for the part and his labor – he was the owner of
the TV repair shop. I kept my promise and went by bus to speak to his
wife at their big home. After visiting with her several times, I helped
her over the phone.

In every case of volunteer work, the "inner voice" directed me in what to do and what to say to help those who sought my help. I always followed through with each case by visiting or telephoning to make sure everything turned out well.

Mr. and Mrs. Lee were fallen-away Catholics, so I helped them to return to church as active parishioners. To express their gratitude to God, Mr. Lee made a big donation to his parish. Mrs. Lee surprised me one afternoon by preparing and delivering a complete turkey dinner on a silver platter with all the trimmings for Thanksgiving.

If God hadn't prepared me for volunteer service through the "Five Silences," I would not have been able to help Mr. and Mrs. Lee. I had to control my emotions and words when Mr. Lee behaved so badly on his first visit. I controlled my mind to excuse him for his rude behavior by thinking he must be very troubled to behave like that to a customer. Otherwise my anger would have made me yell at him and I would have called another repairman. But God helped me to make excuses for him in order to keep my anger under control.

I learned to accept everything that happened as part of God's plan. He had a more important reason for sending Mr. Lee than to fix our TV set. God always has His own reasons for sending a certain person to a job, so we should treat every repairman with respect and say a prayer for him. He may need prayers more than the money he earns from the job he does for you.

One Saturday I told Father Thome what had happened during a family dinner the past week. Tommy asked me, "Ma, what are the 12 fruits?"

I answered, "Banana, papaya, pineapple, guava, orange, apple, grape, grapefruit, tangerine, peach, plum, lychee – but there are more than 12 kinds of fruit."

My husband and three children burst out laughing and kept laughing. I was serious and I didn't know what they were laughing about. I was puzzled. They didn't explain anything to me.

Father Thome told me kindly, "They shouldn't have laughed at you, Florence. They should have explained what Tommy meant. Tommy was asking about the Twelve Fruits of the Holy Spirit. But that's all right. You don't have to know what they are. You already have the Twelve Fruits."

After going to Father Thome for spiritual direction for a few months, I felt God calling me to a contemplative way of life. So I told

Father about my desire for a more prayerful life, and that I felt out of place being out with my family for dinner or at a party. He told me to ignore my desire and to keep going out with my family. His words were: "If you can't lick 'em, join 'em."

But the "inner voice" told me that Father Thome was not guiding me properly. The "inner voice" told me to go out with my family less and less, and only when required by justice or charity, like a birthday dinner for a family member. I knew that charity begins at home, so I went out with the family, but I refused invitations from others. I obeyed the "inner voice."

While making a weekend retreat preached by Bishop James Sweeney, I consulted him about my desire to live a more prayerful life. He told me to just live a normal life as a Christian wife and mother. He said God had called me to live a normal lay life. Again the "inner voice" told me the bishop was not guiding me properly. I relied on the "inner voice" of the Holy Spirit for guidance.

Both Father Thome and Bishop Sweeney were mistaken about God's plans for me. If I had listened to them, I wouldn't be sharing the spiritual lessons of this book with others. Looking back on those 48 years, I see how few priests were qualified to be spiritual directors because they were not spiritual enough.

*To qualify as a spiritual director, a priest must be prayerful and rely on the Holy Spirit every day by consulting him through prayer. He must have the ability to "read" the soul he directs. This ability comes from deep humility and great purity of heart. Finally, he must practice each virtue that he wants another person to practice. I think of a master chef who tests and practices each recipe before teaching another person how to cook that special dish.*

Some priests and religious are not qualified to be true spiritual directors. Some are too worldly. Being spiritual and being worldly don't mix, the way water and oil don't mix. Worldly priests and religious depend too much on book learning and classes. Book learning can lead souls down the wrong path. The Holy Spirit is the only true spiritual director of souls, because He knows all about the spiritual life and all about a soul.

*Christians should rely on the Holy Spirit as their spiritual director instead of another human person. Consult the Holy Spirit before every important decision throughout each day. Every night before bed-time, examine yourself to see whether you offended God and whether you can improve your practice of humility and charity. The Holy Spirit will never misguide you or leave you. A spiritual director can die or be transferred, but the Holy Spirit is always present to guide and help you.*

*A spiritual director is only the human instrument of the Holy Spirit, the source of all spiritual wisdom. Go to the source for spiritual wisdom. Seek guidance from the Holy Spirit. You can get better results by praying before the Blessed Sacrament in silence. Jesus is the Way, the Truth and the Life. Just sitting in calm silence before the Blessed Sacrament for several minutes will move the Holy Spirit to guide you in doing God's will.*

In 1956 Father Thome was transferred to the Marianist novitiate in Santa Cruz, California. Before he left Honolulu, the "inner voice" told me to ask him, "Father, will you continue to guide me through letters? I'm so serious about my spiritual life."

"I know you're serious about your spiritual life, Florence." Reluctantly he agreed to guide me by letter.

I didn't know how to write letters then, but I obeyed the "inner voice" and did my best.

In his first letter he asked me to write out my spiritual exercises. I didn't know the meaning of spiritual exercises. I thought he meant physical exercises. So I asked Mrs. C about them, but she wouldn't explain the meaning to me. She said, "You ask your spiritual director to explain it to you." I was so confused that I didn't answer his letter.

With little education and little religious instruction, I took things in a simple way. For example, when I heard a priest preach about salt losing its flavor and not being good any more, I thought, "Then I would use soy sauce."

I wrote Father Thome only when I needed guidance on a spiritual problem; but I wouldn't get an answer until my problem was over. He always began his letter with: "As usual, I've been busy." By then my problem was over, or the Holy Spirit had already guided and helped me through it.

*Guiding a person is a serious responsibility. A person should not accept this task without the intention and effort to fulfill it faithfully. A spiritual director will answer to God for failing to give the proper guidance according to God's will.*

I did not accept Father Thome's excuse of being too busy, and today I still cannot accept such an excuse. ***Being too busy is the poorest excuse for not doing one's duty to God or to others. We can always make time to answer an important letter or to write an important one. All time belongs to God.*** We should never tell God, "I'm too busy." Someday you may need help from someone, and the person you go to for help may say, "Sorry, I'm too busy."

## Annual Retreats

In one letter to Father Thome, I told him I wanted to make a private retreat of nine days. I usually made that annual retreat at Kona on the island of Hawaii. He suggested that I make a retreat at St. Clare Retreat in Santa Cruz, California. I discussed this retreat with Thomas, who agreed to it.

So in June 1957 I flew to San Francisco. Father Thome met me at the airport and drove me to the Marianist novitiate in Santa Cruz to hear my confession. After that, he drove me to the Brothers' cemetery to pray for the deceased Brothers. On the way back to the car I said, "Let's race to the car. Last one kiss the monkey's ass." He was shocked. But he ran after me and I outran him to the car. I remembered playing that game with neighbors as a child in Honolulu.

Then Father Thome drove me to St. Clare Retreat in the Santa Cruz hills for my nine-day retreat. All my annual retreats were private ones, without a retreat director. I relied on the Holy Spirit to guide me through each retreat.

While on retreat I met Kieran, the caretaker of the buildings and grounds, and spoke to him several times. I kept strict silence during my retreat, but I always placed charity before that silence. I was very businesslike in making retreats, but if someone asked me something, I answered out of charity.

Kieran respected my retreat silence, but I joined him for coffee and dessert after dinner every day, because he always ate alone in a small room next to the kitchen, while I ate in the formal dining room. I felt sorry for him. I could see he needed company and conversation. *Everyone needs kindness and conversation.* Even a dog needs company and being petted. I treated Kieran as a mother would by cleaning the table for him and emptying his ashtray. I also shared my dessert and my spiritual ideas with him.

My sincerity and kindness won his trust. He confided that even though the Sisters didn't think he had a religious vocation, he still had the desire to become a monk. The Sisters didn't think he had a religious vocation because he was only a lowly caretaker.

I told him, "Don't listen to anybody. Go ahead and apply. Try out their way of life if you have the desire. If you don't like it and leave, God won't kill you. If you leave, you can come back to work here or find another job. It's between you and God. Don't give up; keep trying. Just keep praying, and I'll be praying for you. Your desire is a call from God, so you do have a calling to the religious life. Don't lose that desire and calling. Don't give up. You're going to make it."

Because God gave me the job of helping souls answer God's call to serve Him in the religious life, He gave me the ability to identify souls with a religious vocation. I had no training or experience in this kind of work. I had nothing except a loving heart and sincere kindness to win trust and confidence. I was like a patient fisherman with hook and bait who never gives up. Eventually the fish bites. I was also like a doctor who examined a patient, treated her, prescribed medicine for her, and then moved on to the next patient. Because of God's guidance and help, each person I encouraged to serve God in religious life was accepted by a religious order.

I joined Kieran after dinner to share my dessert with him out of charity. Then God used me as His instrument to encourage Kieran to have confidence in God and in himself. I cared about his future and his desire to become a monk. My duty was to encourage him and to pray for him.

Months later, Kieran wrote to thank me for my encouragement and prayers. He had applied to the Trappist Abbey of Our Lady of Guadalupe near Lafayette, Oregon, and he was accepted by the abbot. In that letter he wrote, "You are a doctor of souls, Florence." When I visited that monastery in December 1968 and met him again, he was Brother Kieran, a Trappist monk.

*If a good person has the desire to serve God as a religious, don't interfere. Who are we to stop a person from being a religious, a doctor, a lawyer or a policeman? It's between the individual and God. And we have to respect the free will of people as God does.*

I thank God for the privilege of making annual retreats of nine days at St. Clare Retreat from 1957 to 1963. During my retreats I became friends with most of the Franciscan Sisters who ran the retreat center.

The superior, Sister Carmela, whom I called Mama Carmela, was kind to me. She ordered extra milk, eggs and cheese because of my abstinence from meat and poultry. Mama Carmela told me, "You remind me of the Little Flower, Florence." Three other persons had told me that: Brother Edward Strauss, Mrs. C and Sister Damien Joseph.

After my retreats, each Chinese Sister received permission to see me in private. I never refused to see any Sister who asked to see me. Mama Carmela gave the Sisters permission to see me after they finished doing the dishes from dinner. I helped anyone who knocked at my door.

As each Sister confided in me, I listened carefully and then questioned each one to check her. God helped me to spot a weakness or fault and then gave me the ideas for helping. I could detect what virtue each Sister needed. Then I gave each Sister a certain virtue to practice, such as patience or charity or obedience. Like a doctor of souls, I prescribed a spiritual remedy for each soul seeking help.

For the Sisters who had difficulties in getting along with others in the community, I reminded them that God brought them together so they could practice virtues by getting along with each other. Instead of resenting or backbiting a fellow Sister, they should pray for that Sister, who was there for their sanctification.

The Sisters sometimes fought like the children in a family. Sometimes living together was hard because they weren't of the same flesh and blood. They were strangers from different families and from different parts of the country and of the world. I reminded them that God had brought them together for their salvation and sanctification through the practice of patience, humility and charity.

I loved those Sisters not because they were Sisters, but because of their respect for me and their trust in me. I kept everything said to me confidential. Jesus and the Saint in my soul worked through me to help all those who confided their problems to me.

Whenever I came to make a retreat, all the Sisters stood in a line to greet me. When Father Thome was in Korea, the Sisters volunteered to meet me at the San Francisco airport and drive me to their retreat center in Santa Cruz. In the car on the way to Santa Cruz, one Sister told me that Mama Carmela was happy every time I came, because I gave her a sense of security and peace of mind. She said that Mama

Carmela noticed how well the Sisters behaved and practiced virtues while I was visiting with them.

During one of my retreats, Sister Hubertine read me the poem "Trees" by Joyce Kilmer because I enjoyed their grounds and the view of the nearby forests. She told me I should visit their Our Lady of Peace Retreat in Beaverton, Oregon, because I would enjoy the many tall fir trees there.

Before leaving the retreat center, I emptied my purse of its $40 to $50 as an extra offering besides the usual one for the retreat. Mama Carmela and the Sisters urged me to save the money for the plane fare to California for next year's retreat. I left the money for them anyway.

## First Vows

In 1957 the "inner voice" told me to make private religious vows, but I didn't know what they were or how to make them. I wrote Father Thome: "Something told me to make private vows because God wants me to make them." Then I asked Father for help. So Father Thome answered me by explaining the meaning and seriousness of such vows made to God. He recommended that I make those vows only after thinking it over. I answered his letter with: "Whatever Jesus wants from me, that's all that matters to me." He wrote back: "Pray over it and I'll help you with it."

The "inner voice" also inspired me to tell Father Thome that I must seek my husband's consent because of our marriage vows. Father didn't even think of that. So he wrote Thomas on Eniwetok (one of the Marshall Islands in the South Pacific) to explain the private vows to him and to get his consent. Thomas replied that he understood fully the meaning and seriousness of private vows. He gave consent freely because "Florence is an ardent Catholic." I wrote Thomas myself, and he sent me the same reply.

From then on Father Thome prepared me for making annual vows of poverty, chastity and obedience. They were annual vows, so I could choose whether to renew them for another year or not. Father chose the day of my first profession of vows, December 8, the Feast of the Immaculate Conception. Using the formula of vows Father Thome had sent me, I secretly made my first profession of private vows during the noonday Mass at the cathedral on December 8, 1958.

To the vows of poverty, chastity and obedience, I added the vow to do all things in a more perfect manner. The "inner voice" inspired me to add this vow to help me strive for spiritual perfection. I made my vows secretly and kept the secret just between me and God. No one knew the secret of my private vows to God, not even my children.

That was the way God paved the way and led me step-by-step under the guidance of my spiritual director to give myself completely to God through my private vows. I really wanted to belong to God in a total way.

My love for God and my desire to live a strict life for Him moved me to add the vow of doing all things in a more perfect manner for God. I added this vow on my own and told Father Thome about it. This vow meant making the effort to do everything to the best of my ability. *When done with true love, tasks are done in a more perfect manner. I knew God saw everything I did, so I did everything as well as I could to please Him.*

Living the vow of doing all things in a more perfect manner pleases God more than the vows of poverty, chastity and obedience. Later I learned that St. Teresa of Avila had made a similar vow to God. I tried to do everything in a more perfect manner for God: cooking, cleaning, doing the dishes, serving my family, putting things away, and having the proper posture and table manners. I would never have served others hand and foot like a lowly servant if I didn't do it for God in them. Sometimes I served them with faith that God was in them, because I saw so little of Him in them. At times I saw more of the devil in them. So I did it for Jesus.

*I did everything to please God, and not because I was a perfectionist. Sometimes my children accused me of being too fussy about minor details. But when we offer a chore to God, we should do it well for a perfect God who deserves a perfect gift.*

I recall Dr. Kam Sat telling me, "Your waxed floors are so clean I can eat off of them, Florence. You're a perfectionist." He was wrong. I was not a perfectionist. I kept my kitchen, especially the sink, clean because I didn't want my family to get sick from germs and bacteria. Only lately did I learn how many germs and bacteria there are in the kitchen, especially in dishcloths.

There are so many examples in daily living of how we can do

things with love and with care. One should not only do the dishes well, but also put them away neatly. Move chairs and things to sweep or vacuum completely. Close the cupboard or drawer after getting something. Put things back in their proper places after using them. Turn the lights off when leaving a room. Pick up your own things instead of letting someone else do it for you.

*While crocheting, if I noticed that I skipped a stitch I took apart all the stitches and began over. Even though no one would know about the missing stitch, I did the whole thing over because I knew, and God knew.* With that added vow, I did everything well with thanks and love for a God Who is perfect.

My vow of poverty meant living simply and buying only the things I needed. I lived for God simply, with only the necessities of life. My vow of chastity meant giving up marital sex with my husband. My vow of obedience meant obeying my spiritual director. If he misled me and I obeyed him, God would hold him responsible and not me. I also obeyed my husband in everything except in doing something that offended God. My vow to do all things in a more perfect manner meant doing everything, from the biggest to the smallest, as best I could to prove and express my love for God.

No one knew about my vow to do all things in a more perfect manner, so some people thought I was a perfectionist. I wasn't. It's just that I did everything for God with love and thanks.

## My Mother-in-law

When my mother-in-law needed surgery for cancer, I accompanied her to St. Francis Hospital and prayed for her in the chapel during her seven-hour surgery. The doctors removed part of her stomach and intestines. Someone had to watch her during the night so she wouldn't remove the drainage tube from her stomach or the intravenous tube from her arm. We couldn't afford to hire a private nurse.

Since I was the only one in the family who didn't go to work, I said I would spend the nights watching over her. Thomas drove me to the hospital after dinner, and I spent the entire night with her for three nights. I sat on a chair beside her bed and prayed for her, and checked on her from time to time. I dozed off for short periods.

Late the third night I heard and saw a dead body being wheeled past me in the dim hallway. I got frightened. The next day, exhausted and scared, I told Thomas, "From now on you go and watch over her during the night. She's your mother. Tell Fred and Nancy to take turns with you."

Several years later, I took my mother-in-law by bus to Tripler Hospital twice a week for treatment for diabetes and high blood pressure. She met me in church after the 6:00 morning Mass so we could be at the hospital by 8:00. So I was with her from 6:30 until I got home at 4:00 in the afternoon. I treated her to breakfast and lunch at the hospital cafeteria each time. To take advantage of me, she often invited a friend along, so I had to treat both of them to breakfast and lunch.

One evening after attending a graduation ceremony at Sacred Hearts Academy, I stepped into a shallow hole and cut my right shin on a metal sprinkler. Two mornings later, the cut was infected and painful. I telephoned my mother-in-law to tell her I had to see my doctor, but she insisted that I accompany her to Tripler for her treatment. I took her even though the cut was swollen and painful, with a red line going up to the knee. I didn't get to my doctor's office until after 4:00 in the afternoon. My doctor scolded me for not coming in sooner, and gave me a tetanus shot. I was happier than my mother-in-law when her treatments ended.

That was another incident to show how selfish my mother-in-law was. I could not have given her more respect and love than I did. Yet she never offered to pay her own bus fare. She should have treated me to lunch or breakfast at least once. She had much more money than we had, because of the insurance money and inheritance from her husband plus the thousands of dollars she had gotten back from Tommy and Stephen.

After my father-in-law died, my mother-in-law was alone and lonely and depressed because no one visited her. She telephoned to ask me to pay her regular visits, but I told her how busy I was. I stayed away from her because whenever I saw her I got nervous and my heart started pounding.

Mrs. C said it was my duty to visit my mother-in-law. But I doubted Mrs. C because she was the second person who made my heart go pounding whenever I saw her. When I told Father Read about how my mother-in-law had treated me and about visiting her, he said,

"Florence, stay away from her. She can cause you to lose your faith. Just pray for her." I followed his advice. She could not cause me to lose my gift of faith which I cherished, but she might cause me to lose the gift of charity.

Months later a Chinese relative confirmed the advice of Father Read. She told me in Chinese, "Stay away from your mother-in-law; she's waiting to pounce on you." I pictured a panther pouncing on me. I was glad I had followed Father's advice.

The landlord didn't see my mother-in-law for several days. So he telephoned her son Fred and asked him to check on her. Fred went and found her body on the floor of her bathroom. She had been dead for several days.

The "inner voice" told me, "You don't need to attend her funeral and burial. Just pray for her." So I didn't attend the services. I just prayed for her. During her Chinese funeral and burial I made a holy hour for her in church to pray for her. Afterward I learned from others that it was pouring rain at her burial. Her grave was half full of rain water when her coffin was lowered into it – according to the Chinese, a very bad omen.

I had attended the funeral of my father, grandmother and father-in-law, but not the funerals of my mother, my mother-in-law and my husband. God had His reasons for planning it that way.

I recalled what had happened years earlier after I moved out of my in-laws' home. They always wanted a daughter. When a famous actress from China, Butterfly Hu, came to Hawaii for a visit, my in-laws wanted to adopt her legally, even though she would soon be returning to live in China. They wanted the prestige of having a famous actress as an adopted daughter. They brought in a Taoist priest and official witnesses for the formal ceremony of adoption. My in-laws gave her cash and jewelry after the ceremony.

The next day my mother-in-law went to a dress shop where she knew I had a account. She used my account to charge an expensive bolero sweater of pink angora wool for the actress. When I found that out, I told the shop not to let anyone charge anything with my account. Then I went to face my mother-in-law.

"You had no right to charge the sweater for Butterfly Hu and then put it on my account without my permission. You made a big mistake by adopting her as your daughter. Don't think I'm jealous; I'm not.

She's only a gold digger. How many adoptive parents do you think she has? When you grow old and need someone to care for you, go find Butterfly Hu to help take care of you, because I won't."

Again my words came true. After her husband died, she felt lonely and depressed because no one went to visit her.

An important lesson comes out of my bitter and painful experiences with my mother-in-law. *To you parents-in-law I say that true love for a son or daughter means accepting the person he or she loves. That person deserves respect as a human being and a child of God. Are you so perfect as to give birth to a perfect son or daughter?* Only God knows a person well enough to pass judgment on that person. At the day of reckoning, how would you feel if God told you, "You're not good enough for my Holy Family; you're not good enough for my kingdom?"

## The Shrine

No matter how I struggled financially, I always made sure to pay Audrey's tuition and room and board at St. Louis University. I was always on time with the payments. When I didn't have enough to pay all the monthly bills, I paid the full amount on some of them. Then I telephoned or went to the office to let the clerk know I would pay a smaller amount that month, even if only $5 or $2. The next month I paid the full amount for the bill I had underpaid, and then underpaid the bill I had paid the full amount the month before. The workers never gave me a hard time, because they knew I was honest and sincere enough to inform them by phone or to face them. I always paid off all our bills and debts.

After 4 years of financial struggle, Audrey was finally graduating as a nurse from St. Louis University in 1959. Thomas was working overseas. He wrote to tell me to withdraw enough from our savings for a round-trip ticket so I could attend Audrey's graduation. I had seen a leaflet about the National Shrine of St. Therese in Chicago. After I asked to visit it, he wrote Audrey telling her to be sure to take me to visit that shrine.

It was a 13-hour flight from Honolulu to Los Angeles and another long flight to St. Louis. I arrived there the next morning. Audrey met me at the airport with a corsage. I brought a big box of leis for Audrey and her friends and some anthuriums for the altar of the Sisters' chapel.

Her classmate drove us to my hotel in St. Louis. That evening her friends came late to drive me to the cathedral for the graduation Mass. When we arrived at the cathedral, packed with people, someone stopped us from entering because there was no more room inside, and the procession was about to enter the church through the central door. I went to the side door to beg the usher to let me in. I had come all the way from Hawaii for my daughter's graduation. He said he was sorry, but he couldn't let me in because there was no room.

The "inner voice" told me to wait, and then to follow the man with the red hat, who was last in line. I was short and I could see only the tall pointed red hat. I did what the "inner voice" told me. If I had known the man in red was the cardinal, I would not have dared to follow him into the church. As I followed him down the center aisle of the cathedral, no one stopped me. Blessed Mother must have hidden me with her mantle. Otherwise the ushers would have stopped me.

When the cardinal entered the sanctuary, the "inner voice" told me to go to the right side and hide behind the big statue of Mary. I obeyed and knelt near the big statue. I stayed there the entire Mass with my head down and afraid I would be asked to leave, even though my knees hurt from kneeling so long. With tears of joy I thanked God for my being there to attend the graduation Mass of Audrey. A lady came by to ask, "What's wrong?" I told her," I'm crying because I'm so grateful to God for my being here at my daughter's graduation."

*Anyone responsible for driving a person to an important event should make sure to get that person there on time, and even ahead of time.* Without the help of God and the guidance of the Holy Spirit, I never would have attended the graduation Mass of my only daughter after traveling all the way from Hawaii.

After the Mass, Audrey looked for me at the reception hall. She found her friends who had driven me to the cathedral. She asked them, "Where's my mother?"

"We don't know. She left us before the Mass began."

I was lost and wandering the grounds around the cathedral. Audrey and her friends came looking for me. They finally found me and I told them what had happened. Audrey told me the man with the

A Life Vowed to God

red hat was a cardinal. She also said there was no big statue of Mary near the sanctuary.

The next day Audrey brought me back to the cathedral because she wanted to show me the inside of the cathedral and its dome. We also looked all over the church and in some of the back rooms for the big statue of Blessed Mother. I wanted to prove to her I was right. But we didn't find it. I wondered if Blessed Mother, in the form of a statue, had hidden me during the Mass.

Audrey took me from convent to convent to visit the Sisters. Each time I always made a visit to the chapel first to greet Jesus in the Blessed Sacrament and to pray for the Sisters.

Then Father Pieper and Brother Edward, Marianists, drove Audrey and me to visit their Second Novitiate outside St. Louis. I saw stalks of golden wheat for the first time. I connected the golden wheat with Christ in the Eucharist and the consecrated host I received in Holy Communion. When we arrived, I asked to visit the novitiate chapel. Father Pieper told me the chapel was upstairs. He knew how spiritual I was, so while I spent time with Jesus in the chapel, he entertained Audrey in the parlor.

At breakfast the next morning, Audrey mentioned that there was a musical playing at an outdoor theater, but we didn't have a ride. The title "The King and I" made me want to see it because I connected the title to "Jesus and I." I said, "Why don't we invite Father Pieper and Brother Edward to dinner at our hotel dining room and to the musical afterward? Then they can drive us to the theater." Father happily accepted our invitation.

After dinner Father and Brother Edward drove us to see "The King and I," with Yul Brynner as the king. At the outdoor theater I saw fireflies for the first time. At times I was more interested in watching the fireflies than the musical because I connected the fireflies with Jesus, the Light of the World. When the teacher sang "Getting to Know You," I connected the song to my getting to know all about Jesus.

I wanted to ride a train, so Audrey took me to Chicago by train to visit the National Shrine of St. Therese in St. Clare Church. (When St. Clare Church burned down in 1975, this National Shrine was moved to Darien, Illinois.) It was the first run of a new train called The Bluebird. It reminded me of a bluebird that came to the window of our McCully Street home and sang for me. When I told Thomas and the children about the singing bluebird, they didn't believe me. They said there were no bluebirds in Hawaii. Weeks later, Thomas was sick at home when the bluebird came to our window and sang again. He tried but failed to the catch the bird for me. God let Thomas and the children know I was telling the truth about the bluebird.

On the train I prayed and meditated while Audrey read. At lunchtime I saw a black person for the first time. A black man with a red cap came to announce that lunch was being served. I was afraid to cross the moving platform from our car to the dining car because the train was moving so fast. I just froze. That black man with the red cap offered to carry me over the platform. I was afraid, but I let him carry me over the platform to the dining car. He was gentle and kind. He said, "Enjoy your lunch, ma'am." After lunch he carried me over the platform again.

*In Hawaii God taught me to respect and accept persons of all races. Ever since that train ride, I have prayed for all the races, especially for black persons. I knew the same color of blood runs in the veins of all races: black, white, yellow, brown, red. Every person is a child of God and dear to Him.*

After morning Mass in Chicago, we asked the priest where the Shrine of St. Therese was. That national shrine in honor of St. Therese was her largest shrine in the U.S.A. He didn't know where it was. We had to ask five other persons before we found out how to get there.

The train, called the "El", took us to the edge of the city. We passed many old, rundown houses and poor shacks with barefooted people sitting on the steps of their porches. I prayed for them. After we got off, we walked several long blocks to the church where the shrine was.

As I stood on the threshold of the church, I burst into tears. I felt the tears as tears of gratitude to God for honoring me with such a big, beautiful shrine on earth. It was not me, Florence, standing at the entrance to the shrine, but St. Therese. I was thinking and feeling what St. Therese in my soul was thinking and feeling. I knew and felt everything she was thinking and feeling. The St. Therese in me cried because she was so grateful to God for honoring her with such a big, beautiful shrine here in America.

As I entered the church, someone turned on all the lights in the church. I knew and felt that Jesus was welcoming me, the Little Flower, into her shrine. I was no longer Florence at that shrine, but St. Therese at her own shrine. She cried even more when Jesus turned on all the lights in the church for her. I cried aloud all the way to the sanctuary. Then I saw the many red rose-shaped lights glowing above the entrance to the sanctuary. They were beautiful. I felt the Little Flower as me, and me as the Little Flower.

That was the first time that I felt and knew how completely St. Therese had an abiding influence of my soul and body. The soul, body and tears were mine, but it was really St. Therese herself at her shrine. I was wearing a dress of brown and white, the same colors as the Carmelite habit of St. Therese. The many rose-shaped lights reminded me of the roses that fell at the feet of the pope as he was canonizing St. Therese in St. Peter's Basilica. After my baptism, when I first heard the song about a mockingbird that made me feel and picture myself as a nun in a brown and white habit, I wanted to be buried in that habit.

Audrey sensed that something unusual was happening to me, so she was gentle, kind and patient. When I got over the experience of thinking and feeling as the Little Flower, Audrey asked, "Mom, can I take your picture?" She took lots of pictures of me at the Shrine. I didn't tell her about my secret of being completely possessed by St. Therese. I kept that a secret for God.

Through that event, God gave me a complete revelation for the first time of how St. Therese had taken possession of my soul and body. I had many signs that St. Therese was in my soul and used me in many ways to help people. At the shrine I finally realized clearly and fully that the Little Flower had taken complete possession of my soul and body.

St. Therese must have been with me and watching over me from my birth. That's how the fortune teller in China could read my *sin kwat*, saintly bones. But St. Therese didn't take complete possession of my soul until my baptism. I used to tell Tommy that the Little Flower had a lot to do with my life, but without understanding the meaning of what I was saying. I used to tell Stephen the same thing years later, but with a clearer understanding of its meaning. At the shrine of St. Therese, I had a clear, full understanding of what my "saintly bones" meant – being greatly influenced by St. Therese.

St. Paul said, "It is not I who live, but Christ who lives in me." Using this thought, I could say, "It is not I who live, but St. Therese who lives in me." Ever since that experience at her shrine, I sometimes felt St. Therese in me.

After we returned to St. Louis, Audrey took me on a day's outing on the Mississippi. We boarded *The Admiral*, the best of the steam-paddle ships. That afternoon I had to use the toilet. I walked into the ladies' room and came right out again. The wonderful black lady in charge of the toilet asked, "What's the matter, child?"

I said, "The toilet is brown with doodoo."

She laughed aloud. "That's the muddy water from the river. It's always like that. You'd better go, child, or you'll be sorry. We won't get back till late."

So I went.

In Honolulu I was used to a quiet life in solitude. I needed some quiet time after all the excitement I went through. So Audrey sent me by taxi to make a short retreat at the Kirkwood Retreat. The beautiful grounds had outdoor Stations of the Cross. I could hear the chirping of birds and the rustling of leaves. I finished the retreat with inner peace and spiritual joy.

Father Pieper and Brother Edward came by to drive me to the airport. We stopped at their Second Novitiate on the way to the airport. As we entered the building, I saw a firefly on the glass section of a door. I caught the firefly in my handkerchief. I could see its glow through my handkerchief and played with it. I wanted to take it home with me. But I knew it would die in my handkerchief, so on the way to the airport I released the firefly out of the back window of the car. God played a game with me. It was difficult to catch a live firefly, but God let me catch one.

*I was a child of God then, and now at 83 I'm still a child of God, and still with a sense of humor and playfulness. I crack a smile at Jesus every morning when I get up, no matter how early it is. I have always been childlike; not childish, but childlike. God is so real to me. I call on Jesus for everything. I depend on Him even to help me move my bowels. Jesus has never denied me help.*

As children of God, we should remain childlike before God our Father. Being childlike with Him means to be simple and to be oneself with the simplicity of a child. One should speak to God as a child speaks to a loving father, without formality.

Father Thome met me at the San Francisco airport and took me to the Marianist Novitiate for breakfast. After making my confession, I renewed my religious vows. Then Father drove me to St. Clare Retreat, where I began my nine-day retreat.

## Final Vows

On December 8, 1959, I secretly renewed my vows at Mass for another year. I renewed my vows the third time the following December 8. Father Thome wrote to remind me about renewing my vows each year, but I could never forget the day of my first profession of vows. Each year I reported to Father what I had done the past year. But he never corrected me about anything. I wanted to renew my vows year by year because I knew my husband so well. I have always been careful to keep my promises, especially my promises to God.

In November 1961 I received a letter from Father Thome. He told me Thomas wanted me to make perpetual vows. Thomas was home then, working at Pearl Harbor. He had broken his contract by quitting his overseas job, so he got a job at Pearl Harbor. His high test score got him a job with the second highest rating. Thomas never knew how much my prayers had helped him spiritually and materially all through the years.

I told Thomas the reasons I was against my taking perpetual vows. Father had explained to him how solemn those vows were, and how a dispensation from those vows could come only from Rome. I wanted to take annual vows because they expired at the end of the year. Then I could decide whether to renew them for another year or not. I knew Thomas too well to take perpetual vows.

I also thought it was too soon to take permanent vows. Nuns usually take temporary vows for 5 to 6 years before making perpetual vows. But the "inner voice" told me I must hurry. I didn't question God about it.

Several days later Thomas, Stephen and I were having lunch out. I had nothing to discuss with Thomas except the children and things around the house, so I told him our house needed painting. He became upset and angry. He said that he had just returned from overseas recently, and accused me of burdening him with house chores. He accused me of being a slave driver. Angrily he said that while I was on retreat, he and Stephen would paint the inside of our home.

The next day he brought home round-trip plane tickets to San Francisco to get rid of me for a while, but he said the trip was for my birthday. (No one knew my birth date. Thomas, Audrey and others had gone down to the county department of records, but they couldn't find a record of my birth. I didn't have a birth date, but somehow December 12 became my make-believe birthday. I was happy that it was December 12, because I could celebrate the Feast of Our Lady of Guadalupe instead of my birthday.)

Thomas came home with round-trip plane tickets to San Francisco and put them on the altar. He said, "You're going to make final vows." I didn't like the way he treated me. He should have discussed it with me before buying the tickets. He insisted that I make perpetual vows after making a retreat in Santa Cruz.

Thomas telephoned Father Thome to give him my flight number and the day and time of my arrival. He asked Father to meet me at the airport to drive me to Santa Cruz for my retreat and for my profession of perpetual vows. Thomas also asked him to make reservations for me at a nearby hotel so I could rest up after my retreat. That was the only time he did that. I usually returned home right after every retreat.

I didn't want to go. I thought it was too soon to make permanent vows and everything was too rushed. I had taken temporary vows for only 3 years. My flight was at night, so I attended the noonday Mass at the cathedral and stayed in church to pray. Only a Filipino man was in church. Suddenly I heard a man's voice coming from the tabernacle at the front of the church. It said sternly, "My time is not your time." It was so loud and distinct that it shook me up. I thought the Filipino man nearby had heard it, too, so I looked at him. He kept praying from his prayer book as if he had heard nothing. That was the first time a voice had spoken to me from the tabernacle. The words were meant for me, and I caught the meaning right away: It was time to make my final vows and I should do what my husband wanted. I picked up my purse and left for home right away.

When I got home, while hooking the screen door from the inside, the 3-inch crucifix I wore on a chain around my neck somehow came off the chain and fell on my toe with a thud. (I still can't figure out how it came off the chain.) That scared me. The link that connected the crucifix to the chain was soldered. The surprise was greater than the pain. I said, "I'll go, Jesus, I'll go." Thomas came home early from work and helped me pack. Then he drove me to the airport that evening for my 7:30 flight.

Thomas did force me to take my final vows then, but it was God's will because Father Thome was transferred the following year. *God speaks to us in so many ways. If only we could learn to follow the inspirations of the Holy Spirit. It's a great loss for those who don't heed the voice of God.*

Father Thome met me at the airport and drove me to St. Clare Retreat for my annual retreat. I needed that nine-day retreat for the serious step of making perpetual vows. When we arrived at the retreat house, I could sense the presence of the devil trying to disturb me. I knelt down and asked Father for a blessing to ward off the devil. He saw Mama Carmela coming. Instead of blessing me, he rushed to greet her. He refused to bless me because he saw Mama Carmela coming. Father Thome was a coward and acted out of human respect. As a priest and my spiritual director, he should have blessed me to ward off the devil. *No priest should ever refuse his blessing to someone who asks for it.* Priests have been ordained not only for giving us the sacraments, but also to pray for us and to bless us.

The sisters were happy to see me and made me feel welcome. But a few days before my retreat ended, I became confused and troubled by doubts, because Thomas had pressured me into final vows and because Father Thome didn't give me any guidance. I was disturbed because I didn't know the formula for making my perpetual vows to God. The devil used that confusion and worry to disturb me in a big way and to discourage me.

On December 7, the day my retreat ended, I was so troubled and upset that I cried and went to Mama Carmela. I went to her because I thought she would have the formula I could use for my perpetual vows. Otherwise I never would have told her the secret of my private vows. The Sisters never knew about them. While crying, I told her everything: about my annual vows, about the pressure to make perpetual vows and about the formula for my final vows.

Mama Carmela listened with compassion and then told me everything was going to be all right. She comforted me, reassured me and said the devil often disturbed those about to make final vows. She said that most religious went through what I was going through. Then she got really angry at Father Thome.

"Florence, I'm going to the next room to telephone Father Thome and ask him to come over right away."

"Don't bother Father; he's busy."

I could hear her talking on the phone to Father Thome at the novitiate: "You come over right away. I don't care if you have to hear the confessions of the Poor Clare nuns. You come over right this moment."

As soon as Father Thome arrived, Mama Carmela took him into her office and gave him a lecture. When they came out, Father gave me the formula for my final vows. He told me he would pick me up the day after my profession of vows to take me to a hotel at the beach for a rest. He said that was Thomas' birthday gift to me. Then he gave me his blessing before leaving.

Free of confusion and doubt, I enjoyed peace again. I was eager to make my profession of final vows to God.

During my retreats there I had become friendly with Michael, the new caretaker from Ireland. As I did for Kieran, I went into the small room where he ate so we could talk. After I shared my dessert with him, I cleared and cleaned his table. As I did for Kieran, I brought him a bottle of macadamia nuts every trip. Michael not only enjoyed the nuts, he also showed me how he shared them with his friends the squirrels, which came right up to him and took the nuts from his hand. He never called me "Florence;" he called me "the grand lady from Hawaii."

I knew from the Sisters that since his arrival Michael had never gone to Mass. On December 7, the day before my profession of perpetual vows, after I finished my noonday dinner, I went to keep him company in the small room where he ate.

"Michael, tomorrow is the most important day of my life as a Catholic. Would you be my guest of honor at the Mass tomorrow morning? Since I have no one here, will you be my guest?"

"For you, sure. It would be a privilege and honor to be your special guest on your special day. But I have to go to confession first so I'll be able to receive Communion with you tomorrow."

Michael didn't say a word about being a fallen-away Catholic, and I didn't tell him I was making final vows to God the next morning. During our visit he mentioned he had seen snow in the past and that he missed it. But he also said it hadn't snowed in Santa Cruz for 25 years. Without telling Michael, I decided to pray for snow for him.

In the chapel the next morning, Michael surprised all of us, including the chaplain who offered the Mass. Dressed in a suit and tie, Michael came into the chapel before Mass began and sat beside me. No one knew I had invited him. The Sisters never invited him to Mass.

When it was time for Communion, he escorted me to the rail where we both received Holy Communion together. Seeing this, some of the Sisters had tears in their eyes because they knew Michael had been away from the sacraments for years.

At Mass in the Chapel of the Holy Spirit at St. Clare Retreat, on December 8, the Feast of the Immaculate Conception, 1961, after receiving Communion I professed my perpetual vows of poverty, chastity, obedience and doing all things in a more perfect manner. The "inner voice" told me that God chose Michael to "give me away" to Jesus. I thanked Jesus for Michael, who "gave me away" at my profession of final vows. I also prayed for snow. I told Jesus, "Let it snow, let it snow, let it snow."

I felt the Little Flower in me as I prayed for snow for Michael. Many years later I remembered that the Little Flower had wished for snow for the day she was to receive the Habit. Jesus granted her wish, even though she didn't pray for it. Everyone considered the snow that day a little miracle, because the weather had been so mild.

Until I confided in Mama Carmela about my private vows, none of the Sisters had known about them. So she told all the other Sisters that I was making my final vows at that Mass. All the Sisters were happy to see a lay person make private vows to God. After Mass the Sisters added a place setting at my table in the dining room so Michael could join me for the feast-day breakfast with strawberries and cream, a rare treat for both of us.

The Sisters held a reception for me at 2:00 that afternoon. They used for the first time a tea set for 12 that a benefactor had given them. I never forgot that beautiful set of Royal Doulton china with its pattern of "Old Country Roses." I felt honored and privileged by the reception. The Sisters respected my spirituality of soul. Many years later, God gave me a tea set for four in that same china and pattern. Roses always reminded me of St. Therese, the Little Flower.

Thomas had told Father Thome to make reservations for me at a place where I could rest for three days after my retreat. So Father made reservations for me to stay 3 days at the Hotel Maria Del Mar in a secluded part of the Santa Cruz beach. My return to Honolulu was set for December 12.

The Sisters begged me to stay with them as their guest till then. I could stay in Michael's cottage for free while he was away. Mama Carmela even had Michael clean it for me. But I chose to go to the hotel on the morning of December 9 as planned. I invited Father Thome and Michael to join me for dinner, but only Father came because Michael was away. Father had steak and I had fish.

I was cold the first night because I didn't know how to turn on the heat. Father Thome didn't teach me because he assumed that I knew how. The next morning the maid showed me how to do it. Otherwise it was perfect, because from my room I could see the ocean and beach on the left. My bedroom window faced a tiny chapel on the same grounds where I could attend daily Mass. From my room I could see into the front entrance of the chapel to the tabernacle.

My first meal alone at the hotel was at a small table for two. When I poured my tea, the teapot played the tune "Tea For Two." I thought of Jesus and me as if I were having a honeymoon with Him. I saluted Jesus silently every time I poured tea from that musical teapot.

For me it was a real honeymoon.

The day before my return to Hawaii, I invited all the Sisters to the hotel for tea, ice cream and cake. I wanted to return a treat to the Sisters for treating me to a reception for my profession of perpetual vows. I knew they had lunch at noon, so I asked them to join me at 1:00. I asked the kitchen staff to bake us a sheet cake and to put out several of the musical teapots.

All the Sisters came except Sister Jane, who was taken to the hospital because of illness. The hotel staff baked a white sheet cake and served it with chocolate and vanilla ice cream on a long table in the dining room. There were three teapots that played "Tea For Two" every time they were lifted for pouring. Everyone kept getting small refills just to hear the tune. I made the Sisters laugh when I told them: "Tea for two, and two for tea; Jesus and me, and me and Jesus." We talked, giggled and laughed throughout the simple, joyous celebration.

After my stay of three days, Father Thome drove me to the San Francisco airport. We had a meal there while waiting for my flight back to Hawaii. The "inner voice" told me Father Thome would be sent to the East. I thought he would be going to New York. So I emptied the things from my small Pan Am bag and gave it to him.

I said, "You'll be needing this bag for your trip when you'll be transferred, Father."

"No, I'll be here in the novitiate."

"Here, take it anyway."

"Okay. Thanks."

When I arrived at the Honolulu airport, the joy inside me was so strong that it shone through my face. Stephen kept saying, "You look so good, Mom; you look so pretty" as he kept snapping pictures of me.

The next day when I brought a souvenir to Mary Lum, she said, "What happened to you, Florence? You look radiant. Your cheeks are so rosy." I told her I had just finished my annual retreat, but nothing about my private religious vows. I knew that what she was seeing was not me. When I told Gertrude Welcher I had just returned from my retreat, she called it my "rendezvous with Jesus." She surprised me by using that fancy French expression.

But extra work was waiting for me at home. Thomas had painted the inside of our home and had left ugly streaks on the walls and drops of paint on the wooden floor around the *lauhala* mat in the living room. While I was away, my daughter-in-law Carol came and offered to clean the house and do the laundry before my return, but Thomas told her that he could manage and turned her away to spite me. (Carol told me what had happened afterward.) So the house was dirty, with dust balls here and there, and the pile of laundry was big. When I saw how dirty the house was, Thomas said, "You had your rest already. This is your work. I left the laundry for you to do because it's your job." The streaks on the walls were so ugly when the sunlight shone in that I had to hire a painter to paint the entire house again.

Two weeks after my return I received a letter from Michael saying it had snowed in Santa Cruz after 25 years of no snow. It happened the day after I left California. He enclosed a snapshot of the snow on the ground and one of the Sisters throwing snowballs. God answered my prayers for snow to reward Michael for returning to the sacraments. I thanked God with a heart full of gratitude. God had sent snow for the Little Flower again as He had done when she received the Habit.

I respected Michael and treated him as a son. I invited him to join me at Mass as my special guest, because I knew he had fallen away from the practice of his faith. Because of my respect, kindness and love for him, he accepted my invitation. To bring a fallen-away Catholic back to church and to the sacraments made the whole heavenly host rejoice.

*Never think you're better than a gardener, caretaker, maid or wait-ress. God created everyone equal. Jesus came to serve rather than to be served. He told us it is more blessed to serve than to be served. Remem-ber to treat with respect, courtesy and kindness all those who serve you. The respect, courtesy and kindness you give them are given to God in them. When you demean a person, you demean God in that person.*

If practicing Christians were to see Jesus face to face, wouldn't they serve Jesus humbly with the best of behavior and language? Jesus told doubting Thomas, "Blessed are they who have not seen and yet be-lieve." God has given us the faith to believe that He is in everyone even without our seeing Him.

When I wrote Michael to thank him for his letter and the pictures, I wrote, "I'm glad I wasn't there when it snowed. I would have been so cold."

In his next letter, he wrote, "If you had been here, you would have been frozen and we would have to thaw you out."

It was difficult for me to live the religious vows of poverty, chas-tity, obedience and doing all things in a more perfect manner without a religious habit, without living in a religious community and without a mother superior to guide me. I was praying at Mass when I decided to ask St. Teresa of Avila to be my spiritual mother like a mother supe-rior. I knew Blessed Mother was my spiritual mother, but I put Blessed Mother on a special pedestal. I needed a mother superior to guide me in living my religious vows.

I didn't know anything about St. Teresa of Avila. That same after-noon, as I sat reading my prayer book on the porch, the mail came. There was a brown pamphlet about St. Teresa of Avila. I took that pam-phlet about her as a sign from her that she accepted me as her spiritual daughter. The pamphlet was about some anniversary celebration in her honor.

I believe there are no coincidences in life. Everything that happens is allowed and governed by the Divine Providence of our heavenly Father. I was inspired to ask St. Teresa of Avila to be my spiritual mother and my mother superior. I later learned that she was the founder of the Carmelite Order to which the Little Flower belonged. St. Therese of Lisieux was named after her; so St. Teresa of Avila was both her patron saint and her mother superior.

When someone upset me or when I would go through a period of spiritual trials, St. Teresa's "bookmark" was a real comfort to me:

> *Let nothing disturb you;*
> *nothing cause you fear;*
> *all things pass.*
> *God is unchanging.*
> *Patience obtains all;*
> *whoever has God*
> *needs nothing else.*
> *God alone suffices.*

A year later Father Thome wrote that he was being assigned to Korea. When the "inner voice" told me Father would be transferred to the East, I thought it meant the East Coast. His letter confirmed the thought that he would be going to the East.

On his way to Korea, Father Thome stopped over in Honolulu. I invited Father and a Marianist Brother to have dinner with Stephen and me at the La Ronde Restaurant on October 3, the Feast of St. Therese. While I was seeing Father off at the airport on October 7, he said, "Florence, I know the Holy Spirit will be guiding you."

After Father Thome left for Korea, I realized that God had known about his new assignment years ago. That was the reason God arranged for me to make my perpetual vows after only three years of temporary vows, before Father was sent to Korea. Because Father Thome had directed me in the profession of temporary vows, God made sure he also arranged for my profession of perpetual vows. God is so smart.

After only three years of temporary vows, I was the quickest of all Sisters to have the privilege of making perpetual vows so soon, because of the Saint in my soul.

As my life changed, doing God's will would lead me to live as a stranger among strangers away from Hawaii. God then led me into a life of prayer.

# A Deathbed Desire Fulfilled by God

At 2:00 in the morning Saturday, July 17, 1897, 10 weeks before her death, St. Therese said, "I feel that I'm about to enter into my rest. But I feel especially that my mission is about to begin, my mission of making God loved as I love Him, of giving my little way to souls. If God answers my desire, my heaven will be spent on earth until the end of the world. Yes, I want to spend my heaven on earth in doing good. This isn't impossible, since from the bosom of the beatific vision the angels watch over you."

The next day St. Therese said, "God would not have given me the desire of doing good on earth after my death if He didn't will to realize it; He would rather have given me the desire to rest in Him."

Because of St. Therese's love for God, He fulfilled her deathbed desire by allowing her to have an abiding influence on a soul specially prepared for her so she could continue her mission of making God loved, of sharing her spiritual lessons.

Little Florence was the Little Flower in full bloom. But remember that although St. Therese guided and helped Florence, her handmaid for doing good on earth, Florence had her own identity, personality and free will. St. Therese was surrounded by deep love at home and in the convent. Florence, however, never had much love from her family, husband, in-laws and children. But she had immense love from God the Father, Jesus, and Mary her spiritual mother.

With God's help and guidance, Florence was the one who did all the acts of self-denial, who did all the praying, who endured all the suffering, who made all the sacrifices for love of God. Florence achieved her own holiness. It takes a special person to become the faithful handmaid of a great saint.

Florence based her entire life on love and self-giving – she began her new life with God on February 14, 2000.

# Index

Dear Reader,

If you have any comments about *Soul Within a Peach* or the author, we would appreciate hearing from you. We may use some of the comments to promote the book, and use only initials, city and state to identify the source.

If *Soul Within a Peach* is not available at your local book-store, it may be ordered directly from the publisher. Send a check or money order for $18 per book plus $4 for ship-ping the first book and $2 for each additional book. There is a 25% discount on orders of 4 or more copies.

Attention churches, schools, retreat centers, seminaries, novitiates, centers of formation, and spiritual groups:

Quantity discounts are available on bulk purchases of this book for gift giving, educational purposes, or raising funds.

Please send correspondence or book orders to:


Peace Within Publishing
C/O Frank Amato Publications
P.O. Box 82112
Portland, OR 97282